Contents

CONTRIBUTORS   v
PREFACE   vii
ACKNOWLEDGEMENTS   viii

PART A   Planning and Design of Systems

1   Foodservice Operations
    Peter Jones   3

2   Market Research and Concept Development
    Nigel Hemmington   18

3   Planning and Designing the Menu
    Sean Mooney   45

4   Foodservice Layout and Design
    Nick Johns   59

5   Establishing Staffing Levels
    Stephen Ball   78

6   Developing Operating Standards
    Andrew Lockwood   94

7   Designing Control Systems
    Paul Merricks and Peter Jones   107

8   Designing a Quality Strategy
    Dolf Mogendorff   127

PART B   Managing the Operations

9   Protecting Assets
    Peter Jones   143

10 Improving Employee Performance
    Peter Jones   160

Contents

11 Managing Capacity
John Cousins 174

12 Improving Labour Productivity
Stephen Ball 188

13 Menu Analysis
Peter Jones 204

14 Providing Service Excellence
Andrew Lockwood 216

15 Controlling Costs
Paul Merricks with Peter Jones 231

16 Managing Quality
Nick Johns 245

INDEX 262

Contributors

The Editor, **Peter Jones**, is Head of the Department of Service Sector Management at the University of Brighton Business School. He is the author, co-author or editor of six textbooks and numerous articles, reflecting his research interest in effective operational performance in the hospitality industry. He has also presented conference papers in the UK, the USA and Canada and developed open learning materials for use in the UK and North America. Before taking up his first teaching post, he had worked for multi-national hospitality firms in both the UK and Europe, and owned and managed his own Brussels-based restaurant. He is a Fellow of the HCIMA and was President of EuroCHRIE in 1991/92.

Stephen Ball is Senior Lecturer in the Department of Food, Nutrition and Hospitality Management at the University of Huddersfield. He has a wide range of industrial experience and has acted as consultant for a number of national and international hotel and catering organizations. He has published extensively on productivity in the hospitality industry and has a Master of Philosophy degree for his work on productivity and productivity management in fast food chains. He is editor and chief contributor of *Fast Food Operations and Their Management*.

John Cousins is Head of the School of Hospitality Studies at Thames Valley University, London. His subject is Operations and Strategic Management for the Hospitality Industry. He is the author and co-author of several texts and papers including *Food and Beverage Service* with Dennis Lillicrap, now in its fourth edition.

Nigel Hemmington is Head of Division of Hospitality Management at Cheltenham and Gloucester College of Higher Education. Dr Hemmington's interests are mainly in consumer behaviour related to the strategic management of hospitality operations and he has published a number of articles in this area. Before going into teaching he worked in licensed retailing with John Smiths Brewery and commercial catering with Lyons.

v

Nick Johns is Reader in the Hotel School, City College, Norwich, a Regional College of Anglia Polytechnic University. Dr Johns is well known for his work on the quality and productivity of hospitality operations and has also published extensively upon technical issues such as hygiene and the environment. He has contributed to numerous conferences in the hospitality field, reflecting his wide research interests. Currently he is engaged on a study of recycling in collaboration with the In-Flight Caterers Association.

Andrew Lockwood is Lecturer at the Department of Management Studies at the University of Surrey. His main research interest is in quality service management in the hospitality industry, and he has undertaken consultancy and run numerous courses on this subject in the UK and elsewhere. He is author and co-author of a number of texts, including *The Management of Hotel Operations* and *Readings in Food and Beverage Management*.

Paul Merricks is Principal Lecturer at the Middlesex Business School. One of the co-authors of the first edition of this text, he has continued to research operational aspects of foodservice management.

Dolf Mogendorff is Head of the Department of Hospitality, Tourism and Leisure Management at Glasgow Caledonian University. His main research interest lies in the area of the management of change and innovation and he has published extensively in this field. He has also presented conference papers in the UK and on the continent of Europe. His academic career followed a number of years in hotel management in the UK. He holds a PhD from the University of Aberdeen and is also a fellow of the HCIMA. He was secretary of the Council for Hospitality Management Education from 1990 to 1994.

Sean Mooney is Principal Lecturer in the School of Management, Hospitality and Food at the Blackpool and the Fylde College. He has wide experience in the UK hotel and catering industry and in the Far East, where he taught at the Hong Kong Polytechnic. He has previously published articles on operational aspects of hospitality marketing and capacity management.

Preface

This text is the result of an original idea by Paul Merricks and ten years of debate and discussion amongst a group of colleagues, who informally call themselves the Hospitality Operations Research Group. This group has no clearly defined membership, no subscriptions nor funding, and meets only irregularly, usually at some conference or other. What unites the group however is a *passion* for operations management in the hospitality industry.

It might seem strange to use such a word as 'passion' to describe how a group of academics feel about their subject, certainly a subject as down-to-earth and practical as this. It seems difficult to believe that anyone can get excited by topics such as productivity, capacity, concept development, location analysis, and so on. But it is my experience that is just how these colleagues feel about their work. What makes them feel this way?

First, most if not all of them have worked in the industry before becoming teachers. They have personally experienced the *frisson* of danger that accompanies every single service act, the frustration of things going wrong, the exhilaration of things going right. Each event, each success or failure, has been filed away in order to contribute to their understanding of operations management. Secondly, they have all taught the subject. They comprehend therefore what helps students to understand a topic and what prevents or hinders such understanding. Each, in their own way, has grappled with putting over a subject that requires systematic analysis on the one hand and perception about human behaviour on the other.

As well as passion, the contributors also bring to this text a great deal of *expertise*. The choice of author was based largely on their established track record of research and publication in particular areas of operation management. Each chapter could easily be twice, if not three times, as long as it is, because each author knows so much more about the chapter topic than we are able to include here. Such pruning has been carried out in order to ensure that the coverage of the text is wide-ranging and the balance between topics reflects the focus of the text and level of reader.

The end result of this marriage between passion and expertise is, I hope, one of the most comprehensive, thoroughly researched and innovative texts ever to be written on foodservice management operations. The text is significantly different from that of the first edition (called *The Management of Catering Operations*). The book continues to be centred around the idea that the management of operations requires successful performance in a range of key result areas. In this text, the key result areas and their interrelationship are more fully explained. Furthermore, this text separates out the creation and design of operations from ongoing operational activity in each area. To put it simply: operational success is based on doing the right things in the right way.

Part A of the text explains how to select the right things to do for any type of foodservice operation. These 'right things' include understanding the customer and developing a concept to meet their needs; devising the menu; planning and designing the physical environment; establishing staffing levels; developing operational standards; creating a control system; and planning for quality.

Part B explains how to carry out these things in the right way. Operations managers need to maintain satisfactory performance and take corrective action if things go wrong in a number of areas. These include the assets, menu, employees, capacity, productivity, service, food costs, and quality.

This text is intended for students in the final stages of their management qualification, whether at degree, higher diploma, HCIMA diploma or postgraduate level. It therefore assumes an understanding of the technical aspects of foodservice operations relating to food production and service, as well as a basic knowledge about different sectors of the industry, marketing, human resource management and accounting.

PETER JONES
March 1994

Acknowledgements

We would like to express our grateful thanks to all those individuals and organizations who have helped in the preparation of this book, including British Airways, Burger-King (Europe, Middle East and Africa), Chris Cowls, Philip Gassmann, Bill Flavell, Simon Lake, International Flight Caterers Association, *et al.*

PART A
PLANNING AND DESIGN OF SYSTEMS

1

Foodservice Operations

Peter Jones

INTRODUCTION

The foodservice industry is an enigma. It is one of the fastest-growing sectors of most service-oriented economies, but not the most profitable. It employs many more people than most other sectors, but has a poor image. Despite the fact that eating out is on the increase, the performance of foodservice firms is consistently criticized by the media. The industry is somehow seen as second rate – a poor employer engaged in an activity of little challenge. Feeding people is basically not seen as important. On the other hand, if the industry really performed badly it has the potential to harm very large numbers of people through food poisoning, and if it performs well, it can significantly increase the health and well-being of the nation. This text does not attempt to address this image problem directly. However it does strive to demonstrate that the industry is complex, challenging and increasingly sophisticated. And if this is the case, management too must be up to the task.

This chapter introduces and explains the concept of 'systems' and 'systems analysis'. This idea of the 'service system' is used not only to explore the foodservice industry, but also as the underpinning for the structure of this textbook. The chapter goes on to apply systems analysis, showing how it can be used to identify different kinds of foodservice operation. A number of different classifications of the industry are identified and one is briefly reviewed. The text proceeds to explore the extent to which the management of foodservice is the same for all these kinds of operation or varies according to the operational type. At this point, the concept of key result areas is developed, suggesting that irrespective of type, foodservice managers share similar major objectives. The fundamental principle underlying the text is that to succeed in these key result areas, managers have a choice from a wide range of alternative approaches, techniques, procedures or tools. It is the choice of which of these alternatives to adopt that is dependent on the type of operation. For instance, it is to be expected that all foodservice managers have to schedule employees, but the fast food manager does so differently to the hotel banqueting manager; inventory control is carried out in all foodservice operations, but for an in-flight production unit it is different from that in a steakhouse; or quality standards are fundamental to all, but the specific foodservice standards of a hospital are different from those of a gourmet restaurant.

SYSTEMS AND SYSTEMS ANALYSIS

In order to discuss and evaluate the management of foodservice operations this text adopts a 'systems approach'. A simple system comprises *inputs*, *processes* which transform or combine the inputs in some way, thereby producing *outputs*. In the case of a foodservice operation, for example, inputs would include materials such as raw meat and vegetables; processes used would be vegetable preparation and a range of different cooking methods; so that outputs would result in meals for consumption by customers. To ensure that the desired outputs are produced, there needs to be a 'feedback loop' making the system open, or adaptive to external influences. In our example, such feedback could be customer comments about the food. This basic system is illustrated in Figure 1.1.

The conventional production management approach to understanding management is to map the flow of raw materials through the system.[1] Indeed such flow chart processing has been proposed for services[2] as well as manufacturing-based operations. The challenge of services is the extent to which the participation of the consumer in the service 'event' can be accommodated in a model based solely on materials flow. A distinctive feature of services is that the customer is an 'input' to the system, 'processed' by the system, and an 'output' of the system. Prior to the system operating, the customers' needs greatly influence the original design of the system, as well as causing it to be modified in response to feedback. Thus most services process a combination of physical raw material, information, and the customers themselves. This has led to the idea of the 'service package' or 'service bundle' which can also be modelled as a system. Drawing on the open systems view developed by Murdick, Render and Russell,[3] we have constructed a systems model of service most relevant to foodservice, shown in Figure 1.2. This identifies the specific inputs of a service operation, the productive processes that take place, and a number of possible outputs. The role of the service operations manager is to understand the original design process and then control the system to ensure the desired outputs are achieved on an ongoing basis.

This model is important because it identifies two key features of operations management which underpin the approach of this text. The first basic concept is that of service design. Choices have to be made about how to satisfy stakeholder needs. Stakeholders include customers in particular, but also employees, shareholders, investors, suppliers, and any other significant group that influence the operation's activity. This means selecting specific inputs and particular processes and combining them in such a way as to provide a service operation capable of meeting the identified needs. Successful operations are those in which all parts of the operation fit together efficiently and effectively. Once the service system is designed, it then has to be operated. This requires managers to apply a range of management skills needed to support effective operational activity. This textbook is divided into two parts because of this: Part A takes a strategic perspective by looking at how foodservice operations are conceptualized, designed and set up ready for operations; Part B examines how foodservice operations are managed on a routine basis.

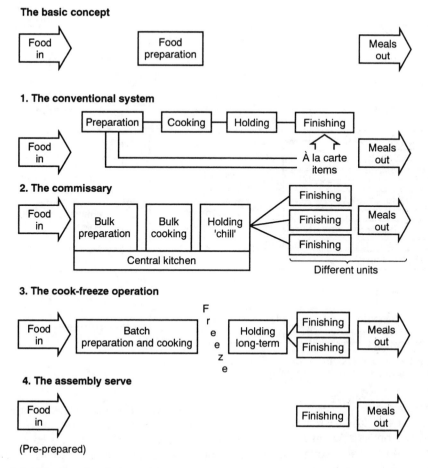

Figure 1.1   Food production systems.

The second basic concept, well understood in marketing, is that in order to understand why things are done it is necessary to look at what is to be achieved. In other words, it is the outputs of any system that explain why certain processes are used and hence certain inputs needed. Merricks and Jones[4] refer to these outputs as key result areas. Lockwood and Jones[5] propose that there are essentially seven of these, common to all service operations: these are discussed later. This textbook reflects this focus on outputs by having chapters in Part B that look at each of these key result areas in turn.

FOODSERVICE SYSTEMS

Having proposed a general model of a service operation, we can now go on to look at specific models of foodservice operations. One of the first basic analyses of foodservice as a system[6] was developed at a time when the systems approach to management was particularly in vogue. This is illustrated in Figure 1.3. It identifies a large number of

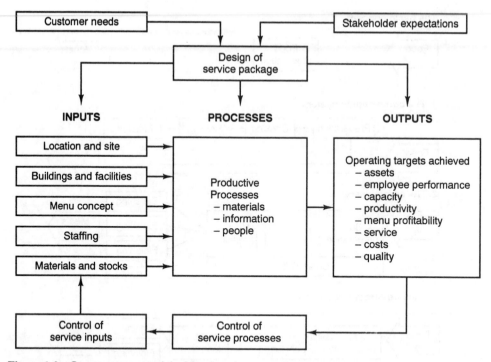

Figure 1.2   Open systems model of foodservice operations.
Based on Murdick, Render and Russell (1993)[3].

different inputs, processes and outputs of the system. For instance, a thin person, described as a 'hungry customer with money', is seen entering the system; and a more portly person is shown as an output, defined as a 'fed customer with less money'. This model described and explained a typical foodservice operation of the 1970s. However, in the 1990s it has some limitations. A major limitation relates to the inference that both production and service processes take place in the same location and at the same time. New technology developed and applied widely during the 1980s makes it possible to serve food to customers many hours after and miles away from where it was prepared. This has been referred to as 'decoupling'.[7] A second limitation is that food production has been modified by simplifying menus and buying in many ready-made raw materials. Fast food is an example of this 'production line' approach to foodservice.

This systems model of a foodservice operation is therefore too simple to fully explain the complexity of all the different types of foodservice operation. Pickworth[8] in a seminal article about foodservice operations helps to explain why. He adopts the concept of the service system and applies it to foodservice. Pickworth defined a service system as an 'operation in which products/services are created and delivered to the customer almost simultaneously'. In some cases a foodservice system is 'dedicated', that is to say it 'is designed to produce a specific range of menu items'. Pickworth uses the example of fast food chains. However, in other cases, a system can be 'multi-faceted', so that it is 'able to produce and serve a broad range of menu items'. An example of this would be a hotel with food production facilities serving a gourmet restaurant, floor service, banqueting and other specialist food outlets. In summary, a dedicated system is

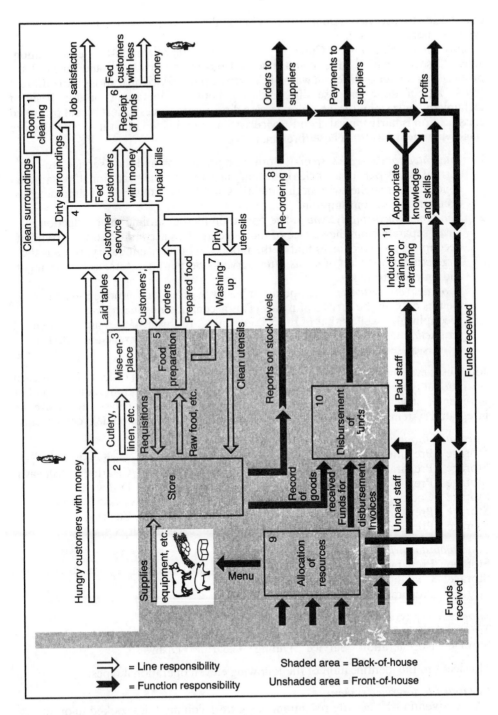

Figure 1.3 The foodservice system.
Source: Cutcliffe (1971)[6].

one specific foodservice system, whereas in a multi-faceted operation there are several systems operating together.

Since the development of Cutcliffe's systems diagram of a multi-faceted operation, Jones,[9] Escueta *et al.*[10], Huelin and Jones,[11] Cousins and Foskett,[12] and Jones[13] have proposed a number of different ways of classifying foodservice operations into different types. All of these propose differentiating between operations on the basis of technology, or systems design, or operational processes. Jones's most recent proposed classification is fairly typical. Foodservice systems are divided into three types, before classifying them further. These three main types are:

1. *Integrated foodservice systems*   Both food production and food service are carried out as part of a single operation. This reflects the 'traditional' restaurant concept and matches with both Cutcliffe's and Pickworth's view of simultaneous production and consumption.
2. *Food manufacturing systems*   The operation focuses around the production of *meals* separate from the service of those meals. This accommodates the trend of decoupling and recognizes that in the modern foodservice industry, there is the large-scale production of *meals* often served by other operators, as with in-flight and on-rail catering.
3. *Food delivery systems*   The operation has little or no food production and focuses only on the service of meals. This accommodates the concept of decoupling, as well as that of production lining. In this instance, little or no meal *production* takes place; meals are either 'assembled' and/or regenerated. The focus is on serving consumers.

Jones uses systems analysis of the processes in each operation in order to look at each operational type. Within each of these main types, there is a different sequence and/or number of stages in the total process. On the basis of this analysis, there are six integrated systems, three food manufacturing systems and two food delivery systems.

Integrated foodservice systems are:
Storage   Preparation   Cooking   Service   Dining   Clearing   Dishwash
Storage   Preparation   Cooking   Holding   Service   Dining   Clearing   Dishwash
Storage   Preparation   Holding   Service   Dining   Clearing   Dishwash
Storage   Cooking   Holding   Service   Dining   Clearing   Dishwash
Storage   Preparation   Cooking   Holding   Service   Dining   Clearing
Storage   Preparation   Cooking   Dining   Clearing   Dishwash

Food manufacturing systems are:
Storage   Preparation   Cooking   Holding   Transport
Storage   Cooking   Holding   Transport
Storage   Preparation   Cooking   Transport

Food delivery systems are:
Transport   Storage   Regeneration   Service   Dining   Clearing   Dishwash
Storage   Regeneration   Service   Dining   Clearing   Dishwash

This leads to the identification of the following eleven operational types:

Integrated foodservice systems:
1A   Conventional à la carte restaurant using fresh commodities cooked to order
1B   Conventional restaurant using fresh commodities cooked in advance
1C   Catering outlet serving only prepared foods, e.g. buffet, sandwich bar

1D Conventional restaurant or cafeteria using convenience commodities served to order
1E Fast food outlet
1F Japanese hibachi restaurant

Food manufacturing systems:
2A Production kitchens using fresh commodities and sous-vide or cook-chill
2B Production kitchens using convenience commodities and sous-vide or cook-chill
2C Home delivery

Food delivery systems:
3A In-flight/some hospital tray serve/on-rail
3B Restaurant/cafeteria/store buying all fully prepared meals from supplier

MANAGING DIFFERENT TYPES OF FOODSERVICE OPERATION

So far the industry has been divided on the basis of the sequence and number of stages in the overall process. If each operational system really is different one from another, other objective criteria for distinguishing between them should be available. In other words, there would need to be differences in the inputs utilized, the specific processes applied, and the outputs expected. Huelin and Jones[14] examine seven key operational features which they suggest do identify inherent differences between alternative systems. These seven criteria included the inputs (type of raw materials, inventory size, and product range width and depth) along with process features (capacity, production batch sizes, and flexibility). Table 1.1 adapts this analysis and applies it to the 11 different systems listed above. Such analysis demonstrates and emphasizes that inputs, processes and outputs vary between operational types; so that although the basic aim of

Table 1.1 Charactistics of foodservice operational types.

	Raw materials type	Inventory size	Product range		Capacity	Batch size	Flexibility
			Depth	Width			
1A	Fresh	High	High	High	Low	Low	High
1B	Fresh	High	High	High	High	High	High
1C	Fresh	High	High	Low	Low	Low	High
1D	Convenience	High	High	High	High	Low	High
1E	Convenience	High	Low	Low	High	Low	Low
1F	Fresh	Low	Low	Low	Low	Low	Low
2A	Fresh	High	High	High	Low	High	High
2B	Convenience	High	High	High	High	High	High
2C	Fresh	Low	High	Low	Low	Low	Low
3A	Fresh	High	Low	High	High	High	High
3B	Convenience	Low	Low	Low	High	Low	Low

Adapted from Huelin and Jones (1990)[11].

a foodservice operation is to process raw materials into meals in order to achieve customer satisfaction, this is achieved in a number of distinct ways.

One significant question therefore remains. Is foodservice, and in particular foodservice management, a single discipline? Or is it so diverse that it is a number of different disciplines – such as food production management, retail management or whatever? If the differences between systems are now so great, then it would be very difficult to talk about 'the management of foodservice operations'. Earlier in the chapter, we identified the importance of outputs or 'key result areas' in understanding why an operation is designed in a particular way and how it should be operated. Lockwood and Jones[15] propose that there are seven key result areas for all service operations. These are:

asset performance
employee performance
customer demand
productivity
service
income
quality

To emphasize that successful operational performance requires the manager actively to control these seven areas, they typically preface these with a 'doing word' such as improving, sustaining, managing, assuring and so on. Their rationale for identifying seven key areas is based on the following argument. There are three main components of an operation: the physical assets of the business (buildings, equipment, financial assets, etc), the human assets (employees) and the customers. Each of these has to be managed effectively. In addition, the combination of each of these with one of the others leads to three more key areas. Customers' interfacing with employees leads to the service key result area; decisions about employing physical plant and equipment or employees to perform operational functions is an issue of productivity; and customers' entering into the physical assets necessitates some kind of transfer of funds from the customer, hence income. Finally, they argue, the combination of assets, employees and customers identifies the seventh and last key result area, namely quality. They illustrate this with a model showing the key result areas as overlapping circles.

Since this model has been developed, it has been reviewed in the context of its relevance to foodservice operations. A major shortcoming of having just three overlapping circles is that there is no place for considering the 'concept', 'meal experience', or 'service package'. To put it simply, where is the menu in a model made up of assets, employees and customers? This text therefore adapts the Lockwood and Jones model by overlaying a triangle which we can think of as the foodservice concept, of which a central element is the menu. This is consistent with the idea of the meal experience[16] in which food is fundamental to the experience along with ten other contributing factors, some of which derive from the assets – decor, lighting, furnishing, from the other customers in the operation, and from the employees, namely service. This is illustrated in Figure 1.4.

PLANNING AND OPERATING FOODSERVICE SYSTEMS

The management of foodservice operations can be considered at two levels. At the strategic level, foodservice operations are conceptualized, planned and developed. An operation will then conform with one of the 11 operational types – it will be in-flight

Figure 1.4   Adapted model of key result areas.
Adapted from Jones and Lockwood (1992)[5].

catering, fast food, home delivery, or whatever. Decisions are made about the type of customer the operation will attract; the location; the menu; the physical layout and decor; the staffing; stock levels and cost forecasts; and the operational systems. These were shown in Figure 1.2 as the inputs to the system. These inputs, the major decisions to be made and the alternative policies and procedures available to foodservice operators are summarized in Table 1.2.

At the operational level, these strategic plans have been actioned and the manager is asked to operate on a day-to-day basis. The emphasis therefore switches from inputs to outputs, i.e. the key result areas. In each of the key result areas there is a range of choices to make about how to meet operational targets. This is illustrated in Table 1.3. Operators within the same sector tend to select the same options, but not always. For instance, fast food operators share a common approach to protecting their assets; hospital caterers utilize the same systems for managing capacity; and the in-flight sector has a specific approach to productivity management. However, in other key result areas it may be the organization, rather than the operational type, that influences activity. Thus achieving improved employee performance through empowerment may be suitable for a number of different types of operation.

The most important features of Tables 1.2 and 1.3 are that each major input and each key result area must *fit*. We can illustrate this very important idea by looking at one of the 11 operational types: the Japanese hibachi table restaurant, exemplified by the Benihana chain. The basic concept is simple. Customers sit on three sides of a rectangular table, into which is set a griddle plate, or *hibachi*. A chef works on the fourth side preparing and cooking meals in front of the customers. The concept appeals to a specific market segment; requires a site of a certain size located near these customers; defines a menu comprising foods that can be cooked in this way; has a distinctive layout, design and Japanese decor; establishes staffing levels based on having the chef in the dining room; requires control systems and quality controls that match

Table 1.2   Key strategic inputs.

Major inputs	Decisions to be made	Alternatives in industry	Industry examples
Concept development	Market segmentation	Mass market	Fast food; licensed trade
		Niche market	Theme restaurants
		Captive market	Hospitals; in-flight
	Location	Population centre	Licensed trade
		Traffic flow	Roadside diners; fast food
		Other	In-flight
	Site selection	Purpose build	Roadside dining
		Adapt	Employee feeding
Menu planning	Menu framework	Wide	A la carte restaurant
		Narrow	Fast food; steak house
	Product depth	Many menu items	Ethnic restaurants; pizza
		Few menu items	In-flight; fast food
	Menu presentation	Large display	Fast food; licensed trade
		Individual menu card	A la carte restaurant
Layout and design	Food production system	Traditional	Restaurants
		Call order	Fast food
		Decoupled	Welfare; travel
	Food service system	Table service	Restaurants
		Counter service	Motorway; schools
		Vending	Employee feeding; travel
Staffing levels	Type of employee	Core staff	Inflight
		Peripheral staff	Outdoor/travel catering
	Productivity levels	Labour-intensive	Licensed trade
		Capital-intensive	Fast food
	Specialization	Highly specialized	A la carte restaurant
		Multi-skilled	Fast food; in-flight
Control systems	Stock management	Make from fresh	A la carte restaurants
		Purchase convenience	Fast food; licensed trade
	Cost control design	Pre-operational control	Liquor and beverage stocks
		Post-operational control	Food stocks
Quality planning	Strategy	Quality inspection	Individual operating units
		Quality control	Welfare; in-flight
		Quality assurance	Restaurant/fast food chain
		Total quality management	Hotel chains

Table 1.3 Operational key result areas.

Key result area	Major concerns	Approaches adopted
Protecting assets	Built environment	Deterrence
		Alarm systems
		Response
	Plant and equipment	
	Materials	HACCP
		COSSH
	People	
	Money	Cash security
		Credit control
Improving employee performance	Individuals	Human resource management
		Employee reward systems
		Empowerment
	Boundary roles stress	
	Teams	Team building
	Organization culture	Task
		Role
Managing capacity	System capacity	Food production
		Food service
	System strategy	Match demand
		Shift capacity
		Shift demand
Managing productivity	Staff scheduling	Full-time
		Part-time
		Casual
	Workload allocation	Specialization
		Flexible working
		Multi-skilling
Menu analysis	Average spend	Menu effectiveness
		Frequency distribution
	Menu item performance	Matrix analysis
		Menu engineering
	Menu profitability	
Improving service	Service process	Service factory
		Service shop
		Mass service
		Professional service
	Service focus	Individual
		Flexibility
		Operational
		Interactive
Controlling costs	Suppliers	Supplier relationship
		Supplier negotiation
		Supplier credit
	Stock	Record keeping
		Stock taking
	Production	
	Sales revenue	
Managing quality	Quality audits	Departmental
		Customer perception
	Quality improvement	Problem identification
		Problem prioritization
		Problem location

this activity. The fit between these things makes this operation distinctive from any other kind of foodservice business, not only in the obvious ways, but in other ways too. For instance, the ratio of restaurant to kitchen floor space is higher in Benihana than conventional restaurants, increasing the potential profitability of the site. Likewise the ratio of chefs to customers is high, although fewer waiting staff are needed. With the fit between these strategic features established, the Benihana chain adopts specific ways of operating within each of the key result areas. Since most, if not all, of the cooking is carried out in the dining room, safety and sanitation issues are managed in a specific way. Having the chefs in contact with the customers means that approaches to employee performance, service and quality are adapted for these specific circumstances. Having only eight seats at each hibachi table results in a distinctive way of managing capacity and controlling costs.

Success therefore depends on the right fit between each of the strategic inputs and all of the operational key result areas. It follows that there are basically three main reasons why foodservice operations may perform badly. First, the overall design of the service package, the basic concept itself, may not work. Secondly, the operational systems put into operating the system may not be appropriate for the concept. Thirdly, management may not meet the standards of performance expected of them. In other words, no matter how good the management is, if the concept is inappropriate and/or the operating systems do not enable the manager to know what is happening and what to do about it, the business will fail. An example of a concept failing, rather than poor systems and poor management, has been Wendys in the UK. This is an extremely successful restaurant chain in the USA, clearly having good systems and management. When the first outlets in the UK were opened, they failed to achieve the sort of success expected of them, largely because the UK consumer did not understand the concept. It is difficult to identify examples of the second type of failure – poor systems – as people are naturally reluctant to give this as a reason for failure. Nonetheless, the widespread criticism received by certain sectors of the industry during the 1980s, notably school meals, hospitals and travel catering, suggests that they had inadequate systems for managing key result areas, especially those relating to costs, service and quality. Finally, poor management is often made the scapegoat for failure, even though the poor strategic planning and weak operating systems actually are the real reasons for this.

As Figure 1.2 explained, a foodservice operation is an open system; it adapts, develops and changes in response to feedback. The underlying causes of change are likely to be that the service package design no longer meets the needs of customers or achieves the objectives of stakeholders in the business. Such adaptation may affect many of the inputs of the operation – the customer base, menu, physical environment, prices and so on. In most cases, however much the operation changes and develops, it will continue to be of the same operational type that it started out as. To move from one type to another really means starting from scratch – reconsidering every single one of those strategic issues identified in Table 1.2. Very few operations have made such a transition. Wimpy in the UK have developed fast food restaurants, as well as continuing their table service operations, thereby moving from type 1A to type 1E. Increasingly, welfare foodservice operations are now a combination of 'food manufacturing systems' and 'food delivery systems' as they adopt centralized food production based around cook-chill technology. Otherwise, major sectors of the industry, and major organizations within it, continue to provide customers with their product/service within the same operational category as they have always done.

CONCLUSION

This chapter discusses four basic ideas that underpin this textbook. First, foodservice operations can best be understood by applying systems thinking and analysis. Key concepts of this approach are inputs, processes, outputs and feedback. Secondly, there are a number of different ways in which foodservice can be broken down into different operational types. The most recent classification suggests there are three main systems which break down into 11 kinds of operation. Thirdly, foodservice operations have to be planned and designed right in the first place. This requires an understanding of the key inputs of the foodservice system. Fourthly, by focusing on outputs or key result areas, *all* foodservice managers share common issues and problems. How they respond to these challenges varies according to the kind of operation they are managing.

The first part of this text examines key inputs from the strategic perspective. Before a foodservice operation begins to operate six major features have to be planned and designed. The *concept* has to be developed in response to customer demand and decisions made about where to locate the operation. The *menu* is planned and designed to match customer expectations and the physical concept. The *physical environment* is determined, with the dual objectives of appealing to the customer and ensuring operational effectiveness. *Staffing levels* are derived from estimates of demand, the conceptualization of the operation, and the physical layout and plant. *Service standards* are established. *Control systems* are adopted in order to ensure the operation meets financial objectives. And an approach to managing *quality* is agreed aimed at ensuring customer satisfaction. The successful operation is one in which all six of these features all fit one with the other – the total 'package' works. Industry examples of outstanding successes obviously spring to mind. Ray Kroc in setting up McDonald's put together a way of doing things that established the world's most successful foodservice chain. TGI Fridays, Pizza Hut and many other well-known restaurant chains have also demonstrated a high level of strategic success. Of course, one rarely hears about the failures! Operations where the menu did not quite fit with the decor; the control system was inadequate; the approach to quality left customers unhappy, tend to sink without trace. Unless, of course, such operations have to be provided for some reason, whereupon they just tend to gain a reputation for being poor. At some time or another catering in schools, in hospitals, on motorways, on ferries, in pubs have all come in for criticism, especially from the authors of good food guides. Today in many cases, foodservice operations of these kinds show the same level of strategic success that the restaurant sector has achieved.

But getting it right in the first place is not the end of the story, only the beginning. Foodservice operations also have to be managed effectively on a day-to-day basis. The second part of this book therefore looks at what managers can do to ensure success each and every day. It does so by looking at each of the key result areas shown in Figure 1.4. These are protecting assets; improving employee performance; managing capacity; improving productivity; engineering the menu; providing service excellence; improving profitability; and managing quality. And although this aspect of foodservice management may appear to be less exciting than strategic planning and design, it really is the most challenging. Making it happen each and every day requires insight, hard work, enthusiasm, dedication and downright determination.

In 1975, I opened my own restaurant in Brussels. Being only three years out of hotel school I did not know a lot about restaurant concept development, and the strategic decisions were made more by luck than judgment. Here is an extract from a review of that restaurant published on 21 October 1978 to give you a feel for the place.

As You Like It is a modest restaurant with scrubbed tables, attractive place settings bearing the Bard's likeness, and a friendly atmosphere. There is variety enough on the menu but, even better, the menu changes at the end of each month. Peter Jones believes that the English dishes need to be made and eaten the same day so he prefers to cook them daily. For that reason the dish of the day is usually British – fish and chips on Fridays. The chef is a Welsh girl with Jones filling in on her day off. Although the menu changes monthly, the food is basically the same – trout, scampi, steak, kidneys, pork chops, lamb cutlets – with the sauce being changed. In order to keep the prices down, Jones tends to buy fruit and vegetables which are in season.

At this time, in 1978, there were 30,000 British people living in Brussels, many not married, under 30 years of age and earning good salaries. The menu, atmosphere, location, style of service, all just fitted with what many of them were looking for. In other words the right strategic choices were made. The hard part was not thinking it up . . . the hard part was making it work for two and a half years. And to achieve that, all the authors in this book believe, understanding key result areas and managing them effectively is the best way to go about it.

REFERENCES

1. Jones, Peter (1988) 'Quality, capacity and productivity in service industries', *International Journal of Hospitality Management*, Vol. 7, No. 2, pp. 104–112.
2. Shostack, G. Lynn (1987) 'Service positioning through structural change', *Journal of Marketing*, Vol. 51, pp. 34– 43.
3. Murdick, R. G., Render, B. and Russell, R. S. (1993) *Service Operations Management*, Allyn & Bacon, Newton, Mass.
4. Merricks, Paul and Jones, Peter (1986) *The Management of Catering Operations*, Cassell, London.
5. Jones, Peter and Lockwood, Andrew (1989) *The Management of Hotel Operations*, Cassell, London.
6. Cutcliffe, G. (1971) *Analysing Catering Operations*, Edward Arnold, London.
7. Jones, Peter (1988) 'The impact of trends in service operations on food service delivery systems', *International Journal of Operations and Production Management*, Vol. 8, No. 7, pp. 23–30.
8. Pickworth, J. R. (1988) 'Service delivery systems in the foodservice industry', *International Journal of Hospitality Management*, Vol. 7, No. 1, pp. 43–62.
9. Jones, Peter, op. cit.
10. Escueta, E. S., Fielder, K. M. and Reisman, A. (1986) 'A new hospital foodservice classification system', *Foodservice Systems*, No. 4, pp. 107–116.
11. Huelin, Alan and Jones, Peter (1990) 'Thinking about catering systems', *International Journal of Operations and Production Management*, Vol 10, No. 8, pp. 42–52.
12. Cousins, J. and Foskett, D. (1989) 'Curriculum development for food production operations teaching for the hospitality industry: a systems framework', *International Journal of Operations and Production Management*, Vol. 9, No. 5 pp. 77–87.
13. Jones, Peter (1993) *A Taxonomy of Foodservice Operations*, 2nd Annual CHME Research Conference, Manchester, April.
14. Huelin, Alan and Jones, Peter (1990) 'Thinking about catering systems', *International Journal of Operations and Production Management*, Vol 10, No. 8, pp. 42–52.

15. Lockwood, Andrew and Jones, Peter (1991) *The Management of Hotel Operations*, Cassell, London.

16. Jones, Peter (1988) *Food Service Operations*, 2nd edition, Chapter 10, Cassell, London.

2

Market Research and Concept Development

Nigel Hemmington

INTRODUCTION

Today's international hospitality industry, including the foodservice industry, operates within an increasingly complex and competitive market environment.[1] In European and North American markets the industry exhibits a number of characteristics of a mature operating environment: falling industry profit margins; emphasis on service as a differentiating factor; emphasis on price, and discounting in particular; a shake-out of capacity, particularly in more traditional sectors of the industry; changing and increased variety of channels of distribution including franchising, consortia, affiliations; and increased international competition.[2] It is within this environment of increased competition that today's foodservice organizations have to operate. This has led to a widespread movement away from product-orientated, mass marketing strategies towards differentiation strategies where foodservice organizations are becoming increasingly precise in matching products to precise consumer demands. As Warren and Ostergren[3] observe: 'Marketing will be the key to success in the 90's. Lip service and slogans will no longer substitute for a real understanding of the market place. No longer can we merely respond to market demands. Instead, we must anticipate them by reading market conditions better and faster than before.'

Through differentiation strategies foodservice organizations seek to achieve competitive advantage by more closely matching products to specific market demands. In the process, organizations also seek to minimize the need for extensive promotional campaigns and remove the need for discounting as a method of product differentiation. There are two key aspects implicit in this move towards a differentiation strategy. First, organizations need to understand consumers both in terms of their needs and their purchasing/consumption behaviour, and secondly, products need to be tailored to meet the specific needs of identified sub-groups of the market. This chapter addresses both of these issues in terms of consumer behaviour, market research, market segmentation, concept development and location analysis.

DEFINITION OF THE CONSUMER

For the purposes of this chapter the consumer is defined as any person who uses, consumes or experiences the product or service regardless of who actually makes the purchase. Thus when a family go out for a meal, although one parent may pay for the meal, all members of the family are consumers. In the same way, employees who enjoy the benefits of a free staff restaurant service, or patients who receive hospital meals in a National Health Service hospital, although not paying directly for these services, are nevertheless consumers. People who actually pay for products and services are defined as customers as well as being consumers.

The highly competitive nature of the foodservice industry means that many meal operations are chasing the business of a limited number of customers, new operations are entering the market every week and less successful businesses are regularly going into receivership. Therefore the survival and growth of organizations depend upon a clear understanding of consumers – what they want, how they choose, how they are influenced in what they choose, what they would prefer if it were available. With this knowledge operators should then be able to make their products accurately match the requirements of their customers.

The need to take a consumer-led approach to business is not restricted to commercial foodservice organizations (i.e. those whose main concern is making a profit). Measures of the quality of service in many of the traditionally non-commercial sectors (now sometimes referred to as the cost sector) are increasingly becoming consumer based. Furthermore, many of the traditionally non-commercial areas of the foodservice industry, such as hospital catering and industrial catering, are becoming more consumer orientated with the introduction of competition through competitive tendering. Thus in the modern foodservice organization the consumer has become the focus of all planning and management decisions, from the first product idea through to delivery to the customer and further product development.[4]

It is interesting to consider how far consumer orientation is likely go when one considers that there are now markets where consumers, in the form of consumer interest groups, are taking a much more proactive and leading role in new product development. Auld and Soule[5] describe a particular case where a consumer interest group has played a key role in new product development in the home finance market. Another consumer group, CAMRA, has had considerable success in promoting real ale and influencing licensed trade operations. It seems likely that such consumer interest groups will develop in other sections of the foodservice market, particularly in areas such as school and hospital meal programmes. There could be significant advantages for providing organization as well as consumers since Auld *et al.* identify two important roles that consumer interest groups can fulfil: as a unified voice for consumers, and as a vehicle for the dissemination of information to consumers about products. Clearly such development may be of mutual benefit.

MODELS OF CONSUMER BEHAVIOUR

Although a relatively new subject, consumer behaviour has become an area of such importance, as described above, that it is now a rapidly developing field of study for both researchers and practising managers. It is also an area where the behavioural sciences (psychology, sociology, anthropology and particularly social psychology) have found an ideal practical application for many of their theories about the behaviour of people and groups. As a result, the analysis of consumer behaviour has been approached in a number of different ways depending upon the behavioural science adopted – e.g. psychology (individual), sociology (groups), economics (money) – and in some cases combinations of disciplines. If nothing else, this range of approaches reveals the importance of the study of consumers and indicates the complicated nature of human behaviour.

It is at least partly because of the complexity of consumer behaviour that the modelling approach has been widely adopted. Models are powerful tools in the description of complex systems, particularly in terms of the identification of variables and the analysis of relationships. Whilst they may take a number of forms (e.g. physical, algebraic) in the description of consumer behaviour, graphical models in the form of flowcharts are the most widely adopted. In terms of a simple classification, consumer behaviour models can be categorized as either monadic – based upon one discipline and therefore focusing on one particular facet of consumer behaviour (psychology, economics, etc.); or eclectic – drawing from a range of disciplines and attempting a more comprehensive description of consumer behaviour.

Monadic Models

The 'Black Box' approach, as illustrated in Figure 2.1, is perhaps the simplest attempt to explain consumer behaviour. It treats the consumer as a 'black box', making no attempt to consider the internal workings of the consumer (physiology or psychology) but rather focuses upon the relationship between inputs (stimulus) to the consumer and the outputs (responses) they produce. Taking a simple cause–effect approach it is possible to adjust input variables and observe the outputs that result from them. In this way it is possible to test, for example, hypotheses about the effect of specific marketing tactics on levels of sales or even micro-economic theories of supply and demand. The value of these models is in their simplicity and the fact that they are firmly based on identifiable and measurable variables. Because of this they avoid the tendency to become involved in the more esoteric and perhaps less operationally useful aspects of consumer behaviour. It is important to remember that at the end of the day organizations are concerned with the results of consumer behaviour rather than the detailed mechanics that lead to those results.

Decision process models look at consumer behaviour as a decision-making or problem-solving process. As such they describe the linear step-by-step stages that consumers go through in their route to purchase and consumption. An example of such a model is shown in Figure 2.2. This is discussed in more detail in terms of foodservice later. Sometimes, particularly when used for marketing purposes, these models are described in behavioural terms as follows:

$$\text{Attention} \rightarrow \text{Interest} \rightarrow \text{Desire} \rightarrow \text{Action} \quad \text{(AIDA)}$$

or:

$$\text{Cognition} \rightarrow \text{Affection} \rightarrow \text{Conation}$$

The decision process models are useful in marketing analysis and planning where an organization seeks to develop strategies appropriate for particular states on the

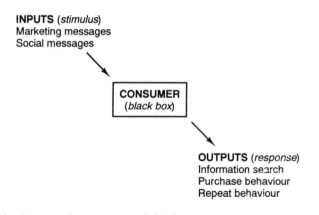

Figure 2.1 'Black box' approach to consumer behaviour.

attention-action continuum. Indeed Lavidge and Steiner[6] have devised just such a model which relates advertising tactics to the AIDA model.

Eclectic Models

Eclectic models attempt a more comprehensive description of consumer behaviour, including both personal and environmental variables, by drawing relevant features from a number of appropriate disciplines. The most significant models of this type are the Engel, Blackwell and Miniard Model; the Howard–Sheth Model; and the Nicosia Model. Whilst these models have the advantage of providing a more comprehensive view of consumer behaviour, they are also much more complex and perhaps overwhelming for the reader. To a certain extent this reduces a major advantage of the model-building approach in terms of simplification and clarification. They are nevertheless useful in market terms for their more complete consideration of the variables that affect the behaviour of consumers.

The Engel, Blackwell and Miniard Model[8] is built around the central concept of consumer behaviour as a decision-making process as follows:

need → recognition → search → alternative evaluation → purchase outcome

Around this core the model builds an internal cognitive continuum (exposure-retention), individual differences, environment influences and stimulus inputs (including marketing inputs). The Howard–Sheth Model[9] takes a similar approach, although it places a greater emphasis on the internal psychological workings of the consumer (perceptual and learning constructs) and takes stages in the AIDA continuum (attention–comprehension–attitude–intention–purchase in this case) as the outputs. The Nicosia Model[10] is different from others in its consideration of the relationship between the consumer and the organization (firm). This model recognizes that while the organization affects the consumer in terms of its marketing and promotional messages, the consumer exerts an influence on the organization in terms of purchasing behaviour. This relationship is particularly interesting in light of the trend towards consumer orientation where the influence of the consumer on organizations is becoming more significant, not just through purchase behaviour but also through market research.

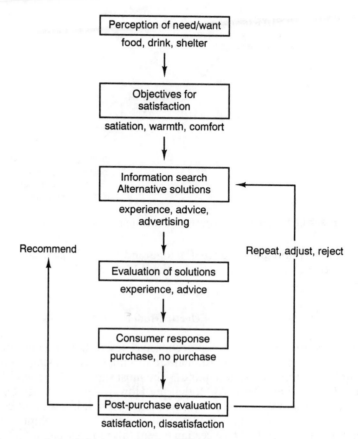

Figure 2.2   Consumer behaviour as a decision-making process.

Aspects of Consumer Behaviour Applied to Foodservice Products

In order to consider consumer behaviour as applied to foodservice products the consumer decision process model as shown in Figure 2.2 will be investigated more closely and will act as the framework for discussion. The starting point of any consumer behaviour process is the perception of a *need*. In terms of foodservice products these needs may be basic physiological needs for food or drink or, as is more likely in modern society, social and recreational needs – the desire to go out with friends, the need for leisure activity. It is common in fact for consumer behaviour to be stimulated by combinations of these needs. An example might be the hungry student who has a social need to dine with friends who may as a group choose to make the meal event a recreational experience at a themed restaurant such as TGI Friday's.

As identified by the model, need recognition will be determined by three things:

1. Memory or previous experience of the situation – many meal requirements are stimulated through routine (the fact that we always eat at particular times) rather than by true physiological needs.
2. Individual differences – psychological, physiological and lifestyle differences will all affect need recognition in terms of foodservices products.

3. Environmental influences – normative pressure of groups will affect need recognition as will social situations, so the need for a drink may be stimulated by particular social circumstances, for example.

Having perceived a need or needs, consumers will conduct an internal memory search to determine the level of previous experience and knowledge of the need situation. Previous experience will usually help determine the *objectives for satisfaction* and a range of available options. It is interesting to note that research by Bettmen and Whan Park[11] indicates that it is not the consumers with the least previous knowledge who do the most processing of available information but rather those with moderate knowledge. They conclude that it is likely that those with the least previous knowledge have insufficient product/market understanding to make sense of all the available data and that they 'give up and seek a simple solution'.

Consumers identify objectives for the satisfaction of needs, usually in very general terms and often subconsciously. In some cases satisfaction in terms of foodservice products will be measured simply in terms of the satiation of hunger and or thirst. It is more common, however, for what appear to be simple needs such as the satisfaction of hunger to be bound up with a complex collection of associated needs such as the need for a social experience, quality, value, hygienic environment, etc. The consumer will at this point informally assess the significance of the different aspects of this bundle of needs with the primary need clearly having overriding importance.

In low-involvement situations, such as the need for a snack on a journey, the internal *search* may be sufficient to make a decision without further action. In high-involvement situations, however, such as the choice of location for a wedding reception, an external search will usually be required. It is at this point that the consumer will be particularly receptive to advertising and promotional messages as well as opinion leadership and word of mouth. The external search will inevitably feed into the exposure-retention continuum at various points, contributing to memory and therefore future internal searches.

The fourth stage in the process is to *evaluate* alternative courses of action in terms of the consumer's perception of the extent to which the previously identified objectives will be satisfied by each course of action. The objectives themselves and perceptions of their likely satisfaction will be influenced by the individual's values, beliefs, attitudes and intentions. As discussed earlier, it is likely that consumers will have a bundle of needs or objectives that they would ideally like satisfied with some having greater importance than others. In most situations the satisfaction of all objectives is unlikely and consumers have to choose the option that they perceive to be the best fit. It appears that some form of compensation strategy is adopted where perceived weaknesses in one aspect are offset by strengths in others. This can be seen in foodservice, where consumers will travel considerable distances for what they perceive to be a high-quality meal (weakness in location offset by quality of meal) and where range of choice may be compromised for speed of service and convenience (such as in fast food).

At this stage a *purchase/consumption decision* will be made. The model appears to assume that purchase will result, but it should be remembered that one of the consumer's options is to choose not to purchase/consume. The outcome of the consumer's decision will be some degree of satisfaction or dissatisfaction depending upon the extent to which expectations have been met. These outcomes will then feed into the individual's attitudes and beliefs about the products, the supplying organization and the reliability of information/knowledge.

A key issue at the outcome stage of consumer behaviour is the concept of cognitive dissonance. Dissonance arises where information seems to conflict with the chosen course of action, i.e. created by information about the positive features of a rejected option or negative features of a chosen option. This creates discomfort which the consumer will seek to minimize through a change of decision, a change of attitude leading to different choices in the future, or focusing on the positive aspects of the chosen alternative whilst ignoring the positive aspects of rejected alternatives.

MARKET RESEARCH

By implication, the adoption of the consumer-orientated approach requires the flow of information between consumers and organizations. Market research is primarily concerned with the flow of information about consumers to the organization and may be defined as 'the disciplined collection and evaluation of specific data in order to help suppliers to understand their customers' needs better'[12] or, as the Market Research Society defines it, 'the means used by those who provide goods and services to keep themselves in touch with the needs and wants of those who buy and use goods and services'.[13]

Scope and Objectives

As defined above, market research underpins much of the decision making within organizations and should serve to mould the work of the foodservice organization, particularly in terms of products, to the requirements of the consumer. For it to be effective in this role, market research needs to be an ongoing monitoring process rather than an *ad hoc* occasional activity. This is recognized by many of the larger foodservice organizations, where the market research function has become part of a much wider integrated marketing and management information system.

The scope and associated objectives of market research are potentially wide and may, for instance, address the following areas:

- Market identification and measurement (demographics) – in terms of the total market and significant segments of the market; maturity of market.
- Analysis of market characteristics – consumer attitudes, activities and needs; consumer search and purchase behaviour; desirable product features; market trends.
- Analysis of the competitive environment – existing provision by market segment and geography; analysis of market share; competitor strengths and weaknesses.
- Critical success factors – key aspects in terms of production and delivery systems, support and associated services, costs and pricing.
- General market projections (up to five years) – underlying growth trends, including demographic forecasts; maturity of market and market provision; market share; consumer trends; product trends; environmental changes – political, economic, social and technological (PEST analysis).

Market Research Process

Whilst some market research data will be generated as part of the organization's wider management information system there is no doubt that there will still be a need for research which addresses specific market issues. Although such projects will all be different, a general research process for such projects can be identified, as in Figure 2.3. There are two generic classifications of data which may be collected in market research: primary data (field research), which are original data that have been generated specifically for the project by such methods as experimentation, observation or questionnaires; and secondary data (desk research), which are existing published data that may have relevance to the project in hand in terms of statistics or previous similar market research work. These sources of data should be seen as forming a hierarchy: internal secondary data are always researched first in order to establish the factors relevant to the research/problem environment. Where this initial research fails to reveal appropriate courses of action, external secondary data should be researched in order to establish whether the same, similar, or analogous market research problems have already been investigated. Again, where this process fails to reveal applicable courses of action, the final approach is to generate primary data through specifically designed market research. Whilst this hierarchical approach to data collection is logical in terms of research method, it is also the most cost-effective since primary research is invariably the most expensive and external secondary research is usually more expensive than internal secondary research.

Secondary Research Sources

Secondary research, or desk research as it is sometimes known, has the advantage of being economical, relatively fast and non-reactive in that it does not disturb or distort that which is being investigated. It is also extremely unlikely that there is no relevant information on a market research area, especially when underpinning theory and analogous situations in other markets or industries are investigated. Even where this secondary research fails to provide answers, it will almost certainly provide guidance on suitable approaches for subsequent primary research. It is essential therefore that the starting point of all market research should be secondary research even where it is the intention from the outset to conduct primary research.

The answers to some market research problems may be found within the files of the organization itself. Most organizations fail to make full use of data and information that is routinely collected, or fail to generate data that could be readily collected, because internal record systems have not been designed in a form that is useful for market research. As noted earlier, many of the larger and more sophisticated foodservice organizations have realized this and are now collecting market data as part of a wider management information system. This has been greatly facilitated by advances in information technology, particularly computer-based systems and electronic point-of-sale systems (EPOS). Foodservice organizations are now able to gather and manage large quantities of data on things such as: sales of meal items by number of units, by types of meal items (e.g. starters, main courses, sweets), by sales value, and even time/date of sale; long-term sales history and projections; customer origin and frequency of purchase (particularly for corporate customers where there are order and credit

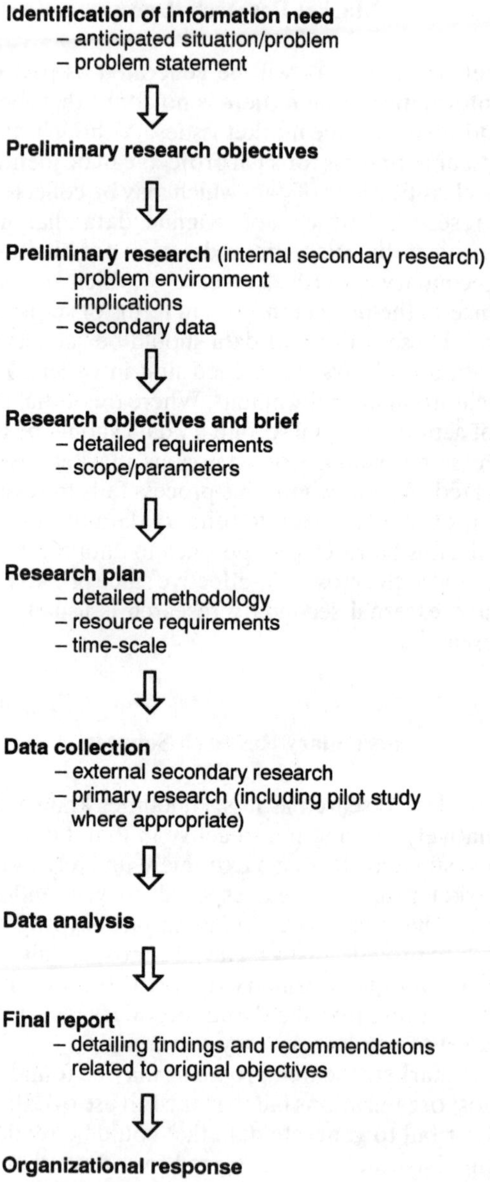

Identification of information need
  – anticipated situation/problem
  – problem statement

⇩

Preliminary research objectives

⇩

Preliminary research (internal secondary research)
  – problem environment
  – implications
  – secondary data

⇩

Research objectives and brief
  – detailed requirements
  – scope/parameters

⇩

Research plan
  – detailed methodology
  – resource requirements
  – time-scale

⇩

Data collection
  – external secondary research
  – primary research (including pilot study
    where appropriate)

⇩

Data analysis

⇩

Final report
  – detailing findings and recommendations
    related to original objectives

⇩

Organizational response

Figure 2.3 The market research process.

records); and advertising and promotional expenditure analysed by media, product type and market.

External sources include material published by government, trade and professional associations, market research companies, consultancy companies, stock market analysts, research organizations and educational institutions – to name a few. Indeed, there are so many sources of external secondary data that this chapter can only give some guidelines to indicate the sort of material that is available. There are a number of general guides which can be used to find sources relevant to particular subjects, such as *Where to Find Business Information* and *Compendium of Marketing Information Sources*. Databases, either 'online' (accessed via a personal computer and a modem link) or CD-ROM (Compact Disc Read-Only Memory), offer the benefits of searches through large quantities of data using keywords. Databases currently available include: *Profile* (full-text media articles from daily newspapers such as the *Financial Times*, *Daily Telegraph, Guardian, The Economist*); *ICC Viewdata* (company accounts) and the *1991 Census* (complete data from the 1991 census).

The government collects data through the Business Statistics Office and the Office of Population Censuses and Surveys which are brought together through the co-ordination of the Central Statistical Office. As an indication of what is available from different government publications *The Guide to Official Statistics* is invaluable whilst the booklet *Government Statistics: A Brief Guide to Sources* lists various ministries and departments, including telephone numbers, responsible for specific economic and social data. Some government publications commonly used in market research include *Annual Abstract of Statistics and the Monthly Digest of Statistics* (information on the economy, population and industrial output on a monthly and annual basis), *Economic Trends* (general economic background to markets) and *Social Trends* (demographics, spending, leisure trends, etc.).

Market research companies and stock market analysts produce and sell a wide range of market reports for general use. These reports are usually quite general because they are aimed at wide markets but they do provide good introductions and basic descriptions of markets and sectors. A full international listing of these reports in published in *Marketsearch/The International Directory of Published Market Research* with a brief description, price and contact details of the publisher. Organizations that publish reports on the hotel and catering industry, or specific sectors of it, include Key Note, Jordans, Euromonitor, Mintel and Retail Business (Economist Intelligence Unit). *ADMAP* is a monthly journal that provides information on advertising media with regular analyses of advertising expenditure by product and media; Media Expenditure Analysis (MEAL) also publishes detailed information on advertising expenditure on media by product and individual advertisers.

Trade and professional organizations often produce useful information in the form of yearbooks and directories and also occasionally commission market research reports. The Hotel, Catering and Institutional Management Association (HCIMA) provides a number of services for members including an annual directory which includes lists of organizations within the industry, a monthly journal called *Hospitality* and an extensive library from which it will carry out keyword searches. The European Caterers Association (ECA) and the British Institute of Innkeeping (BII) publish similar information with specific focus on the catering and licensed retailing industries. The British Hospitality Association (BHA) publishes an annual report which includes a statistical analysis of the hotel and catering industry and also commissions *ad hoc* surveys, such as the UK Contract Catering Survey 1993. The trade press, such as *Caterer and Hotelkeeper, Hospitality, Voice* and *Hotel and Restaurant*, is mainly useful for monitoring day-to-day changes in the industry. In addition, they often report on new research which through their identified sources may then be followed up.

Primary Research

Whilst the advantages of secondary data are the relatively low cost and speed of access, there are potential disadvantages in terms of how specifically such data address the issue – and therefore the extent to which they actually apply to the situation. Other possible disadvantages may include the fact that the data are also freely available to competitors and that they will have been gathered some time ago and therefore may be out of date. Primary data, although more expensive and time consuming, will provide exclusive information tailored to a particular issue. As such, primary data are usually concerned with the habits, attitudes and requirements of particular groups of consumers. It is not within the scope of this chapter to provide a detailed description of all aspects of primary research methodology: it will therefore concentrate on introducing the main techniques and principles of primary research as they apply to market research projects.

In all research it is essential that a logical method of enquiry is adopted in order to ensure the validity of the study. The testing stage, when the fieldwork is done, is also a key point when appropriate scientific method should be adopted. The key features of scientific method are that changes in only one independent variable should be tested at a time (price for example); the dependent variable (number of customers per shop) should be measured before and after the change in price; a control group (another restaurant) which is not exposed to the changes in price should also be tested to ensure that any changes in the number of customers in the test restaurant are in fact due to the change price and not some other extraneous factor (e.g. general changes in demand).

The three main methods of gathering primary data are experimentation, observation and surveys (questionnaires, interviews, etc.). *Experimental research* is firmly based in scientific methodology where phenomena are exposed to controlled changes and the observed differences before and after are measured. This method was developed in the physical sciences and is most appropriate in areas where all variables can be controlled. In behavioural sciences like market research, however, it is virtually impossible to control all variables and therefore experimentation is less widely used. Nevertheless, there are situations, particularly when market-testing products, where experiments are used; the example of price changes and demand discussed above is one such example.

Observation as a research technique is useful in determining and measuring behaviour such as pedestrian traffic flows and restaurant location, customer flow patterns in foodservice operations and meal consumption behaviour (e.g. plate waste). The advantage of this approach is that it is firmly based on actual behaviour and can be used where there is likelihood that customers will not accurately remember their behaviour or may be too embarrassed to answer questions. The major problem with this technique is that the observation itself may actually distort behaviour; but hidden observation involves moral questions in terms of the invasion of privacy, Christenson[14] reports a study where periscopes were used in a public lavatory! Indeed, the Market Research Society Code of Practice actually states that people may only be observed where they would expect to be observed.

Survey techniques are certainly the most common way of generating primary data in market research and are particularly useful in investigating consumers' knowledge, beliefs, attitudes and preferences. All surveys are based upon some form of questionnaire as the mechanism for generating data, although the questionnaire may be administered in a number of ways including face-to-face interviews, over the telephone, or by post. The data produced through surveys may be either qualitative or quantitative. Qualitative research is exploratory, creative and diagnostic in that it seeks to identify variables associated with issues, e.g. consumer attitudes. As such it can provide the information, particularly the precoded responses to questions, that forms the basis of a structured, quantitative questionnaire. To encourage the generative process, qualitative research tends to be relatively unstructured in order to allow the free expression of views and ideas. The techniques used to generate qualitative data include in-depth interviews, group discussions, and indirect projective techniques such as sentence completion and ambiguous pictures.

Quantitative research seeks to assign values or numbers to variables and thereby quantify their significance. In order to do this, quantitative research tends to be highly structured with a clear sequence of questions most of which will have precoded responses. Because of this structured nature it is essential that appropriate precoded responses for the questions are identified. Quantitative research should therefore always be preceded by qualitative research which identifies the variables that are appropriate for the particular sample being investigated. The techniques used to generate quantitative data are invariably based upon questionnaires, which again may be administered in personal interview or telephone interview, or by post.

Personal interviewing offers a number of particular benefits in market research. It ensures that the right number and type of respondents are sampled; it allows for a more dynamic interaction with respondents which helps where shown material is necessary and can help where sensitive issues need to be drawn out; and it ensures the quality of the data in terms of the level of respondent understanding and full response to all questions. There are, however, potential disadvantages particularly in terms of the cost of interviewer time, the danger of interviewer bias and potential reluctance of respondents to discuss sensitive issues.[15] The costs of travel and time make personal interviewing expensive, and by the mid-1970s it seemed logical to use telephone interviews. There was a problem, however, in that telephone ownership was concentrated in the more affluent parts of society, which made telephone interviews unsuitable for most forms of social research until the late 1980s and early 1990s – by 1990 domestic telephone penetration approached 90 per cent.[16] At about the same time, Computer Assisted Telephone Interviewing (CATI) developed, and further increased the popularity of this approach to the extent that by 1990 telephone interviewing had overtaken personal interviewing.[17] The advantages of telephone interviewing are similar to personal interviewing although the costs are significantly less. There are still potential problems of sample bias, however, and there are suggestions that respondents rapidly tire of telephone-administered questionnaires.[18]

Postal (self-completion) surveys have the major advantage of relative low cost, particularly in terms of time; they also have the potential to cover geographically dispersed populations, and there are no problems of interviewer bias. The major problem, however, is one of low response rates, typical 40 to 69 per cent but sometimes as low as 20 per cent,[19] which may lead to non-response bias. The key issue, therefore, in the design of postal surveys is how to elicit the maximum level of response from the sample. Features such as an appropriate covering letter, incentives (e.g. discount vouchers for meals), return envelopes, questionnaire design (short and simple to complete) and follow-up letters are all used in attempts to maximize response rates. The highest level of response occurs where recipients have an established relationship with the sending organization. Many foodservice organizations have seen the advantage of collecting the names and addresses of customers and developing brand loyalty through special offer coupons and other meal offers. The market research potential of such specific sampling frames is considerable, although their inherent bias should also be remembered.

Sampling

In market research it is rarely practical, in terms of cost or time, to conduct a complete enumeration (or census) of the survey population. Because of this, a sample of the population is selected to give representative and unbiased data about the population. The aim is to ensure that the results of the survey should be as close as possible to those that would have been obtained had the whole population been surveyed. In practice, all samples over- or underestimate true population values to varying degrees. A good sample design, however, should enable inferences to be made about the population with acceptable margins of error, known as the sampling error. The magnitude of the sampling error is determined by the size of the sample and the sample design.

The size of a sample depends upon the nature of the population, levels of non-response, the type of information required and the cost. Where populations are relatively homogeneous it is possible to use smaller samples, but where they are heterogeneous larger samples will be necessary to cover the range of attributes. Non-response should also be allowed for in that the sample should be sufficiently large to accommodate the expected non-response rate.

Analysis of sub-groups of the sample requires that the sample is of such a size that it ensures that the smallest sub-group will be adequately represented for meaningful analysis. The degree of accuracy required in the results can also be used to determine sample size; in general, the larger the sample the greater the precision. Where random sampling is used, it is possible to calculate the size of the sample necessary to give the required level of accuracy. It should be remembered, however, that in order to double the precision of sample survey estimates, sample size has to be increased four times. The law of diminishing returns applies and it soon becomes too expensive for minimal improvements in precision. It is thus important to decide on the balance between the sample size, and therefore cost, and acceptable levels of accuracy. There are a number of methods of sampling suitable for market research. These are fully discussed by Buttle.[20]

Simple random sampling is where n samples are selected from the population (N) with each having an equal chance of selection. This is normally done by numbering the sample population from 1 to N and then drawing n random numbers for 1 to N from random numbers tables. These numbers are then those selected from the sample. *Systematic random sampling* is used where a large population is to be covered. To select a sample of n items it is necessary to calculate the sampling interval k by:

$$k = \frac{\text{population size } (N)}{\text{sample size } (n)}$$

A random number is then taken between 1 and k and every k'th item is selected through the sampling list $n - 1$ times.

Where populations have characteristics which may be used to improve the sample design (e.g. gender, age), *stratified sampling* should be used. In proportionate stratified sampling, the population is divided into groups, or strata, and random samples are selected from each. Where it is known that the strata in the population are unequal in size, these inequalities may be built into the sample through disproportionate stratified sampling where more items are selected from large strata and fewer from small strata. In this way the sample should more accurately reflect the characteristics of the population. Where samples are to be taken from very large populations it is often the case that geographical groupings can be identified (e.g. counties, local authorities). In order to avoid the selection of a dispersed sample, which would be expensive to survey, *multi-stage sampling* can be adopted where a first-stage random sample of the groups can be made and further stages added as required. Stratification may be used at each stage to ensure adequate coverage. *Quota sampling* is another approach where the sample is specifically designed to reflect known characteristics of the population (usually gender, age, social strata). This is achieved through the use of interviewers who are given specific numbers (quota) of interviews to carry out within each identified group. This method ensures that particular sample characteristics are guaranteed without the risk of possible distortions associated with non-response in stratified samples.

Market Research into Consumer Attitudes

Attitudes may be defined as the individual's 'covert feelings of favourability, or unfavourability, toward an object, person, issue, or behaviour'.[21] As such they are unidimensional and represent only the affective (like/dislike) psychological constructs of the individual, beliefs representing the cognitive (knowledge) constructs, and behaviour representing the conative (action) constructs. This unidimensional view of attitudes, beliefs and behaviour has important marketing implications since it implies a causal flow of the type:

$$\text{Beliefs} \rightarrow \text{Attitudes} \rightarrow \text{Intention} \rightarrow \text{Behaviour}$$

In this view beliefs contribute to the formation of attitudes, whilst intentions are the immediate consequences of those attitudes. Behaviour, as the result of intention, is one step removed from attitude. In consumer behaviour terms this implies that where a consumer learns something new about a product which forms a belief, this belief will give rise to an attitude which will in turn give rise to a predisposition to act in terms of purchase/consumption.

From the above it is easy to see how theorists and practitioners have been excited by the possibilities of using attitudes to explain and predict consumer behaviour. The nature of the attitude–behaviour relationship has, however, been the subject of some debate, particularly since the work of a number of researchers seemed to cast doubt on the existence of any direct relationship at all.[22] Early pessimism about the predictive validity of attitude has recently given way to a view that there may be a strong attitude–behaviour relationship where respondents have direct experience of the behavioural object, where appropriate measures of attitude are used (specifically attitudes to performing the behaviour in question rather than attitudes to the behavioural object itself), and where large research samples are used. It would seem therefore that attitude measurement could be an extremely valuable technique in market research supporting many phases of marketing decision making. As Lutz states, 'Marketers who understand that causal [attitude–behaviour] sequence, and who use it in decision making, have a powerful ally in their battle for superiority in the market place.'

Attitude-based techniques have only rarely been used in the investigation of foodservice consumers. Law *et al.* have investigated the attitudes of high school students to school lunches using attitude statements,[23] whilst Carlisle *et al.* have looked at the connotative meanings of food for high school children in Alabama.[24] Likert-based scaling techniques have been used in a number of studies. Hemmington, Kipps and Thompson developed a Likert scale in their investigation of the attitudes of London schoolchildren to school feeding[25] which was further developed by Hemmington and Chapman in a study of the attitudes of parents and schoolchildren to school meals in Gloucestershire.[26] The study of school meals in Gloucestershire is particularly interesting because it was specifically commissioned as market research to support marketing planning within the school meals service. The results of the research identified a number of specific issues that were important to parents and children as consumers (e.g. healthy eating, social role of school meals, dining environment). These issues were addressed by the service in a number of operational and marketing strategies which, despite a price increase at the time, resulted in an increased uptake of school meals of 5 per cent. This represented an increase of some 3,750 meals per day.

MARKET SEGMENTATION

It is increasingly being recognized that there is no such thing as *the* customer. Whilst the 1960s and 1970s were typified by mass production and volume sales, the 1990s consumer is more sophisticated and individualistic. 'Today's search is for something special, something different, something which reinforces the buyer's own sense of identity as a person, an individual, as someone separate from the herd.[27] The total population is therefore made up of people with a wide range of different characteristics. So most, if not all, foodservice concepts are aimed at a specific kind of people or 'market segment'.

Such segments may be identifiable on the basis of demographics, socio-economic background, life-style, purchase behaviour, or some other measurable characteristic, as illustrated in Figure 2.4. Basic demographic variables that may be taken into account when defining a segment may include age, sex, race, religion and family size. One particular, now somewhat outdated, approach to segmentation is the concept of socio-economic group that divides the population into six categories on the basis of their social class and occupational status. More complex classification systems include sub-dividing the total population on the basis of the development of the family status or family life-cycle, and commercially developed segmentation approaches such as ACORN and SAGACITY. ACORN stands for 'A classification of residential neighbourhoods' and has been used by some restaurant chains, such as Berni Inns.[28] On the other hand, SAGACITY identifies a four-stage family life-cycle, sub-divided into further categories on the basis of income and socio-economic class (white collar and blue collar). Life-style segmentation is also known as psychographics, and focuses on the activities, interests and opinions of customers. It is expensive to establish segments on this basis as it requires a large-scale research survey for each category of product or service. One way to avoid the research cost is to assume that group membership may have the necessary life-style to match the product. For instance, holders of American Express or Diners Club cards may be targeted by specific types of foodservice operator. Finally, segmentation can be based on the benefits the consumer perceives as receiving from the product or service they purchase. This emphasizes a key aspect of segmentation, namely that the market segments itself – it is not the marketer or foodservice organizations that does so.

Geographic
Region	Continent, country, county.
Location	Transportation network, retail areas, leisure facilities, etc.
Population density	Urban, suburban, rural.
Climate	Tropical, Mediterranean, temperate, etc.

Demographic
Age	Under 5, 5–11, 12–18, 19–34, 35–49, 50–64, 64+.
Sex	Female, male.
Family life-cycle	Young single; Young, married, no children; Young, single, children under 6; Young, married, children under 6; Young, married, children 6 or over; Older, married with children; Older, married, children left home; Older, married, retired; solitary survivor.
Income	Annual income under £5,000; £5,000-10,000; £10,000-15,000; etc.
Occupation	Professional; Managers, technical, proprietors; junior managers, sales, clerical; skilled manual/craft; manual, operative; retired; students; unemployed; etc.
Education	Type of school, highest qualification, etc.
Race/nationality	British, North American, Asian, Afro-Caribbean, etc.

Geodemographic
Combinations of geographic (neighbourhood) and demographic variables – classifications include: ACORN,
PiN,
Super Profiles,
MOSAIC,
DEFINE.

Psychographic
Social class	Registrar-General's social classification Jicnar's social classification
Life-style	'Environmentally concerned', 'health orientated', 'style conscious' etc.
Personality	Gregarious, introspective, authoritarian impulsive, ambitious, etc.

Behavioural
Benefits sought	Qualtiy, variety, economy, service, social interaction
Use frequency	Never, rarely, occasional, frequent, heavy
Occasions	Functional, regular, special (celebration), 'distress purchase'
AIDA	Attention – Interest – Desire – Action
Attitudes	Enthusiastic, positive, indifferent, negative, hostile.
Values	Diet, health, vegetarian, vegan, 'living lightly', quality, economy

Figure 2.4 Segmentation variables for foodservice markets.
After Kotler (1988)[28].

Once the approach to segmentation is decided on, it is necessary to investigate the segments further. Market segments can be tested in a number of ways in order to establish some key characteristics:

- Is the market homogeneous? Will everyone in the segment behave in the same way and respond in a uniform manner?
- Is the market identifiable? Can the segment be identified in terms of its size, location, and specific characteristics?
- Is the segment accessible? Is it possible to reach consumers in this market through relevant means of communication?
- Is the segment substantial? Will the total sales and projected profit margin provide an effective return on the investment – both the investment in the new concept and the marketing of it?
- Is the segment recognized by the consumers themselves? Although psychographics or benefit analysis may identify a clear segment, if customers themselves do not wish to be associated with this grouping, they may reject the new product or service rather than publicly acknowledge their group membership.

CONCEPT DEVELOPMENT

Levels of competition in the foodservice industry mean that, in order to remain competitive, organizations must pursue ongoing concepts and product development programmes. Any existing product portfolio is vulnerable to the effects of change, particularly as products move through their product life-cycles, but also as a result of changing consumer needs, changes in the competitive environment and new technological developments. The development of new concepts is therefore fundamental to the continuing health of foodservice organizations. It should nevertheless be remembered that the development of new concepts and products is fraught with risk and that the failure rate of new products is disturbingly high.[28] It is interesting to note Johnson and Scholes' observation[29] that the most successful organizations following product development strategies appear to succeed because of their general management approach rather than particular product development activities. They identify the following features that characterize these successful organizations, they are more market focused; they concentrate on developing products that build on core organizational skills; they are good at selling ideas internally; and they involve cross-disciplinary teams (including customers and suppliers) in new developments.

Concept development in foodservice may be categorized as follows:

- New concepts – concepts that create a complete new market, e.g. delivered meals, Benihana.
- New market concepts – new concepts that enter an established market, e.g. new fast-food concepts such as waffles.
- Modified concepts – existing concepts adjusted to provide greater consumer satisfaction, may include further market segmentation, e.g. Deep Pan Pizza Co.
- Repositioned concepts – existing concepts, perhaps modified, targeted at new market segments, e.g. sushi bars from Japan to USA to Europe, fast-food operations into schools and hospitals.

- Extended concepts – existing concepts which are modified, or extended, to appeal to wider market segments, e.g. McDonald's addition of chicken and fish items, to its menus.

Organizations usually adopt combinations of the above with specific approaches largely determined by organizational strategy and policy. Whilst the development of completely new concepts offers the potential for the greatest rewards it is also the strategy with highest risk of failure; and whilst modification, repositioning or extending concepts have lower associated risks, they are also likely to have a lower reward potential. Clearly, foodservice organizations have to consider the balance of such factors in determining the strategy they adopt in the development of their product portfolio. Although there are a number of approaches to concept development, as outlined above, it is still possible to identify a generic concept development process as illustrated in Figure 2.5.

Foodservice Design Specification

Having analysed the market and identified a suitable segment with reasonably homogeneous needs, information on consumer needs, wants and drives is used to develop the design specification. This document describes in detail all the significant parameters that the foodservice concept must satisfy. It should be noted, however, that it describes what the organization is trying to achieve in terms of the satisfaction of consumer needs; it does not describe the final concept. In addition to consumer-based parameters, the design specification will also include aspects relating to the organization's requirements in terms of mission (the sort of business it sees itself in), strategy (how it intends to develop that business) and policy (the general guidelines for operation that it sets for itself), and it is also likely that it will include external considerations such as competition and legislation. Hollins and Hollins[30] provide an exhaustive list of elements that may be considered in the development of a design specification for services.

In terms of foodservice design the key elements of a specification would include:

- Product characteristics – usually expressed in terms of consumer demands rather than actual product characteristics themselves, e.g. functional/experiential, variety/focused, active/passive, bright/subdued, loud/quiet, fast/relaxed, public/intimate, etc. These demands are subsequently interpreted into product characteristics through the concept development process;
- Price – related to customer acceptability and commercial viability;
- Level of consumer participation – particularly in terms of service delivery, related to consumer perceptions of price/service ratio;
- Location – related to access by and to the market segment;
- Availability – in terms of time, related to consumer demand.

The importance of the design specification to the final success of new products is illustrated by research[31] which indicates that market success, measured in terms of market share, is directly related to the length of the specification from which it was designed. This is almost certainly because the elements of the design specification in effect form the objectives of the concept development process. Clearly the better and more precise the objectives, the more likely it is that they will be achieved.

Market research
–definition of market segment in terms
of geography, demographics and
needs/drives

⇩

Design specification
– detailed requirements to which concept
must conform including locational
requirements

⇩

Concept development
– interpretation of specification into
foodservice concept, creativity

⇩

Concept specification
– development of detailed specifications for
concept including menu, service, theme
and operational methods

⇩

Concept testing
– trials and experiments to test and refine
concept specification incl. scaling up

⇩

Marketing and operational strategy
– in light of specifications, development
and testing

⇩

Market testing
– market acceptability, sales forecasts,
advertising and promotion campaign

⇩

Implementation
⇩

Monitoring, evaluation and review
– position analysis

Figure 2.5   Foodservice concept development.

Concept Development

The development of foodservice concepts must be constrained by market needs as
defined by the design specification. A number of key consumer requirements for the
concept having been determined, the satisfaction of these requirements through
features designed into the foodservice concept becomes the objective of the concept
development process. The aim is to design what people want without restricting ideas

about the different ways in which this might be achieved. It is at this stage of the process that creativity can play a critical role in the development of new concepts. Indeed creativity is actually encouraged by using consumer needs as the starting point for idea generation, rather than jumping straight to traditional solutions or existing product interpretations of demand. With foodservice systems there are a number of ways in which particular consumer needs can be met and by using consumer needs as the starting point a full range of these options can be considered, often for application in situations where they have not been considered before.

When a number of ideas have been generated, the next stage in the concept development process involves the assessment of the ideas and the selection of the most suitable for further development. Clearly the idea of assessing concepts is to spot the poor ideas and drop them so that efforts can be focused on the idea, or ideas, that seem to be the best. This is not easy, and there are many examples of organizations that have developed the wrong idea: the Sinclair C5, or the BBC's Eldorado, for example! The usual method of assessing concepts is to rate them all against a number of criteria, particularly those contained within the design specification. Kotler suggests a product screening approach which looks at the product idea, the target market, competition, market size, development time and costs, production costs, rate of return and match with company objectives and resources. Hollins and Hollins have developed a 'concept assessment matrix' specifically for service concepts. This approach focuses on five stages:

- Safety and legislative requirements – this is an area of particular relevance to foodservice and any concept that has any potential safety or legislative problems will need to be eliminated or redesigned to remove them.
- Strategic requirements – concepts rated according to the match between the concept and organizational strategy, objectives and resources.
- Market requirements – concepts rated against the key market requirements as identified by the design specification.
- Combination – whilst one concept will probably look the best at this point, others will have good points that could be built into the chosen concept.
- Specification – finally concepts will be rated against the detailed design specification.

Foodservice Concept Specification

As a result of the assessment process a suitable concept should have been identified for further development. The organization should now have a clear idea of this concept and it should be possible to generate a detailed concept specification. Unlike the design specification, which was expressed in terms of consumer needs, the concept specification is expressed in terms of the product and its features which are the organization's interpretations of consumer needs.

Kotler suggests that a product is made up of a core conception, tangible conceptions and augmented conceptions. In the foodservice industry the core product is either the satisfaction of hunger, or the opportunity to socialize, or both. It is these two 'benefits' that a customer receives. The tangible product is the translation of the concept into its physical form. In the fast food sector, BurgerKing has six different restaurant designs available for franchise, from a mobile unit up to a major high street location. Finally, the augmented product is all those elements of the product which make it complete, many of which are intangible. On the basis of this, it is possible to identify a wide range of different types of foodservice operation, each with their own unique set of core, tangible and augmented product elements. Such operations differ in terms of location (which we shall discuss shortly), menu type (see Chapter 3), layout and design (see Chapter 4), service style, service level (See Chapter 7), and degree of specialisation. When all of these criteria are taken into account, there are many more foodservice types than the 11 identified in Chapter 1. This is because marketing, as well as technological, criteria are now being taken into account. The result is that there is a foodservice concept or operation for every possible context. Whilst foodservice concept specifications will include descriptive information on the product (menu, price list, theme, design, location), they will also include process details relating to the total service delivery system from resourcing to methods of production to foodservice and customer care. This will in effect be the first draft of a total operations manual and will form the basis of the concept testing stage.

Concept and Market Testing

The detailed concept specification forms the basis of further development through the testing of prototypes of the foodservice concept. This involves testing all parts of the total concept and will usually be carried out in an incremental way with small components, such as specific meal items and design ideas, being tested initially. Meal items should at this point be tested by trained food tasters to ensure that taste characteristics are as determined in the specifications. As components are tested and the specifications confirmed they will be put together so that eventually it is possible to test the complete concept as a whole. In this way the ideas and specifications are tested and refined into a coherent and practical foodservice concept.

Once a full concept prototype has been developed a consumer test can be conducted with a representative sample of the target market. Consumer reaction to the concept must be closely monitored, preferably using a range of techniques to elicit as much market information as possible. Discreet observation of behaviour is essential and should be backed up with more overt interview and questionnaire techniques such as word association, rating scales and quality rankings. It is essential that at this point both the concept and the market are as close as possible to the anticipated real-life situation since it is on the basis of this test that decisions about full market testing of the concept will be made. In the case of smaller foodservice organizations the concept would probably go from this stage to full implementation. With larger organizations, where the concept is being developed for multiple outlets, further market testing is usually undertaken.

Market testing involves the launch of the concept in a limited number of outlets, thereby simulating on a small scale the full-scale launch. The purpose of market testing is to gauge how consumers react to the actual concept under real-life market conditions and how large the market is likely to be, specifically in terms of the numbers who try the concept, the numbers of repeat consumers and the numbers who develop some form of brand loyalty. Market testing is also particularly useful in determining the effectiveness of advertising and promotional strategies. This is the ultimate way of testing foodservice concepts and should provide the closest and most accurate evaluation of the concept related to its market.

Despite the potential advantages of market testing, there is some scepticism about its true value, particularly in terms of the impossibility of controlling variables and therefore attributing results. There are also concerns about the costs of market testing, but these are largely erroneous since successful concepts should not lead to losses and unsuccessful ones are far less costly than failure in a full concept launch.

FOODSERVICE LOCATIONS

The location decision is critical to the success of foodservice operations, not just in terms of the consumer, but also because a mistake in the choice of location is almost impossible to correct. Whilst other aspects of the product such as meal items, decor or promotion can be relatively easily adjusted or even changed, once a location has been developed the organization is either stuck with it or will have to bear the substantial costs of withdrawal. Since location is an integral part of the total foodservice concept, location criteria should be identified in the concept specification. The location decision is based on an analysis of the number of people belonging to a specific market segment, or market segments, in the vicinity of the potential site. Factors are taken into account that identify the market structure and 'trade area' or catchment area. The market structure refers to how the population in terms of market segments is spread over a location, for it is extremely unlikely that any location will be occupied by a single market segment whilst the trade area identifies how this population is liable to behave, based on factors that assist or prevent usage of the potential foodservice outlet.

Market Structure

Market structure is made up a number of characteristics comprising the population density; the population mix in terms of demographics such as age, gender and ethnic background; economic characteristics including range and nature of employment, wage levels and unemployment; and other factors that influence development. There are three basic levels of population density: urban, suburban and non-urban. However, since foodservice outlets do not necessarily depend on people who live in the area, but may serve people who work in the area or are passing through, just knowing the population density has some limitations. For instance, the City of London supports a large number of outlets even though very few people live in the City. As a result most of these outlets close after 8.00 pm at night and do not open at weekends. Likewise, some motorway service restaurants are surrounded by areas of extremely low population density, but nonetheless have very high levels of usage. As well as knowing the total population it is necessary to understand the mix of the population in order to establish how many people in the target market segment live in the area. Certain locations are known to have population mixes that are untypical of the population as a whole. For instance, the proportion of older, retired people is greater than elsewhere in towns on the south coast of England such as Eastbourne and Bournemouth, or in states in the USA such as Florida. The same potential imbalance of local populations is true of socio-economic groupings, ethnic origin, and other consumer characteristics. The importance of demographic analysis is that it helps to establish both the potential aggregate demand and the social behaviour of consumers, and hence their eating-out habits.

Such demographic imbalance may be partly related to the local economy and infrastructure of a region. Historically, the nature of local industry was often based on the availability of raw materials. Mining is based around coal deposits, steel making near iron ore, textiles near ports, and so on. As economies develop and global trade expands, there can be major shifts leading to significant changes. Such changes can partly be managed by government intervention through setting up assisted area status, or free trade ports, and so on. The economic profile of a location influences social behaviour, but in addition levels of disposable income and hence spending patterns. It is not enough to have sufficient numbers of consumers with an inclination to eat out; the economy has to provide them with enough disposable income to allow them to do so. This simple message certainly struck home to restaurateurs during the early 1990s in the UK, as the economy entered a period of extended recession.

Trade Area

As well as market structure, location analysis also takes into account the potential trade area. A typical benchmark for this has been a radius of three miles around a fast food outlet in the USA, and five miles for a restaurant.[32] However, drawing a circle around a potential site is not sophisticated enough to establish the true area from which most customers will be attracted. For instance, none of the consumers in a Little Chef or Happy Eater are likely to live within five miles of the outlet, whilst many customers using the 'local' will live within walking distance of the pub. The trade area will be affected by the topography or 'lie of the land', layout of road networks, psychological barriers, infrastructure, employment concentrations and level of competition. The geography of an area can either help or hinder the movement of people. Rivers, hills and mountains create barriers, whereas valleys and relatively flat land facilitate movement. In many cases, the regional transportation network reflects this natural topography. However, roads and railways may not only enable movement, but also hinder it by in themselves creating barriers. As well as by physical barriers, consumers may also be influenced in their movements by psychological barriers. For instance, they may be reluctant to travel to or through areas where the population is different to themselves.

There are essentially two methods of quantifying the trade area, the empirical approach and gravitational theory. The empirical approach involves observational methods such as identifying natural boundaries such as rivers and 'consumer spotting' where the origin of consumers is plotted on an area map. Gravitational theory is based upon Reilly's law, which relates the frequency with which residents will trade in specific areas to the population size of the area and their distance from the area. This can be used to identify breaking points between areas and therefore the boundaries of the catchment area. In addition to analysing the raw potential of an area, it is also important to analyse competition and the extent to which the needs of the target market are already being catered for by existing operations. An index of saturation can be calculated to compare the potential of different areas in terms of the total market value and the level of competition as follows:

$$\text{Index of saturation} = \frac{\text{customers in area} \times \text{expenditure per person}}{\text{restaurant space allocated to product in area}}$$

Types of Location

Melaniphy analyses a number of locations, both for fast food outlets and for restaurants in the USA, each with their own specific characteristics. For instance, the market structure of a major suburban restaurant will largely be made up of managers and residents, with 40 to 55 years being the dominant age category; whereas an ethnic suburban restaurant will tend to attract local residents with an average age of around 30 years old. Trade area also varies for each type of location. For cxample, a downtown fast food outlet will have a trade area of one to two blocks from which over 80 per cent of its custom will come, compared with a highway interchange location which will draw over 40 per cent of its customer from outside a ten-mile radius. For the former outlet, traffic flow would comprise only pedestrians; for the latter at least 15,000 cars per day. Twelve generic types of foodservice location can be identified as follows:

- Transportation nodes – airports, railway, stations, ports.
- On-board transportation – rail, aircraft, ferries, ships.
- Town/city centre – town centre locations usually associated with traditional high street retailing.
- Roads – motorway services, roadside facilities, out-of-town road links.
- Retail/shopping centres – shopping centres, arcades, malls, out-of-town retail areas.
- Leisure facilities – theme parks, leisure centres, sports clubs, health clubs, parks.
- Tourist attractions and resorts – unique destinations, heritage sites.
- Education – schools, colleges, universities.
- Health care – hospitals, nursing homes, day centres.
- Hotels – hostels, guest houses, inns, hotels, country house hotels.
- Industrial/commercial areas – industrial parks, central business districts, technology parks, in-house company locations.
- Residential areas – small local retail areas, traditionally dominated by licensed retail operations such as public houses and social clubs.

The above is not an exhaustive list of potential locations and certainly with the growth of foodservice into more specialized areas such as oil rigs, more specialized locations will evolve often with their own specific characteristics. It is also interesting to note that there is a direct consumer – location relationship, and for some market segments this relationship is so close that there is virtually no location decision to be made, e.g. hospitals, schools, transportation.

SITE SELECTION

Once an area has been selected as a suitable location for a foodservice outlet, the specific site for the operation needs to be selected. Methods of site selection have evolved from traditional judgemental methods to far more scientific methods based upon quantitative statistical approaches.[33] This has been facilitated by greater experience of site selection which enables the site attributes of similar successful foodservice operations to be identified. These attributes can then be used as the criteria for the selection of new sites. Conversely it is also important to analyse the reasons for the poor performance of less successful or failed sites. In general the more sites analysed and the greater the database, the more reliable the model is likely to be. Larger foodservice organizations have a clear advantage in terms of access of data from many outlets.

Melaniphy identifies 16 different kinds of site based on US practice. In the UK some similar types of site are identifiable. For instance, in the USA, many foodservice operators believed that McDonald's site selection criteria were so good that rather than conduct detailed feasibility studies themselves, they simply selected sites adjacent to this market leader. In the UK anecdotal evidence suggests that fast food operators seek high street locations close to Marks & Spencer outlets. Locational characteristics for other kinds of restaurants are less clear cut. In the USA, cities and even quite small towns are typically laid out in a grid pattern with clearly defined business, shopping and residential areas. British cities have evolved over long periods of time with their street patterns influenced by factors such as the extent and nature of bombing during the Second World War, and streets in the centre of small towns have remained unchanged for centuries. Thus for a significant number of public houses, their location has remain unchanged for at least a hundred years.

The selection of a specific site, especially for outlets depending on motorized custom, depends upon understanding key criteria such as traffic flows, traffic counts, visibility, access, utilities, competition and consumer behaviour. In considering traffic patterns account may need to be taken of the road width, number of lanes, speed limits, parking restrictions, intersections and permitted turns, carriageway barriers and traffic lights. All of these will affect both the volume of traffic and how this varies during the day. However, a site also needs to have access from the traffic flow and visibility so that passers-by are able to see the outlet in time to make a decision. Sites on corners or brows of hills are therefore rarely suitable. Even then errors can be made. A senior executive with 30 years of experience in the UK roadside dining market was responsible for opening two new outlets in 1991. One was on a site adjacent to a roundabout with one of the highest traffic counts of any site, the other on a major road in East Anglia had one of the lowest. The operating performance of the former is significantly worse than the latter because a high proportion of its passing traffic is travelling less than two miles. The East Anglian restaurant has a passing trade of consumers travelling long distances and is ideally located to cause them to stop for a break.

CONCLUSION

In any competitive activity such as the foodservice industry, those who succeed are likely to be those who are able to most clearly define the objectives for success. They are the ones who can then focus all their organizational efforts on the achievement of those clearly defined goals whilst at the same time avoiding expending resources on less fundamental activities. In all commercial activity it has become clear that the essential goal for success is consumer satisfaction. It is no longer sufficient to create products in the hope that they will sell through traditional marketing/selling techniques. In almost all areas of business there are many operators competing for a limited number of sales and indeed it is now common for supply in many markets to exceed demand. In these situations customers will be able to choose those products that most closely meet their needs.

Thus, operations that are able to provide consumers most closely with what they want and are able to make them aware of it will be the ones that benefit from repeat custom and the free publicity that comes from the recommendations of satisfied consumers. They are the ones to which custom will come readily and which will have less dependency upon expensive marketing and promotional campaigns. They will also be the ones that do not need to become involved in discounting activities, already identified as a characteristic of mature or saturated markets, to promote sales. Thus, those businesses that are able to define clearly the needs of the consumers whom they intend to satisfy will have a distinctive competitive advantage over their rivals.

Understanding the market segment or segments helps ensure that all aspects of the foodservice product fit the customers it serves. For many years, the licensed house sector of the industry failed to see young people, under the age of 18 years, as a potential market. Unlike the rest of Europe, UK licensing law prohibited the sale of alcohol to under-18s, and under-14s were not permitted to use licensed premises. As a result few, if any, facilities were made available to encourage families to frequent pubs. However, during the 1980s, enlightened licensees recognized the potential of this market; and many pubs now provide play areas, children's rooms, lounges and other facilities aimed at attracting parents with children. In the 1990s, many of the large brewery chains are developing their outlets to conform to product and price specifications aimed at specific market segments – such as the 'disco pub' aimed at 18- to 25-year-olds. Fifield believes 'customers are only too happy to tell us where they are, what they want now and what they might want in the future. The only thing an organization needs is someone there to hear.'

REFERENCES

1. Crawford-Welch, S. (1992) 'Competitive marketing strategies in the international hospitality industry', in Teare, R and Olsen, M., *International Hospitality Management; Corporate Strategy in Practice*, Pitman, London, pp. 95–109.

2. Crawford-Welch, S. (1991) 'Marketing hospitality into the 21st Century', *International Journal of Contemporary Hospitality Management*, Vol. 3 No. 3 pp. 21–27.

3. Warren, P and Ostergren, N. W. (1990) 'Marketing your hotel; challenges of the '90s', *Cornell Hotel and Restaurant Quarterly*.

4. Townley, R. R. (1989) 'New products needed by the foodservice industry: a survey of important trends critical for the development of new products for today's demanding foodservice consumer', *Journal of Foodservice Systems*, Vol. 5, pp. 113–124.

5. Auld, J. W. and Soule, D. J. (1992) 'The role of a consumer interest group in new product development; a case study of Canadians for home equity conversion', *Journal of Consumer Studies and Home Economics*, Vol 16, pp. 331–343.

6. Lavidge, R. J. and Steiner, G. A. (1961) 'A model for predictive measurement of advertising effectiveness', *Journal of Marketing*, Vol. 25, pp. 59–62.

7. Fishbein, M. (1967) 'Attitude and prediction of behaviour', in Fishbein, M., *Attitude Theory and Measurement*, Wiley, Chichester.

8. Engel, J. F., Blackwell, R. D. and Miniard, P. W. (1990) *Consumer Behaviour*, Dryden, Hinsdale, Ill.

9. Howard, J. A. and Sheth, J. N. (1969) *The Theory of Buyer Behaviour*, Wiley, Chichester.

10. Nicosia, F. L., (1966) *Consumer Decision Processes*, Prentice-Hall, Englewood Cliffs, NJ.

11. Bettmen, J. R. and Whan Park, C. (1991) 'Effects of prior knowledge and experience and phase of the choice process on consumer decision processes; a protocol analysis', in Kassarjian, H. H. and Robertson, T. S., *Perspectives in Consumer Behaviour*, Prentice-Hall, Englewood Cliffs, NJ, pp. 182–202.

12. Chisnall, P. M. (1992) *Marketing Research*, McGraw-Hill, New York, p. 6.

13. The Market Research Society (1984) quoted by Cowell, D., *The Marketing of Services*, Butterworth-Heinemann, p. 81.

14. Christenson, L. B. (1988) *Experimental Methodology*, Allyn & Bacon, Newton, Mass.

15. Robertson, E. (1990) 'Face-to-face Interviewing', in Birn, R., Hague, P. and Vangelder, P., *A Handbook of Market Research Techniques*, Kogan Page, London, pp. 129–146.

16. Weitz, J. (1990) 'Telephone Interviewing', in Birn, R., Hague, P. and Vangelder, P. (eds), *A Handbook of Market Research Techniques*, Kogan Page, London, pp. 147–163.

17. Ibid., p. 149.

18. Cox, R. and Brittain, P. (1988) *Retail Management*, Pitman, London, p. 41.

19. Wood, L. and Mouncey, P. (1990) 'Postal Research', in Birn, R., Hague, P. and Vangelder, P. (eds), *A Handbook of Market Research Techniques*, Kogan Page, London, pp. 170.

20. Buttle, F. (1987) *Hotel and Food Service Marketing*, Cassell, London, pp. 58–60.

21. Lutz, R. J. 'The role of attitude theory in marketing', in Kassarjian, H. H. and Robertson, T. S., *Perspectives in Consumer Behaviour*, Prentice-Hall, Englewood Cliffs, NJ, p. 319.

22. Borgida, E. and Campbell, B. (1982) 'Belief relevance and attitude – behaviour consistency; the moderating role of personal experience', *Journal of Personality and Social Psychology*, Vol. 42 No. 2, pp. 239–247.

23. Law, H. M., Lewis, H. F., Grant, V. C. and Bacheman, D. S. (1972) 'Sophomore high school students' attitudes towards school lunch', *Journal of the American Dietetic Association*, Vol. 60, pp. 38–41.

24. Carlisle, J. C., Bass, M. A. and Owsley, B. W. (1980) 'Food preferences and connotative meaning of foods of Alabama teenagers', *School Food Service Review*, Vol. 4, No. 1, pp. 19–26.

25. Hemmington, N. R., Kipps, M. and Thomson, J. (1984) *The School Meals Service in the Inner London Education Authority*, University of Surrey, Guildford.

26. Hemmington, N. R. and Chapman F. (1992) 'Planning for change in a regional school meals service: an attitudinal assessment', in Teare, R., *Managing Projects in Hospitality Organizations*, Cassell, London, pp. 33–76.

27. Fifield, P. (1993) 'Market segmentation' in *Standpoint*, Winchester Consulting Group.

28. Kotler, P. (1988) *Marketing Management: Analysis, Planning, Implementation and Control*, Prentice-Hall, Englewood Cliffs, NJ.

29. Johnson, G. and Scholes, K. (1993) *Exploring Corporate Strategy*, Prentice-Hall, Englewood Cliffs, NJ.

30. Hollins, G. and Hollins, B. (1991) *Total Design: Managing the Design Process in the Service Sector*, Pitman.

31. Hollins, G. and Hollins, B., op. cit.

32. Melaniphy, J. C., (1992) *Restaurant and Fast Food Site Selection*, John Wiley.

33. Thompson, J. S. (1980) 'Site location research for fast food restaurants', *Journal of Foodservice Systems*, Vol. 1, pp. 115–126.

3

Planning and Designing the Menu

Sean Mooney

INTRODUCTION

The word 'menu' has two quite separate meanings. It can mean the product range that a foodservice outlet offers; or the piece of literature or display used to communicate the product range to the customer. In this chapter, we look at how the menu in its first sense, as a product range, is *planned*; and how the menu in its second sense, a card or display, is *designed*. The chapter begins by examining the overall role the menu plays in the achievement of planned outcomes, especially customer satisfaction and operating targets. It then goes on to consider the various factors that should be taken into account at the early stages of the menu planning process. The critical factors involved in the design production of printed and other forms of menus are then examined, with consideration being given to the need for variety, creativity and flexibility in menus. The chapter ends with a review of some key issues relating to menu planning and design: the cost of the menu; ethical concerns; and the need to monitor and evaluate menu performance.

A menu can be presented in print or formats such as boards and backlit boxes. It is an extremely important marketing tool as it facilitates the process of communication between foodservice operator and the customer. It is essentially a list or a representation of what the customer is being offered. In reality, more often than not, the menu also serves as a limit on what a foodservice operation is willing and able to prepare and serve. It may also dictate the talents of the production and service personnel, as well as determine the space and equipment requirements of an operation. Nonetheless, the principal role of the menu is as a marketing tool. A well-designed and well-produced menu contributes to foodservice management's chances of success. It is, after all, the only piece of print advertising that the customer will almost certainly read when using the operation.

All sectors of the foodservice industry operate in an increasingly complex business environment, therefore a planned and structured approach to menu planning and design is essential. Even small independently owner-managed operations, to compete and thrive, should adopt a professional approach to menu planning. Management time and effort need to be invested wisely in this aspect of the research and development process to ensure that new and emerging market segments are developed and that the menu's position at the centre of the foodservice marketing efforts are fruitful.

THE ROLE OF THE MENU

Since the menu is at the heart of the foodservice operation's marketing activities it must not only complement an operation's other marketing activities but be designed with its own marketing objectives clearly specified. The major objectives associated with effective menus are commonly regarded as fourfold.

First, the menu must be co-ordinated with and seek to further the goals of the marketing concept. As discussed in the previous chapter, this means that the foodservice operation selects its market position as its response to its understanding of the needs, desires and behavioural characteristics of its targeted customers. If market needs are correctly analysed, financial success will naturally result. Conversely if customers are not being satisfied, business volumes will suffer and failure will be the inevitable result. Market research, conducted in-house or externally, over regular periods will provide strong, though not infallible, indication of customers' needs, wants and perceptions. The menu therefore must be designed to appeal to its target audience(s) and also blend with the operation's overall trading format, customer services, and communications policies. Miller[1] suggests that menu and marketing strategies are closely aligned to the Maslow hierarchy of needs behavioural model. This model suggests that at one end of the hierarchy there are individuals who have a want for food, and their selection and purchase motivation will be to obtain food and/or beverage to satisfy hunger and/or thirst. At the opposite end of the hierarchy is the individual who has very complex needs for menu items, method of preparation, presentation and environment for dining satisfaction. This model helps in understanding the vast range of dining concepts and aligning them to the needs of the market place. Some of the 11 operational types identified in Chapter 1 tend to satisfy the first kind of customer, notably cafeterias and fast food operations; the more sophisticated consumer will seek out full-service restaurants or the Benihana concept.

Secondly, the menu should act as a means to influence customer demand for menu items. The menu planner can influence customer demand using a variety of tactics such as the menu item descriptions, position of items on the menu, clip-ons and creative artwork. Popular or profitable items can be highlighted or given more prominent positioning to draw customers' attention to them. This attempt at influencing menu outcomes is a part and parcel of the foodservice manager's armoury. The menu should strive not only to maximize sales overall, but also to increase the sales of higher-profit items in order to increase overall profitability. This is explained in further detail in Chapter 13, which discusses the concept of menu engineering.

Thirdly, the menu should contribute to the establishment and maintenance of a positive perceived image of the foodservice operation. Image is a particularly important aspect of the restaurant's micro-environment. The menu, along with aspects such as ambiance, interior design, in-house facilities and personnel, has a contribution to make. The menu is often the initial communication vehicle the customer encounters on entering an operation. So it is important that the mechanics of the communication process are understood by the planner in order that the customer receives a clear, unambiguous message. This message should be derived from the corporate direction currently being followed by the foodservice operator and be in harmony with all strategic activities, particularly marketing. The menu's role in the formation of an enduring corporate communications strategy is critical.

Fourthly, the menu is a conduit for gaining competitive advantage through branding of products. Many successful foodservice operations have menu items for which they are noted. Examples are easily recognized amongst the major players in the fast food sector, such as McDonald's and BurgerKing, where signature items such as the Big Mac and the Whopper are promoted heavily to create a distinct competitive advantage. The general principles underlying signature items, or branded products, can be effectively used by operators in most sectors to enhance the perceived image of their products and create a distinct competitive advantage for their operations. For example, Gardner Merchant, the UK's leading contract caterer, has a branded range of sandwiches using the title 'The Signature Series'.

Additionally the menu should be used to increase repeat visits and purchases. This can be best achieved by including items that have consistently proven to be popular. It is also important to refresh and revitalize the menu to avoid so-called menu fatigue, customer boredom with menu items, and enable the operation to continue to attract new customers. To do this effectively requires, at both the strategic and tactical level of operations, the setting up of an integrated customer profile database to identify trends that are pertinent to the operation and then the menu to be altered to take advantage of these changing consumer tastes. The database should include, as appropriate, demographic, socio-economic, socio-cultural and purchase behaviour information. Whilst this may sound rather complicated and time-consuming for the smaller operator, especially when compared to what the very large operators invest in their databases, it is not that difficult. The real strength and advantage to the operator is in the discipline which the process imposes by ensuring the adoption of a proactive approach to the management of the operation.

TYPE OF MENU

There is an extensive range of menu types found in the foodservice industry. Basically, however, the menu continues to be a list of dishes, sometimes grouped together into a number of separate courses. The classical menu framework, illustrated in Figure 3.1, remains a useful reference point from which to commence the study of menus and their construction. This proposes a sequence of 13 courses. Before the development of cafeteria service, the advent of fast food, and evolution of theme restaurants, there were basically three kinds of menu. The restaurant à la carte menu provided a wide range of individually priced dishes, usually cooked to order, within the classical framework. The table d'hôte menu, on the other hand, had a set price for the meal, and was usually three or four courses, often of dishes made for that meal service. The third menu type is the banquet menu, planned in advance for an agreed number of people. In multi-faceted operations, such as hotels, more than one kind of menu will be adopted. In other situations, for example the provision of meals in the workplace, the range of main course dishes offered on a daily basis is fairly restricted, and variety is achieved by the use of cyclical menus.

During the twentieth century, the classical menu framework has evolved considerably. The foodservice industry has developed a myriad of differing concepts where

1. Cold hors d'oeuvre   8. Sherbet

2. Soup   9. Roast and salad

3. Hot hors d'oeuvre   10. Vegetables

4. Fish   11. Sweet dish

5. Main course   12. Savoury

6. Hot entrée   13. Dessert

7. Cold entrée

Figure 3.1 The classical menu framework.
Source: Eugen Pauli (1979) *Classical Cooking the Modern Way*.

many of the principles and rules underpinning the traditional menu formats have been significantly adapted or dispensed with. Modern menus are generally much simpler than the à la carte menu format and with fewer menu selections, but their origins clearly stem from the classical framework. Figure 3.2 breaks down menu items into the generic categories more representative of foodservice operations today. There appears to be an increasing trend in some sectors of the foodservice industry away from the logical sequence of dishes illustrated above to a style which is more eclectic. For example, TGI Friday's menus are organized on a wide range of food categories starting with nachos, soups, salads, entrées, desserts, combination dishes, Friday's Lite, sandwiches, pasta and pizza, steak and ribs, chicken, seafood, beverages, and desserts. Whether this trend will confine itself to the heavily branded, informal concept is difficult to predict. What is clear, however, is that whatever type of menu format is utilized it must communicate a clear selling message to the customer and provide food service management with the means to do this in a flexible and cost-effective manner.

FOOD	BEVERAGES
Starters/Appetizers	Non-alcoholic
Main course	Cockails
Vegetables and salads	Beers
Desserts/sweets	Wines
Speciality items	After-dinner drinks

Figure 3.2 Potential menu item categories.

INFLUENCES ON MENU PLANNING

This section identifies those factors that foodservice management need to consider during the early stages of the menu planning process and discusses their relative importance within the context of the market. Perhaps the most obvious factor is the customer. To be successful a menu must always aim to satisfy the customer; therefore the foodservice operations manager must fully understand consumer behaviour to ensure that the menu product/service offering is what is wanted by the targeted customer group.

Customer service needs to be viewed as an integral component of the menu planning process. Arnold *et al.*[2] have suggested that there are two aspects of service to be considered in relation to the securing of competitive advantage; those of a qualifying service and those of a determining service. A qualifying service is a service that an operator must offer simply to qualify for customer consideration. This may be because it is very important to customers or because most competitors offer the service and customers consider it to be the norm, as for example accepting payment via credit cards. A determining service is a service that actually determines customers' restaurant preferences and choice. A restaurant with a unique product or product range may have many of the features of all restaurants, but be selected because of its unique determining feature. In the case of menus, menu items may have a similar role. Some will be 'qualifying dishes', placed on the menu because they are expected to be there; whereas others will be 'determining dishes', providing something unique and of appeal to customers.

Once the targeted customer group's desires are determined, a further consideration is the range, availability and cost of the required food and beverage ingredients that will make up the assortment of products that are to be offered. Many items are seasonal, and some items may be difficult to obtain in a fresh or other state at a reasonable price over a stable time period. Consistent and reliable sources of supply must be located. For most operators this is a major task of strategic significance and is discussed in Chapter 7 (page 114). Clearly the sourcing and the purchasing of commodities has an important impact on the menu planning process.

Distinctive competences, such as the skills and expertise of production and service employees, must also be considered. However good the planning of the menu, if employees are not able to prepare meals to the specified standard, the operation will not be successful. For example, if new menu items are being introduced, the existing employees' talents and skills, necessary to prepare, present and serve each item, need to be reviewed and retraining provided if necessary. For many years, hotels in particular have served menu items from a range of different international cuisines or carried out promotional themed events. For these non-traditional dishes, many kitchens employ chefs from the Far East in order to ensure the authenticity of the food.

The layout and the design of the whole foodservice operation also need to be examined. The kitchen and dispense area are of particular importance. A detailed analysis of both capacity and capability is necessary. For example, all the necessary equipment must be available to produce the full menu. Significant changes to menus may even require modifications to the layout of the kitchen and service areas. However, the more specialized the concept and dedicated the system, the more difficult it is to adapt. Hamburger chains which, in response to changing consumer tastes, have experimented with diversifying their product range, have found if difficult to do so owing to layout and equipment constraints.

The menu should be planned to appeal to all of the five senses. In attempting to do this, the menu planner has to ensure that no one method of cooking dominates. Food's characteristics, including its sensory properties, play an important role in its acceptance by customers. With food in particular, every item listed should be contrasted with every other item using each of the senses to determine suitability for selection to the menu. There should be variety with regards to taste – variations of flavours and preparation styles; sight – contrast of colours and shapes; smell – aromas; feel – contrast of consistencies and textures; and hearing – selling the 'wow' factor as with a sizzling steak or a popping champagne cork. Trends such as the growing demand for spicier foods have to be monitored and if need be incorporated on to the menu. In devising new menus for in-flight meals, airline caterers go to extensive lengths to research menu items as the olfactory and sensory characteristics of food and drink change in a pressurized aircraft in flight.

Finally the menu should provide customers with the opportunity to select a nutritionally balanced meal. Some foodservice operations have a greater obligation than others to satisfy the nutritional needs of their customers, for instance in hospitals and schools. As the nutritional quality of food becomes a more important issue for customers generally, foodservice operators cannot afford to ignore this aspect of the menu planning process, particularly at the initial stages of menu development as it will perhaps save a lot of criticism and concern at a later stage. A case in point is the growing debate in the UK and elsewhere in the developed world concerning the lack of availability in schools of properly balanced meals. Cooper[3] revealed the details of recent research findings in America which suggest that poor diets are placing many children at great risk in later life from diseases such as cancer, heart problems, osteoporosis and obesity. The causes of this apparent neglect are complex and have built up over a number of decades. They are reflected in some instances by the changing life-styles of parents and the difficult choices faced by school governing bodies in determining priorities when allocating scarce resources.

MENU DEVELOPMENT

Traditional menus are planned on the basis of clearly established principles using the established framework of courses and repertoire of dishes available within each category. These principles remain hardly changed since the days of the great Escoffier, who worked at the Ritz in London during the 1880s. However, as we identified above, there are many sectors of the industry, focused at specific market segments, that have invented their own style of menu. The apparent simplicity of some of their menu offerings can be deceiving as they are, especially in the case of the mature and successful brands, highly engineered and complex products.

Feltenstein[4] and Khan[5] discuss at length the process of developing and bringing on to the market new restaurant concepts and new menu items. These processes have been adapted from other areas of commercial activity and their main significance is that they are structured and bring with them the imposition of what is a highly disciplined set of routines. A typical approach is illustrated in Figure 3.3. This type of disciplined approach is being utilized more frequently by foodservice management in many sectors of the industry. It is not only necessary where major sums of capital are being invested in the research and development process, but also in the smallest operation as the margins between success and failure narrow.

Once a framework is established the foodservice manager can begin the process of selecting potential menu items for each of the menu's categories. Sources of information are numerous and varied. The most commonly utilized sources are trade journals, cookery books, the operator's own experience, and understanding of existing and potential customer bases. When sufficient items are collected, these can be ranked

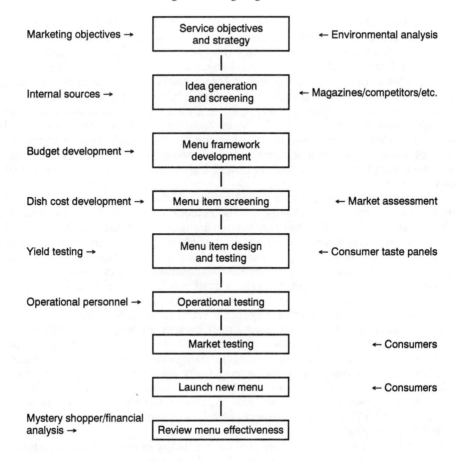

Marketing objectives → | Service objectives and strategy | ← Environmental analysis

Internal sources → | Idea generation and screening | ← Magazines/competitors/etc.

Budget development → | Menu framework development

Dish cost development → | Menu item screening | ← Market assessment

Yield testing → | Menu item design and testing | ← Consumer taste panels

Operational personnel → | Operational testing

Market testing | ← Consumers

Launch new menu | ← Consumers

Mystery shopper/financial analysis → | Review menu effectiveness

Figure 3.3 Model of new menu development.

against set criteria such as customer popularity and profitability. Feltenstein recommends the use of a task force approach to this part of the process. This process of ranking, which should include both quantitative and qualitative analysis, will eliminate those items which do not satisfy the foodservice operation's objectives. Menu items can then be developed. This involves recipe formulation, operational specification and testing, preliminary market testing and ultimately the planning of the marketing and roll-out campaign.

Other factors which also need to be considered in the overall process are the key trends which are taking place in the market generally, as these are often indicators of what will be demanded in each specific operation. Information on trends can be obtained from a combination of specific market research data such as Keynote and Mintel reports, census data, an on-going objective analysis of customers, and the local competitive environment. Increased demand toward more healthful food, 'grazing' or snacking, and so on, are examples of trends which foodservice operators are required to take on board and to evaluate in terms of the impact to their operations. Other trends to consider, some of which may be structural, might include those which allow for regional differences and uniqueness.

The complexity of this process can be illustrated by examining one of the UK's most successful restaurant chains. Exchange restaurants were the first American themed restaurant chain to establish a presence outside London. Each unit is named after an individual American city or state. Exchanges are geared up for families and large parties, which many operators in the mid-scale market recognize as that which offers the greatest potential for growth in the future. One-fifth of Exchange customers are children and a special children's menu, Diner Saurs, has been designed and developed with this market segment in mind. The menu offers a wide selection of dishes, 16 of which are from the main menu and cater for the most sophisticated of tastes. The concept's market positioning strategy does, however, have a considerable degree of flexibility built into it, to ensure that other important target markets are not driven away.

All promotional activities are planned and co-ordinated from the centre. Promotions are planned to coincide with holidays and celebrations in the USA. For example, a recent 'Savour the South' national campaign featured Cajun dishes with discount offers on particular menu items. The menu framework is eclectic, with a choice of over a hundred dishes. The main emphasis is on Tex-Mex and Cajun type food, with a number of items having a high degree of theatre purposefully built into them to add to the degree of variety and excitement of the overall product service offering.

Menus are changed three times every two years, depending upon market trends. Customers are very much part of the process as formal and informal customer feedback is elicited on a systematic basis. Sales are rigorously analysed and suppliers are also involved to find out what is new and selling well. Trends such as the move towards increased preference of chicken over beef; changes in the way people eat, with more emphasis on 'grazing'; the growing popularity amongst customers for sharing a selection of dishes in the centre of the table, rather than ordering three formal courses; the demand for spicier food; a gradual increase in the size of parties; these are all influences which Exchanges have recognized and incorporated into their menus and operating strategies.

New dishes are given a thorough trial period before being launched throughout the chain. Initial testing takes place in four of the chain's units to gather customer reaction. New items which show the necessary potential are further tested and revised before being included on the chain's menu. Dishes not selling are removed and replaced at regular intervals and items which require adjustments are modified.

Its menus are also clearly an integral part of their customer communications strategy. They play a key role in the concept's overall visual merchandising appeal. They reinforce the concept's market positioning statement, arouse interest and move the customer towards purchase and communicate a co-ordinated offer to the target customer group effectively. The next section looks at effective communication through the menu in more detail.

DESIGNING THE MENU

Design is a concept which is difficult to define. Dawson[6] suggests that design involves creativity, seeks to optimize profitability and consumer satisfaction, is ubiquitous in a corporate environment, and comprises elements of performance, quality, durability, appearance and costs. This provides the menu designer with a very useful working definition from which to start. If the menu is designed badly it can damage a business as surely as the steepest recession. But such design is not easy, especially when one considers the short time during which menus are usually read. And yet, the menu, like most forms of advertising, is expected to perform a variety of functions such as informing, entertaining, persuading, reminding, complementing, reassuring, reinforcing, and attempting to add value to the overall product/service offering by changing attitudes to it.

The overriding objective of a well-designed menu is to ensure that what is presented to customers is clear and makes it easy for them to decide what they want to eat and drink. Whilst there are no hard and fast rules governing what constitutes a good menu there are a number of good design principles to follow. At the beginning it is necessary to consider the image the menu is supposed to portray. This should be in keeping with the rest of the concept. If an outlet has an image of fun and informality, then it is unlikely that a formal, upmarket, conservatively styled menu will work. The design of the menu cover in particular plays a major part in getting the perceived image across.

The range of written information on menus will normally include the name of the operation, the title ('menu' or 'wine list'), opening hours, a welcome, specific order instructions, as well as the menu items and their descriptions. For example, every Brewers Fayre menu gives the customer 'how to order' directions because of its very individual service delivery system. Also included may be statements related to an operation's customer quality policy, pricing policy, and payment policy. The information about prices in particular must be accurate in order to comply with the Trades Description Act. Registered trade marks and logo will normally be included where applicable, as may phone and fax numbers.

Clearly there is a complex message here to be communicated. The desired effect can usually be achieved by the correct use of graphics to create perceptions of the restaurant, as well as to manipulate customers' buying decisions. Effects such as underlining, boxing, shading or circling particular menu items draw attention to specific items, as indeed can lengthening the description or enlarging type size. Adequate spacing between menu items is necessary to avoid the feeling of clutter. Menu copy that is surrounded by a white background will emphasize the black print and make the menu easier to read. Varying the type size will also enhance the overall appeal of the menu. The print font used should be easily distinguished and read by the customer. The food items that are listed on the menu should be organized in a logical sequence so that the customer can determine rapidly and easily what is on offer. The menu has to be given some symmetry and form. It should look balanced to the eye. This can be achieved by using different sized print and by grouping the categorized menu items together.

Inserts or clip-ons listing daily specials are a good merchandising tactic and are commonly used throughout the foodservice industry usually to accentuate specific high-profit items. Sales generated from high-profit daily specials listed on an insert can often form a major part of food turnover. Inserts can be remarkably easy to produce. They can be printed in-house with the help of a computer and good-quality laser printer to give a high degree of consistency in terms of appearance. They can also be handwritten and if done so creatively can be most effective, especially where individuality is seen as being a desirable feature of the restaurant. Ideally, where inserts are in use they are probably better presented on the same quality of paper as the menu itself. In some situations it may be possible to get away with running them off on a less costly paper or card. Inserts can also be used to create a perception of variety and change, which many customers seem to expect from restaurants today. Simple devices like dating the insert

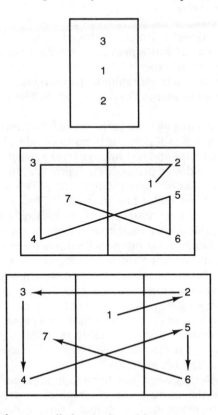

Figure 3.4 Gaze motion theory applied to 1-, 2- and 3-page menus.

or printing the day of the week on it give customers the impression that something different or out of the ordinary is on offer. This tactic also helps create the sense that the food is fresh and bought in the market that day.

There are other ways to guide customers toward higher-profit items. The location of specific items is a critical aspect of using the menu as a profit tool. It is known, for example, that the human eye tends to read a menu in a predictable pattern. What catches the eye last and what the eye's attention is subconsciously directed to remain uppermost in the customer's mind. These ideas are known as 'gaze motion theory'. This theory, when applied to the printed menu, suggests that there is a hot spot where the eye falls first. When higher-profit items are prominently featured in this hot spot, their sales will increase. What is also implicit in all of this is that each positional slot on the menu has differing degrees of 'heat'. The menu designer must therefore analyse and grade all the space on the menu and allocate menu items accordingly. It is important to ensure that the popularity of certain menu items and the profitability of others remain balanced, otherwise customers may react unfavourably. Gaze motion theory is illustrated in Figure 3.4 illustrating how the typical menu is scanned. On the classic magazine-style or two fold menu, the prominent space is on the upper right-hand side. On the three and single page menus, the hot spot is in the centre of the menu. If there are items that are popular but are less profitable then the lower left hand side of the menu is the place to position them.

Whilst the principles of gaze motion theory appear to be extensively utilized, they are by no means suitable for all contexts. Menus that have an extensive array of items spread over several pages present some problems in that positional bias may not be so easily ascertained. TGI Friday's menu runs to eight pages and is organized by food category. Whilst gaze motion rules could be applied to the individual pages, it is likely some of the impact of positioning of the higher profit items in the dominant spaces is negated due to the length of the menu. In smaller, upmarket operations the opposite might apply. For example, there is a trend toward so-called 'free form' restaurants where the menu is arranged in what is a seemingly haphazard fashion in order to create the perception of variety. The idea is similar to the 'mix and match' concept, where the customer apparently chooses at random until the whole meal comes together. It thus gives customers the impression that they have more to choose from and are more in charge of their own buying decisions.

The organization of the menu by category and the strategic positioning of items within categories, assisted by illustration and symbols, is not the only way to influence the customer choice. Language also has an important role to play. The primary function of the copy used on the menu is that of all forms of communication: it must ensure that it is meaningful, familiar and attractive to the targeted audience. The menu designer attempts to move customers, like any advertiser does, through a persuasive sequence of attention, interest, desire and action, or AIDA. Assisted, as indicated above, by the subtle use of graphics, artwork and so on, the menu writer needs to give considerable attention to the style and content of the menu copy. With menu copy, there now appears to be a movement away from the use of the over-elaborate language that was evident in the 1980s towards more simplified presentations with straightforward wording. The type of expressions that should always be avoided are cliché descriptions such as 'exciting', 'enhanced with', and so on. Over-indulgence of such terms can put customers off, especially when their expectations are not met. The menu writer has essentially two broad choices; to have descriptions or not. On the one hand there will always be some operators who will wish to cultivate the server-customer relationship by adopting a very minimalist approach, leaving the server to do the describing. This approach has implications in terms of the skills required, labour costs and the training in communication skills that will be necessary. It is clearly not a tactic that would suit all operators but nevertheless is an option available in spite of its limitations. On the other hand, if the descriptions used are inadequate or are simply over the top, not only can customers feel overwhelmed and confused but they may keep the server at the table longer than necessary, thus causing a reduction in productivity. The writer must also consider more practical issues, for example clarifying to the customer the use of distinctive ingredients, such as garlic, and adapting to customers' heightened awareness of the dietary values of foods.

ISSUES OF MENU PLANNING AND DESIGN

Although there are some basic principles that underpin the planning and design of all menus, different foodservice operators face a range of issues. These are the frequency with which the menu should be changed, the cost of the menu design, ethical issues, and measurement of menu effectiveness.

Frequency of Menu Modification

There was a great deal of logic about restaurants that offered both an à la carte and table d'hôte menu. The former was an extensive list of items that changed rarely; the latter a short list of dishes planned only for that day. This afforded the foodservice manager maximum freedom to take advantage of seasonal produce. A daily list of dishes allows more cost flexibility. This also works well in operations with a captive market or regular clientele, such as hospitals, schools and employee feeding. Such menus are often planned over a cycle of three to six weeks in order to assure quality through standardization. Food offered, whilst changing substantially each day, will need an element of constancy. So while particular dishes may change each day, the food categories will not, In simple terms, it is likely that the wider the product range the less frequent is the need to modify the menu.

Cost of Menu Production

An additional important factor which the food service manager has to contend with is the cost of producing the printed menu. There are a wide range of variables that can impact on the cost of the menu, and the foodservice manager has always to remember that the menu must above all things be both readable and attractive to the customer. With the advent of desktop publishing, the foodservice manager today need depend less on the services of external printers than ever before. It is quite feasible for an upmarket hotel to produce menus of good appearance for a range of outlets within the unit. With a computer and a good printer, the daily table d'hôte style menu, for example, can be relatively inexpensive to produce. Miller[7] suggests that there are a number of advantages to be achieved by creating menus with desktop publishing. The most important of these are the ability to change menu items quickly in response to new customer demands; greater opportunity for experimentation by adding new items or repositioning existing ones; increased ease of incorporating specials and other price changes into regular menu offerings; lower costs for production and flexibility in menu design; and the potential for adding considerable variety to an outlet's special-events promotions. This type of technology is increasingly being used to create menus that do not change every day and it can easily offer foodservice managers more flexibility than the permanent-type menu does.

A further aspect of the overall cost picture is the type of material to be used. Management often have to consider experimenting with different alternatives in order to find the best mix for their operation. Laminated paper offers advantages in terms of flexibility, durability, presentation and perhaps overall cost. However, laminated paper does not suit every type of operation, especially the upscale full-service type of restaurant. Unlaminated paper, in smaller operations, is often preferred because lamination tends to give the menu a cheaper feel. An additional way to gain flexibility is the magazine-style stock cover frequently seen in hotel restaurants. The material used might be leather or a similar fabric, with a cord down the centre that holds a paper insert; the same cover can usually hold both the lunch and dinner menus. Most suppliers offer a wide range of alternative ways of customizing hard covers at little extra cost. Hard covers typically last up to two years so are an attractive and flexible alternative to the paper-type menu.

Ethical Issues in Menu Planning and Design

As we approach the beginning of the next millennium it is interesting to note the increasing debate and interest in ethical issues within the business community generally. The foodservice industry has long recognized the importance of accuracy in describing its products on the printed menu and by visual or oral representation to customers. Not to do so in this industry, where survival depends so much upon customer satisfaction, would be foolish. Misrepresentation of product and service offerings is most effectively regulated by the sanction of customer dissatisfaction and loss of patronage. In addition, there is an increasing and considerable range of legislation waiting to trap the careless and unwary operator. For instance, a case in 1993 resulted in a fine of £1,750 for contravention of the Trade Descriptions Act when the pub's menu claimed it was selling 'home cooked' food, whereas the trading standards officer was informed by the chef that the item was in fact a factory mass-produced item, heated in a microwave and served to the customer. Problems can, however, be avoided by rigorous questioning at the planning and design stage, regarding representation of a number of areas to ensure that the menu is accurate and fully truthful in every aspect. These areas are quality and quantity, point of origin of menu items, merchandising terms used, means of preservation, food preparation methods, product identification, price, brand names, nutritional claims, visual and verbal presentation.

Measuring Menu Effectiveness

The importance of maintaining standards is a major priority for any foodservice operation. Regular testing to determine whether the menu has accomplished its objectives should be carried out. This requires management to establish performance criteria for each menu item and indeed for the menu as a total package. This enables the operator to evaluate actual performance against the predetermined criteria and allow the menu to be further developed as appropriate. A menu item may have quite particular performance criteria, for instance a high level of 'theatre' built into it, such as fajitos brought to the table on sizzling hot skillets. Even this element needs to be evaluated.

Different methods are used to evaluate menu effectiveness. Analysing the number of items sold daily or by meal occasion within each menu category is perhaps the most common approach. Modern electronic point-of-sale restaurant billing systems can be programmed to provide foodservice management with this information in an easily readable format. The details of menu analysis and menu engineering are developed further in Chapter 13. Many of the larger commercial foodservice organizations now use mystery diners as an additional method of ensuring that they remain competitive. A mystery diner visits a unit and experiences what is on offer. The advantage of the mystery diner is his or her independence of the host organization and anonymity to the unit managers. Every aspect of the operation that has an interface with the customer is graded, including the menu. If a menu item falls below an acceptable level the unit manager is informed and is expected to take the necessary action. A follow-up is normally carried out to ensure that the corrective actions taken have been effective. The importance of considering in detail, at the planning and design stage, the menu evaluation process cannot be overstated as many operators fail to give this aspect sufficient attention.

CONCLUSION

In this chapter we have introduced the reader to the notion that the menu planning and design process has a close relationship with the foodservice organization's marketing and operational strategies. The idea of a structured and disciplined approach to the planning and design of the menu that involves the setting of objectives and rigorous performance criteria is recommended for all foodservice operations. The menu is at the heart of the operational aspect of customer communications and is a vital component of the customer's purchasing decision process. The menu reflects the market positioning the operator wishes to convey to the customer. It should attempt to give a true reflection of the restaurant's product/service offer in order to reinforce, clarify and strengthen customer perceptions rather than confuse customer expectations. The menu planning and design process incurs costs and will need to be evaluated in terms of the benefits derived.

Part of the benefits of good customer communications is the increased perception of added value. The menu is used to make clear the intrinsic qualities inherent in the product/service offer, the extra it brings the foodservice operation in terms of customer satisfaction and the level of customer service it provides. The incorporation of attributes of taste, variety and excitement are fundamental elements of the process which need to be emphasized to help build sales and traffic momentum.

Lastly, the monitoring and evaluation of the menu's performance, using predetermined criteria, is perhaps the most critical stage of the planning and design process. Here, the success or otherwise of the menu is confirmed by evidence of key success factors such as increasing sales revenue in real terms by increasing customer visit frequencies and customer transactions per visit, adding value to the customer offer, making customer choice effective, improving customer perceptions towards new offers and improving contribution from the restaurant's overall product/service mix. If the overall result is that the menu is in tune with the restaurant's theme and is organized in a way that best suits the established cost and pricing parameters, it is likely that it will do the job for which it is designed. If it is not, then it is also very likely that the expensive and difficult process will need to be repeated.

REFERENCES

1. Miller, J. E. (1987) *Menu Pricing and Strategy*, Van Nostrand Reinhold, New York.

2. Arnold, D. R., Capella, I. M. and Smith, G. D. (1983) *Strategic Retail Management*, Addison-Wesley, New York.

3. Cooper, D. (1993) *The Food Programme*, BBC Radio, 22 October.

4. Feltenstein, T. (1986) 'New-product development in food service: a structured approach', *Cornell HRA Quarterly*, November pp. 63–71.

5. Khan, M. A. (1992) *Restaurant Franchising*, Van Nostrand Reinhold, New York.

6. Dawson, J. (1989) Module 13, *Locational Strategy, Site Utilisation, and Store Design*, Module 7: MBA Distance Learning Programme, Institute for Retail Studies, University of Stirling.

7. Miller, S. G. (1988) 'Creating menus with desktop publishing', *Cornell HRA Quarterly*, February pp. 32–35.

8. Sangster, A., (1993) 'Brewing giant in court fine for frozen food con,' *What's Brewing*, November, p. 10.

4

Foodservice Layout and Design

Nick Johns

INTRODUCTION

This chapter examines the relationship between foodservice systems and the layout and design of the facilities in which they operate. All parts of a system, divided into a number of sub-systems, have an influence upon each other and upon the way they work together. Thus the whole organization is like a spider's web; a break or change in any thread will be felt along all the others. Kitchen and restaurant facilities represent important sub-systems in the operation – sensitive threads in the foodservice web. Foodservice processes usually involve a kitchen and a restaurant or service facility, but there are many variations on this theme. In Chapter 1, it was proposed that there are basically 11 different systems to found in the foodservice industry, each of which has a unique set of sub-systems and operating parameters. For instance, a cook-chill system may have a large central kitchen with a number of small satellite units for regenerating the food, whereas call-order and vending units have their own individual special needs. There is also a relationship between an operation and the premises in which it is located. As discussed in Chapter 3, the restaurant decor must match the design of the menu, along with the style or speed of service and other operational characteristics. For example, customers at a roadside cafe expect a bright, informal, cheerful environment; a full-service restaurant usually requires a different approach, because its clientele take longer over their meals and expect a more formal style of service. Similar considerations apply also to the layout and allocation of space. Kitchen layout has to take account of production capacity: high volume production usually necessitates efficient flow and transfer of materials. The design must also match the needs of the staff team, providing spaces for specialists to work, an office for an executive chef and so on.

GENERAL CONSIDERATIONS

Customers require a high-quality meal experience, one which meets their needs and tastes at that time. In order to achieve this the objectives of foodservice operations must be clearly identified at the beginning of the design process. Customer orientation is

Table 4.1 Typical foodservice sub-systems.

Kitchen	Restaurant	General
Goods delivery/receipt	Table preparation	Toilets
Raw materials storage	Service	Washrooms
Preparation	Consumption	Cloakrooms
Cooking	Some preparation	Bar
Chilling/freezing	(e.g. guéridon)	Lounge
Regeneration	Clearing	Waiting area
Hot-holding		
Portioning		
Wash-up		
Waste disposal		

probably the most important issue in designing any foodservice operation. Service organizations must provide what their customers require, where it is needed and in the way the customers want it. The capacity, efficiency and quality of the operation will be markedly affected by the layout and design and this should be a consideration from the start. The sub-systems necessary to provide an adequate foodservice operation must be identified and integrated. A foodservice operation must therefore be able to provide food of the required standard in sufficient quantities so that service is timely. Payment should be free of delays. The food itself must be appealing, wholesome and safe to eat. The surroundings should harmonize with the operation concept, the menu and the style of service.

The layout of a foodservice operation depends upon the *nature of the processes*, or sub-systems, which must be accommodated. The classification in Chapter 1 of the industry into 11 operational types, assumes there are a maximum of ten main processes in any foodservice system. A more detailed analysis of sub-systems is shown in Table 4.1. Integration of these is a key consideration. Their positioning should take account of likely movements of workers between them. Flow of raw materials, partly prepared foods and finished products should be as linear and logical as possible. There should be no need for delays in processing or service (for example, caused by waiting for lifts) and storage capacity should be conveniently located. The layout should also take into account the preferences of the production team, so that there is harmony between the social and technical sub-systems of the operation. Good layout and integration of production and service functions is also essential to the hygiene, health and safety of the operation.

Design of a foodservice facility must allow for adequate *capacity* in the processing, transport and storage of raw materials, process intermediates and finished products. The actual nature of the process will bring different requirements within these three categories. Trade-offs may be possible between different functions. For example, a conveyor-belt transport system may remove the need for large batch production. A continuous production system coupled with a conveyor belt may remove the need to store large batches of service-ready food. The style of the process itself also affects capacity. Short processes with few stages, such as fish and chip take-aways, tend to have smaller storage needs than complex, multi-stage operations, such as in-flight meal production. Processes based upon pre-cooked materials, such as fast food stores, may be able to operate a just-in-time system of delivery, thus avoiding much material storage.

Facility design should seek to minimize *non-productive work activity*, such as unnecessary movements of personnel, equipment or materials. This objective will partly be met if the facilities are integrated as described above, but other issues to consider are traffic flows and the widths of passageways. Heights of working surfaces and equipment items may be critical, and so are floor levels. Steps, cambers and flooring irregularities may bring personal accidents, spilled trolleys and other risks. Multi-level restaurants can offer diners a delightful experience, but delays, loss, waste and confusion caused by inadequate lift facilities may ruin the perceived quality of the experience. Design efficiency extends beyond the kitchen. Efficient use of space can maximize restaurant revenue generation, whilst well-designed decor makes a good selling environment. Restaurant layout can improve the teamwork, morale and efficiency of service staff. Kitchens that are designed to be visible to customers combine three functions: besides producing the food they merchandise their products, and at the same time increase customer confidence about the quality and safety of the food.

Another important design aspect is the availability of toilets, bars, cloakrooms and other services. For example, the ventilation system should ensure that stale food smells cannot enter the eating area. Lighting should match the mood of the establishment, but must be sufficient for cash transactions and security where these are required. *Hygiene* and *health and safety* are important aspects of quality. Kitchen layout should be such that 'clean' elements (cooked foods, washed plates) can be kept away from 'dirty' elements (toilets, outdoor clothing, raw meat, etc.). All areas should be designed for cleanability as far as possible, for example, kitchen floors should be of slip-resistant tile or of edge-welded vinyl, coved to the wall. Foodservice premises should also have 'ecological' pest control features[1] such as oversite concreting, pest-proof drains and outlets, and external paths adjacent to walls.

KITCHEN DESIGN FACTORS

Foodservice operations essentially contain two types of process.[2] 'Production' operations output a tangible product without the customer being aware of the process by which it is made. 'Service' operations generally have no tangible product, and the customer is not only aware of, but actually participates in, the process. This chapter follows the traditional view that foodservice contains both 'production' and 'service' processes. In this case the kitchen usually comes into the former 'production' category. Aesthetics and customer perception are therefore comparatively unimportant in most traditional kitchen design. The main requirements are efficiency, quality, health and safety. However, if the kitchen is to be open to the view of customers, this may impose constraints upon its design.

Kitchen Space Allocation

Space is at a premium in most kitchens, because it represents an opportunity cost in restaurant space or other revenue-earning customer facilities. However, facilities must be designed on an adequate scale, because subsequent extensions and enlargements are usually very costly. Space is required in the kitchen for personnel to work and to move about, for locating equipment, and for the transport and storage of materials. Kitchen

Table 4.2   Kitchen space allowances per meal served.

Maximum no. of meals served in busiest period	Range of space requirement per meal (metre^2)
100	0.66–1.20
200	0.54–1.00
300	0.46–0.88
400	0.41–0.75
500	0.37–0.66
600	0.34–0.60
700	0.32–0.52
800	0.29–0.47
900	0.26–0.42
1,000	0.24–0.40

Table 4.3   Table kitchen space allowances recommended for different styles of foodservice operation.

	Mean kitchen space allowance per meal served (metres^2)			
Approx. nos. of meals	200	300	600	1000
Cafeteria	0.58	0.42	0.35	0.30
Hospital	1.00	0.76	0.72	0.65
Hotel	1.00	0.49	0.42	0.33
Industrial restaurant	0.58	0.33	0.26	0.23
Full service restaurant	0.65	0.40	0.40	0.37

space can be allocated approximately on the basis of the maximum number of meals that are to be served during the busiest period. The space requirement per meal decreases with increasing overall numbers. As a 'rule of thumb' the production of 100 meals requires an area per meal about three times that for 1,000 meals.[3] The relationship is shown in more detail in Table 4.2.

Kitchen space allowances usually also vary with the type of operation. This may be due to its diversity. The more types of cooking activity, the more space tends to be needed to accommodate different operations and items of equipment. Operations serving several different types of meal, such as breakfast, lunch and evening meal, usually require more space than those which normally service just one or two meal types.[4] Room service and the supply of vended meals may also increase space requirements. Typical variations in space allowances for different types of operation are shown in Table 4.3.

Other factors affecting kitchen space requirements include the type of raw materials and equipment used and the diversity of the menu. Kitchens which use pre-prepared foods generally require less space than those using raw items. The level of preparation activity is reduced and considerably less waste produced. Pre-prepared foods tend to have less diverse storage needs than raw ones. In an ideal situation, raw vegetables, fruit, meat and dry goods would all require different storage conditions; frozen and chilled items need just two. Raw foods also have a wide range of optimum shelf lifetimes. An operation using, for example, sous-vide meals can work on a standardized shelf life. If deliveries are suitably regular, the space requirements of such a system can be reduced to a bare minimum. Added benefits are reductions in inventory and administration costs, as well as better food hygiene control.

In general, machines (which stay in one place while they carry out preparation or assembly tasks) require a smaller space allocation than personnel, who need 'elbow room' to work. However, machines are less versatile than people (see also Figure 5.1), and tasks which would be quite simple in human terms may demand complex equipment. Any saving in space also has to be weighed against increased investment of long-term capital. The pace of technological innovation in foodservice equipment means that there is a continuous improvement in the efficiency and productivity of all mechanized processes. In particular, cooking and reheating equipment, such as ovens and brat pans, are now able to achieve extremely efficient rates of heat transfer. Ovens are also able to handle increasingly larger batch loads. These two effects mean that equipment space requirements are decreasing, because fewer items are needed to achieve a given capacity.

In general, an extensive menu requires a greater space allocation than a limited one. A large menu tends to need a large raw material inventory and to put pressure on storage facilities. A large number of diverse cooking and preparation activities may need a lot of space, for personnel or equipment, or both. There may also be demands for extra space for in-process storage while items cool or thaw, or wait their turn for mechanical processing. An extensive menu usually requires a large range of crockery and cutlery, which must be stored before, after and during use. Many of these aspects can be controlled by carefully designing and limiting the menu. The amount of space required in a kitchen also of course depends on the way it is utilized. Important issues in this respect are the placement of work-centres relative to one another and the layout of work flow. Careful layout and design can control the direction and volume of work flow traffic and therefore reduce the loss of productive space to traffic lanes. These issues are discussed in more detail below.

Placement of Work-Centres

A principal objective of kitchen planning is ergonomic efficiency, that is to say the optimum use of workers' activity within the environment. One way to achieve this is to make movement between the different sub-systems or work-centres of the operation as efficient as possible. It is hardly ever possible to locate all of these close together, so priority lines of movement must be drawn up. The shape of the kitchen and the space allocated to each work-centre may also impose constraints upon the layout. A number of techniques are available to the foodservice manager and kitchen designer, including relationship charts, relationship diagrams and flow diagrams.

Relationship charts help the designer to analyse the spatial interaction between work-centres. Their use in kitchen layout planning is associated with the work of Avery.[5] A typical relationship chart is shown in Figure 4.1. Numbers at the intersections between work-centres indicate those which should ideally be located close together. The chart may be produced by an individual or by a working party set up to propose a layout. An alternative is to ask the food production team to rate the importance of locating the various centres together, using a questionnaire or interview

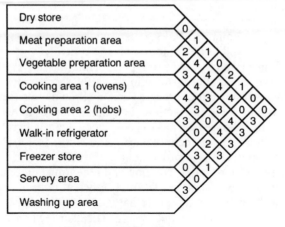

Key to proximity ratings

Very important   4
Moderately important   3
Desirable   2
Occasionally needed   1
Not needed   0

Figure 4.1 Work-centre relationship chart.

proforma. Scores are averaged and the results entered on to a diagram similar to that shown above, called a consensus chart. Relationship charts can be used to make decisions about the locations and distances between work-centres.

Relationship charts provide numerical estimates of ideal work-centre proximities; they do not give a visual picture of how the centres should be located. Designers usually convert their information to a more accessible form by drawing an activity relationship diagram, based upon the chart. The different sub-systems or work-centres are drawn in as circles, joined by the number of lines indicated in the appropriate box on the relationship chart. Work-centres which are linked by a large number of lines should be placed close together, as shown in Figure 4.2. It is possible to evolve an optimum layout for the work-centres by drawing a series of such diagrams. String diagrams[6] are another type of activity relationship diagram, usually produced for a limited, localized series of operations. For instance, they may be used to analyse one particular preparation of cooking activity. Observations of the operation are recorded on a plan of the work area, using strings to indicate human movements. Operations monitored in this way can often be made more efficient by moving the activity centres about to reduce the amount of string required. String diagrams are an effective tool in the design of small one-person foodservice units such as back bar systems or call-order counters.

An alternative way to analyse the layout of work-centres is by a flow diagram, which can record the flow of raw materials, intermediates, finished products or personnel through the operation. Various types of diagram are available, using boxes, symbols, coloured lines, etc. to indicate the flow of specific materials.[7] Flow diagrams may not always help to improve the ergonomic efficiency of an operation, but they should always be drawn up as part of the analysis. They provide additional useful information about the movement of the food, and may identify contamination routes and other risks.

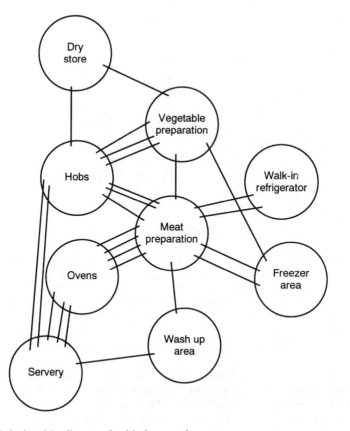

Figure 4.2 Relationship diagram for kitchen work-centres.

Movement of Materials and Personnel

Movement is essential for work. Space is required by personnel for sitting or standing, to perform the actions demanded by the work, to move themselves from place to place and to move equipment and materials about. The latter may include raw items, process intermediates and finished products. It is important to distinguish clearly between the different ways space is to be used. In practice there are three categories: work space, work aisles and traffic lanes, defined as follows:

Work space refers to the actual space where the work is performed. It includes the 'elbow room' required for manipulating materials, but not floor space.

Work aisles are areas where workers stand or sit to perform work. They permit access to and from the work space and provide for work-related movement, for instance from tables to ovens. Aisles may also permit a number of workers to operate as a team, passing items to one another, or sharing equipment.

Traffic lanes are major routes along which work flows. They are usually designed to be as straight as possible and should be wide enough to permit quick, safe passage of trolleys, trays and groups of personnel. Traffic lanes may be required for raw materials, process intermediates and finished products, but they will also be needed for transport of waste, clean and dirty crockery, cutlery and pots. Separate traffic lanes should be

Table 4.4 Typical allocations for work space categories.

Category	Space (mm)
Work space	600
Work aisle	750
Traffic lane	900

provided for designated 'clean' and 'dirty' items; for example, waste disposal should have a lane of its own. These three different categories of space are used to build up the typical work-centre patterns shown in Figure 4.3. Typical space allocations are shown in Table 4.4.

Arrangement of Traffic Lanes

Work aisles and traffic lanes must be arranged in such way that conflicts of purpose do not occur. Usual practice is to keep them separate; for example, traffic lanes are often laid out at right angles to adjacent work aisles, as shown in Figure 4.3(a). Such a layout is typically found in large-scale foodservice operations, especially cook-chill production units. Traffic lanes should as far as possible avoid routes with steps, stairs, cambers or lifts. From a health and safety point of view it is important that passages remain unobstructed, and this may be a problem with traffic lanes which are comparatively infrequently used, such as those for waste removal, or receipt of goods. Parking of trolleys, storage of equipment or depositing of waste in these areas may be discouraged by placing such traffic lanes away from convenient open spaces or by locating them within sight of the manager's office.

Arrangement of Work-centres

Kitchen operations invariably involve the manipulation of food prior to cooking or processing, therefore work-centre layout often includes tables or surfaces as well as large equipment items. Two layout options are available for this type of space: side-by-side and back-to-back. A side-by-side layout requires considerable unproductive human movement, because the workstation is spread out. To some extent this may be avoided by having the equipment at right angles to the preparation table, as shown in Figure 4.3(b). This makes it difficult for workers to share equipment and may also be impossible to achieve if a number of similar stations have to be fitted into a single area. Space may be saved by locating work-centres side-by-side along an aisle and also by allowing two neighbouring preparation stations to share a central cooking station, (see Figure 4.3(c)).

A back-to-back workstation, like that shown in Figure 4.3(d), demands less human movement than a side-by-side arrangement. However, most of the movement involves turning through 180°. Depending on the tightness of the turn this may cause accidents or back injury. The space between the back-to-back work positions must never be a designated traffic lane. Some spatial advantage may be gained by arranging work stations into a U configuration. A variation of the back-to-back layout is the 'back bar' design of operation shown in Figure 4.4. This approach is often used for small, call-order operations and permits the food to be prepared and served by the same

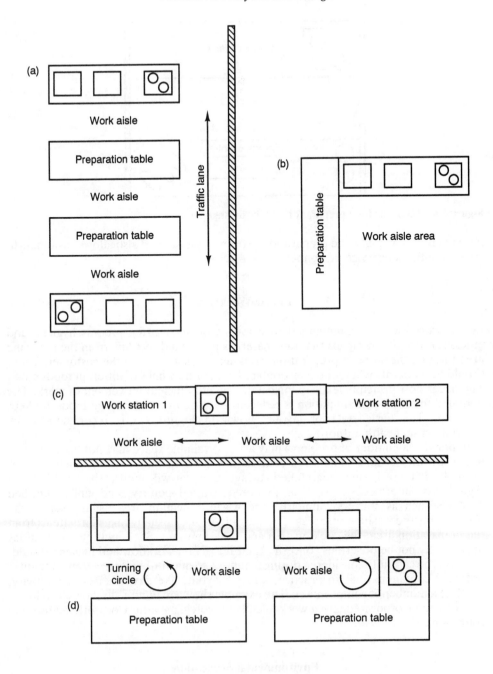

Figure 4.3 Various kitchen work-centre layouts. (a) Traffic lanes at right angles to work aisles; (b) cooking equipment at right angles to preparation table; (c) two workstations side by side sharing central equipment; (d) back-to-back workstation arrangements.

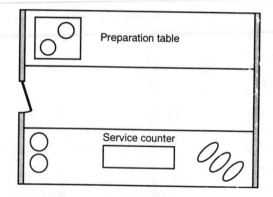

Figure 4.4 Back bar food preparation/service arrangement.

individual. It may make the preparation extremely visual, and also allows customers to interact with foodservice personnel.

Linear Workflow

Linear workflow is recommended as a means of maximizing process hygiene and efficiency. Broadly it means that raw materials pass in a direct line from the receiving area through the store to preparation, cooking, the servery and the customer. There should be no points where the flow doubles back, or flow lines of different foods cross. The linear flow principle leads to logical design and efficient movement of work. The potential for cross-contamination is reduced, because raw and cooked foods are kept separate. The basic style of layout shown in Figure 4.5 is recommended by environmental health authorities.[8]

In practice a number of problems may arise. Available space may not be suited to a linear layout, because some work-centres may have to fulfil several functions. For example, if there is only one chilled storage room, it will tend to be used for raw ingredients, intermediates such as prepared, stuffed poultry, and chilled finished products such as starters. Similarly, the waste collection area usually serves the preparation and washing-up areas. The washing-up area usually takes dirty items from the preparation area, the cooking area and the restaurant. Such multiple interactions may or may not be of serious concern. Their impact on workflow and hygiene should, however, be carefully considered during planning, to maximize efficiency and minimize potential contamination. In practice, kitchen layout, like any other design activity, involves a number of compromises. The example shown in Figure 4.6 shows how linear flow can be incorporated into a workable plan involving a variety of work-centres and traffic lanes.

Environmental Separation

The different functional areas of a kitchen must frequently be kept environmentally separate. It may be necessary, for example, to insulate the manager's or executive chief's office from a high noise level in the food preparation area. This can be done with fibreboard partition and double glazing. The restaurant, too, must be protected from

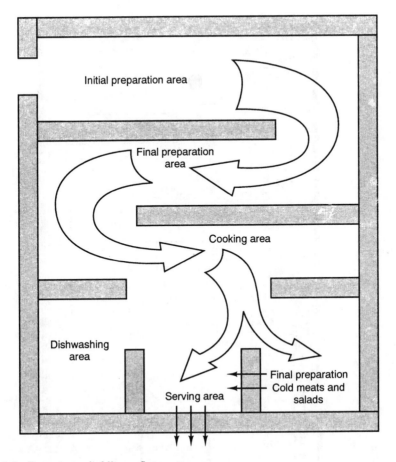

Initial preparation area

Final preparation
area

Cooking area

Dishwashing
area

Serving area

Final preparation
Cold meats and
salads

Figure 4.5   Recommended linear flow pattern.

kitchen clatter, which would spoil the meal experience. All parts of the kitchen, but particularly areas housing cold-holding equipment, should be protected from solar heat gain. Cold rooms should be located together as far as possible. Walls separating them from the kitchen must be well insulated to maximize thermal efficiency and to prevent condensation from forming. This is particularly important where dry and cold stores are located side-by-side. Humidity levels are important: ventilation or extractor systems should be so organized that air passes through storage areas into the more humid parts of the kitchen, not vice-versa.

From the food hygiene point of view, a foodservice operation can be divided into 'clean' and 'dirty' areas. The latter are defined as anywhere where personnel, equipment or food might become contaminated. Typical dirty areas are lavatories, washrooms, raw meat and vegetable stores and preparation areas, storage or collection points for waste, the dish-washing area and the restaurant. 'Clean areas' are locations where cooked and ready-to-eat foods are handled and stored, such as hot-holding, plating-up, cooking and salad assembly areas. By definition any contamination of clean areas is harmful. Clean and dirty areas can be physically separated with either barriers or shoulder-high partition walls, and staff should not be obliged to move back and forth

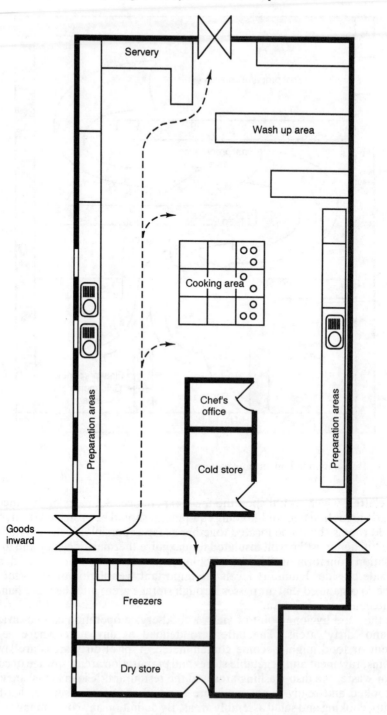

Figure 4.6   Practical kitchen layout using the linear principle.

between them. The significance of hygienic layout, work flow and process design should be explained at staff induction and training sessions. personnel can be encouraged to wash by installing hand basins wherever they must pass between dirty and clean areas. Notices should urge staff to 'Wash your hands before passing this point'. Hand basins should be installed between locker rooms and food handling areas so that employees can wash their hands after changing their street clothes.

RESTAURANT DESIGN FACTORS

The restaurant embodies the 'service' aspect of a foodservice operation. It has no tangible product, and the customer is an integral part of the process. Therefore aesthetics and customer perception are the foremost issues in restaurant design. However, this is not the only concern; the practicalities of laying and clearing tables, cash transactions and security also need to be considered. Space, flow and facilities are therefore important restaurant design issues.

Aesthetics centre around the desired atmosphere or ambiance – the blend of decor, lighting and music which best enhances the meal experience. The objective of design is to resonate or harmonize with the product concept, menu and style of service, so that the complete service package is appropriate to customers' needs. Considerations include the length of time customers will spend over their meal. For instance, fast food restaurants may best be served by bright, primary or pastel colours and bold patterns. Furniture may be more functional than comfortable, with washable plastic surfaces or chromium plate. Lighting may be bright and music brisk, to achieve a cheerful atmosphere. In more formal restaurants customers may enjoy lengthy meals, amidst subdued colours and lighting, restrained patterns, furniture designed to provide comfort, and moody, reflective music. Between these two extremes there are many shades of style. In addition, a theme approach may mean enhancing the meal experience with specific artifacts. For example, seafood restaurants may decorate with fishnets or buoys; units offering Mexican-style food may feature sombreros and ponchos. A successful style often requires a careful balance between the tasteful and the outrageous.

Restaurant Space Allocation

Restaurant space is usually made up of the number of intended seats, plus 'elbow room' for customers and access for service. More formal styles of operation tend to require greater space allocations. For instance, more space is required for table service than for self-service, and there is a noticeable trade-off between productivity and quality. Space must also be allowed for service stations, if these are required, and for traffic lanes to permit service and clearing. Restaurants frequently use moveable furniture, partitions, service stations, and even such decorative features as planters and fish tanks.[9] This makes it possible to maximize the use of space and to react quickly to changes in demand. Typical space allocations are shown in Table 4.5. These space allocations refer only to seating areas and do not include other customer requirements such as cloakrooms and lobbies.

Place settings should allow customers sufficient room at the table. This is usually estimated at 900 mm per person. The arrangement of tables is also important. Figure

Table 4.5 Typical restaurant space allowances for different styles of foodservice operation.

Situation	Approx. allocation (metres^2 per person)
Cocktail party/reception (standing)	0.46
Cafeteria (seated)	1.20
Luxury restaurant (seated)	1.70
Industrial staff restaurant (seated)	1.60
Coffee shop (seated)	1.30
Bar and lounge area (seated)	1.70

4.7 shows how different arrangements can affect the use of space. In practice the picture may be complicated by other factors such as the shape and orientation of the room or the requirements of daylighting or the view. Use of wall space or dining counters will improve the productivity of restaurant space, but will also affect the meal experience and the harmony between facilities and product concept.

Work flow needs are often not as clear in a restaurant as they are in a kitchen. However, there are always two aspects to be considered: service/clearing and customer flow. The service process requires adequate access from the servery and to the washing-up area. Traffic lanes should be clearly identified and 900 mm should be allocated between any two seated individuals bordering a lane. Designation of traffic lanes should take the role of satellite service stations into account, as well as the movement of trolleys for sweets, carvery or guéridon work. Sharp turns and corners should be avoided. Customer flow is more likely to be a problem in self-service operations. A clearly laid out, logical flow is important and barriers may be needed to ensure that customers pass through the layout in the expected way. Choosing food, paying for it and disposing of waste and dirty crockery should be as simple as the design can allow. Traffic lanes of at least 900 mm are needed, as customers tend to be less adroit than trained staff, and may have bags or luggage with them. Self-service counters effectively have to permit customers the maximum range of choice in the minimum time.

Numerous layouts are available, as shown in Figure 4.8. A linear arrangement (Figure 4.8(a)) allows all customers access to all foods, but the flow is limited to the speed of the slowest customer. Double and multiple counters (Figures 4.8(b)–(d)) may increase the flow rate satisfactorily, but slow customers, and slow replenishment of *bains-marie* from the kitchen, can still cause hold-ups. U-shaped counters, such as that in Figure 4.8(e), permit more efficient use of space. A back bar unit as was shown in Figure 4.4, is effectively a style of linear self-service counter; it is effective because the volume of service is limited by the volume of production. Free-flow counters may also be used, for example where customers are able freely to select buffet or carvery items from tables surrounding, or dotted about, the room. Many kinds of restaurant, such as Harvester, Pizza Hut and AJs restaurants, feature such self-help salad bars.

Food Courts

A recent development in restaurant design is the food court style of operation, used in motorway rest areas and, increasingly, in shopping malls. A series of small food outlets surround a central seating area. Each outlet usually specializes in a particular style of food, so that it is possible to offer customers a choice of ethnic dishes, salads, healthy options, etc. These may be operated by a single foodservice firm, or the space leased out

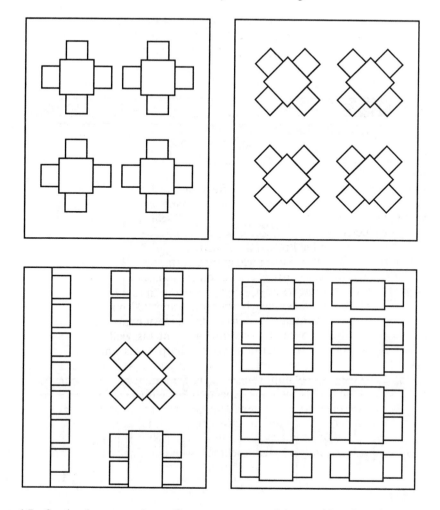

Figure 4.7 Seating layouts and use of restaurant space. Square tables give a less regimented layout, but seat fewer people than rectangular tables or wall or bar arrangements.

to a number of different operators. They represent a good opportunity for brand franchising, so fast food chains in particular have developed an operational configuration for such locations. Each outlet is usually arranged on the back bar principle and has its own till. In this way it is possible to provide the customer with a comprehensive range of foods and to give rapid service. The central seating area, which must be regularly serviced and maintained, often contains a bar or drinks counter.

Customer Facilities

Foodservice customers and staff usually require toilet facilities both by necessity and by law. Basic legal requirements are still as shown in Table 4.6. Disabled cubicles and nappy changing facilities should also be considered, particularly where family groups

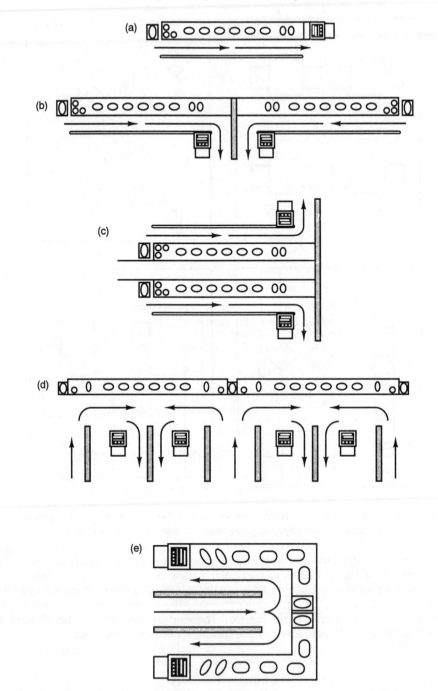

Figure 4.8 Self-service counter arrangements. (a) Linear counter; (b) double linear counter; (c) double parallel linear arrangement; (d) multiple choice–multiple till arrangement; (e) U-shaped arrangement.

Table 4.6 Staff and public sanitary accommodation.

No. of male/female staff	WC's	Urinals	Wash-basins
Hotels, restaurant, shops			
1–15	1	–	1
16–30	2	not	2
31–50	3	speci-	3
51–75	4	fied	4
76–100	5	–	5
Male public			
1–100	1	4	3
101–200	2	8	5
201–300	3	12	7
etc.			

are expected. Hot and cold water and drying facilities should be provided. The volume of service may also dictate the style of hand drying: hot air requires less maintenance than paper towel dispensers, but may cause queues. Cloakrooms should be accessible, but if not permanently manned they may generate security problems. Space should be adequate for the number of guests expected at any given time. The lobby or waiting area is often combined with the bar. It is the first point of contact for the customer and therefore very important in terms of style and concept. The till or cash desk may present special problems in a formal style of restaurant. It must be sited unobtrusively, yet it should be well lit, to maintain security and accuracy in cash transactions. This may be a problem where lighting is kept low to provide atmosphere.

THE DESIGN PROCESS

The theme of this chapter has been the necessity of integrating facility design with other aspects of the operation: the concept, the menu, the staff team. In addition, layout and design have to take account of the shape of the building and the space available in it. All this requires a well co-ordinated planning team, consisting of some or all of the following individuals: owner or administrator of the operation, architect, foodservice design consultant, interior designer, mechanical or electrical consultant, and equipment supply/installation company representative. The planning process should start with a brief containing a detailed specification of the foodservice concept and process, as discussed in Chapter 2. Decisions about capacity and quality should already have been made and the service style clearly understood. The concept of the operation should include types of raw materials used and production processes envisaged, as well as the roles of production and service staff. The nature of the interface between customers and service staff should also be well defined.

The brief provides the basis for the architect and specialist design consultants to produce an outline of what is needed and a broad estimate of the likely cost. Funds can then be allocated and the design consultants will work within their respective budgets to produce a detailed plan which is acceptable to the owner of the business. Close teamwork is essential; in particular, it is advisable to consult the production and service personnel who will actually work in the facility when it is completed. Final plans will contain precise estimates of cost, an artists's impression, and detailed drawings, including the layout of services and equipment. It is of great importance to plan the positioning of the latter. Otherwise there may be health and safety or hygiene hazards, in the form of trailing cables, or water and waste running over the floor to reach a drain. The final plan will also include equipment lists and precise details of finishes and decoration.

Building contractors may be chosen by the team from prior experience, or by tender. It may be important to maintain close supervision during construction, so that the facility is actually built to the intended specification. Small details can bring major problems later if they are neglected. For instance, kitchen floors must incorporate a fall or camber downwards towards drainage points, so that spilled water can escape. A reverse fall can result in a permanent pool in one corner. If planned layouts of equipment and services are not faithfully translated into practice the facility may not fulfil its intended function in the foodservice system.

CONCLUSION

A foodservice facility is an integral part of the foodservice system, and its successful design has implications for the achievement of key results areas. This chapter examines general principles of foodservice facility design in terms of capacity, efficiency and quality considerations. The layout and design of facilities are closely related to the intended foodservice concept and style, to the menu and to the working needs of the foodservice team. Foodservice operations consist of a number of sub-systems, each of which may require a different work-centre. Integration of these centres can be achieved by optimizing interactions and at the same time minimizing unnecessary traffic between them. Kitchen design is discussed in terms of space, placement of work-centres and the movement of materials and personnel. Various arrangements of work space and equipment are outlined and the virtues of linear work flow and environmental integrity are discussed. Restaurant design assumes a meal experience in which the customer interacts to some degree with service personnel and to other customers. Aesthetic aspects are very important, together with the efficiency and productivity of the service process. Use of restaurant space is related to the style and standard of service, but also to the flow of food, cleared plates and customers. The chapter reviews the design process and the function of the design team, who are responsible for co-ordinating the complex interactions of the system. It is essential that the design of the foodservice facility fits into the patterns established by marketing and operational experience.

REFERENCES

1. Johns, N. (1991) *Managing Food Hygiene*, Macmillan, Basingstoke.
2. Johns, N and Wheeler, K.L. (1991) 'Productivity and performance measurement and monitoring', in Teare, R. and Boer, A. (eds) *Strategic Hospitality Management*, Cassell, London, pp. 45–71.

3. Fuller, J. and Kirk, D. (1991) *Kitchen Planning and Management*, Butterworth-Heinemann, Oxford, Ch. 9.

4. Kotschevar, L. H. and Terrell, M. E. (1985) *Foodservice Planning: Layout and Equipment*, 3rd ed, John Wiley, New York.

5. Avery, A.C. (1973) 'Equipment arrangement for greater worker productivity', in Pedderson, R.B. *et al.* (eds), *Increasing Productivity in Food Service*, Cahners Books, Boston, pp. 57–87.

6. Harris, N. D. (1991) *Service Operations Management*, Cassell, London.

7. Johns, N. op. cit.

8. Mendes, M. F., Lynch, D. J. and Stanley, C. A. (1978) ' A bacteriological survey of kitchens', *Environmental Health*, Vol. 86 No. 10, pp. 227–231.

9. Lawson, F. (1987) *Restaurants, Clubs and Bars: Planning, Design and Investment*, Architectural Press, London.

5

Establishing Staffing Levels

Stephen Ball

INTRODUCTION

One of the most important planning considerations involved with a foodservice operation concerns the establishment of appropriate staffing levels to provide the goods and services that it sells or supplies to the consumer. With staffing costs representing a substantial element of operating costs in the foodservice industry, it is vital that managers accurately establish staffing levels and then control the subsequent staffing costs within predetermined financial limits. Staffing levels should be not greater or less than is required to complete the tasks to the set quality and quantity standards within an operation. Staffing levels and costs therefore need to be consistent with both the catering and financial policies of the operation.

In order to establish the overall complement of staff for an operation, managers require a knowledge and understanding of the tasks to be done within the operation, a clear idea of demand at particular times, the establishment of work standards to be achieved and a recognition of the level to which individual staff can be expected to perform. In other words, such aspects as work study, the setting of productivity standards and volume forecasting are relevant. The difficulties of forecasting customer demand and some of the methods available for forecasting are explained within this chapter, as are the nature and some of the ways of determining standards. Establishing staff levels also involves staff scheduling. This, along with work study, is mentioned in this chapter and developed further in Chapter 12. The way a job is designed within a foodservice operation offers a way to provide satisfaction for staff while increasing productivity for the operation. Appropriately designed jobs can also reduce the need for staff and hence affect staffing levels. Job design can be applied in the planning of a new operation and is therefore examined in this chapter. Equally, job design could be used to restructure work at some point after the operation has opened. It is therefore referred to again in Chapter 10.

Labour costs for most foodservice operations generally lie between 25 per cent and 35 per cent of total sales. In some cases, for instance in many fast food operations and bar, it could be less than 25 per cent and in other operations more than 35 per cent; for instance, labour costs associated with food production in 4 or 5 star hotels or in hospital catering departments. Labour costs are basically the product of hourly rates of pay and the numbers of hours worked. It therefore follows that if hourly rates of pay are not too dissimilar between operations, any differences in labour cost from one foodservice operation to another will be caused by differences in the number of hours worked or staffing levels in the operation. Any differences in hours worked between operations may relate to the effectiveness or management control or to a range of other factors. This chapter commences by analysing some of the main factors affecting staffing levels.

FACTORS INFLUENCING STAFFING LEVELS

There are many varied factors affecting the levels of staffing in foodservice operations. Some operations have planned their system from the outset to exploit these factors actively so that their staffing needs are minimized. Others have focused upon them to reduce their need for additional staff, rather than on increased recruitment activity, when labour shortage problems have occurred.[1] The factors influencing levels of staff are essentially associated with the components of the foodservice delivery system. In order to examine these factors in a structured way the sequence of components included in Pickworth's service delivery system model[2] is drawn upon.

Market Demands

Nearly all foodservice operations employ variable-cost staff or staff with a variable cost element. Variable-cost staff are those whose numbers are related to the volume of business. As business volume increases for whatever reason, either during the day or over a period, it becomes necessary at some point to use more variable staff. The reverse should also be true when business volume decreases. Typical examples of these kinds of staff are waiting staff, dishwashing staff and certain food preparation staff. Staffing levels must reflect the level of demand.

Market Strategy

There are two key marketing concepts which can affect staffing levels: the degree to which the service is customized to the consumer, and the level of service provided. Most often, but not always, these go hand in hand: when one is high, so too is the other. A foodservice delivery system with a high degree of customization will work to satisfy an individual customer's needs. Service levels are associated with both the judgements made by the consumer of the *quantity* of the benefits received from a service and the *quality* of benefits received. In most fast food operations customization does not prevail and service levels are low. The degree of customization is greater in cafeterias, where there is usually the opportunity to choose from a wide variety of menu items, and where there is a modest increase in service levels. Customization and service levels are even greater in conventional à la carte restaurants with full table service. Generally, and other things being equal, as the degree of customization and the level of service increases there is a corresponding need to increase staff input.

Production Strategy

There are a number of design considerations related to production strategy which may impact upon staffing requirements. The issue of particular importance here relates to the make or buy decision. A restaurant could buy-in prepared foods or produce menu items in-house using one of a variety of systems (see section below headed 'Production and Service Processes') from basic ingredients. In the former situation prime cooking is done off site, perhaps by a manufacturer. For the restaurant labour costs could be kept to a minimum as it would largely require only unskilled kitchen staff, and cooking would be more a matter of reheating and finishing. The use of catering packages, which either partially or entirely use pre-prepared menu items, has enabled pub retailing companies to realize labour and productivity benefits. Bass Taverns, for example, has benefited from using catering packages because, amongst other things, they have enabled production and merchandising to be controlled, have reduced skills reliance where appropriate and also have had roll-out potential throughout the company. On the other hand, restaurants preparing all menu items from basic ingredients would require more highly skilled staff and probably additional staff to take responsibility for the more complex purchasing, receiving and storing activities. The make or buy decision at its most general level revolves around the issues of cost versus control. There are different food, labour, operating costs and capital implications associated with both, whereas control may be facilitated by buying-in but creativity lost.

Menus and Sales Mix

Menu items offered can also affect labour costs and staffing levels. This can be because of the number of individual items on the menu, the flexibility of the menu, the complexity of menu items and the amount of kitchen preparation time required to produce them, the style of service needed for certain menu items, and the availability and use of part-prepared and convenience foods. Consider, for example, the size of the product range. Fast food operations were typically characterized by limited menus and a core product, such as hamburgers, fried chicken, fried fish or pizza. Restricted menus built around core menu items not only reduced the staff skill requirements of operations but also facilitated high customer to staff ratios. However, in order to maintain existing custom and gain new custom, many operators have had to extend menus. The standard McDonald's menu, for example, now has 25 per cent more items than in 1980. Such product diversification could, if not carefully managed, result in increased staffing. Conversely, streamlining menus can reduce staff requirements. The takeover of Sweeney Todd's by BrightReasons led to a considerable rationalization of the menu size and offered the opportunity, all other things being equal, for reduced staff needs. Menu planning, and in particular the limiting of numbers and varieties of menu items, can be of considerable importance in the control of labour costs. Staffing will be affected by whether menu items are served in/on disposable or non-disposable ware. When the latter are used, dishwashing equipment and staff will be required.

Technology and Equipment

The amount of human labour has been substantially reduced in some foodservice operations, especially in restaurant chain operations, by the substitution of technology, including equipment, and manufacturing solutions. McDonald's has been systematically planned, designed, organized and controlled in such a way that it can be likened to a manufacturing operation. It has adopted the production line approach to service. Jones[3] has claimed that this approach to foodservice delivery has potentially the greatest impact on efficiency, productivity and profitability. McDonald's is driven especially by organized preplanned systems, or soft technology, rather than being reliant upon the discretion, attitude or skill of its employees. Operatives use advanced equipment in order to produce efficiently and quickly a standardized product of a reliable quality. One of the key ingredients is the breaking down of the total job into tasks, which in turn are broken down into the smallest and simplest of steps, some of which can be mechanized while the remainder require minimal skill. The application of this technocratic approach to service contexts has been referred to as the industrialization of service by Levitt[4] and has been employed by Kentucky Fried Chicken, Pizza Hut, BurgerKing and many other chain operations. The chains generally have been much more aware of the advantages which advanced technology can give their multi-unit systems and of the subsequent staff savings. But mechanization is not confined to the chains and the large operations: relatively simple and cheap ways of mechanizing have also been utilized in traditional foodservice operations.[5]

Equipment research and development has also focused on labour reduction in order to make operations more efficient, the benefits of which can be passed on to the consumer. The need for automated and labour-saving equipment has become even more pressing, given the current shortage of suitable workers in the UK and other countries. A good example of a labour-saving device was the introduction by Arby's, which recently entered the UK, of a conveyor belt system, called Vittleveyor, in some of its US outlets. This carried food horizontally and vertically, increasing efficiency and enabling a greater turnover of customers. Computers and communication systems are being increasingly used as their costs decline and they become more sophisticated. In some table service restaurants remote waiter stations and point of sale devices are being used to speed orders to the kitchen, thereby freeing staff time. Arby's has used a computer device that allows customers to order their own food. Another labour-saving example relates to the development of an entirely automated operation using assembly line robots.[6] At the same time as equipment and other technologies reduce the need for labour they can also lower the required skill levels. An example is one-piece baking machines that thaw, proof and bake at the push of a single button.

Staffing levels are influenced by the extent to which a task can be mechanized. The decision whether to mechanize, or to rely upon the abilities of a person, or to use a combination of equipment and a person's ability to undertake a foodservice task essentially relates to the consideration of a variety of aspects. Table 5.1 shows a framework for analysing tasks in order to aid this decision. In analysing the cashiering function Strank[7] explains that there is a role for both point-of-sale equipment, because of its calculation and data storage abilities and reliability, and a cashier, owing to the

Table 5.1 Comparison of characteristics and abilities of people and machines.

People		Machines
Relatively slow	Speed	Capable of very high
Reaction speed of 1 second		speeds
		Reaction speed almost
		instantaneous
Highly variable	Power	Constant and consistent
Not suited to routine tasks	Consistency	Ideal for precise, repetitive, tasks
Can only do one thing at a time	Complexity of	Can perform several
	task	tasks simultaneously
Good at remembering principles		
and strategies	Memory	Good at 'remembering' large
		amounts of data
Slow and may make errors	Calculation	Fast and error-free
Capable of identifying mistakes		
Limited range of senses but capable		
of	Sensory abilities	Wide range of sensory
highly complex interpretation		data, e.g. electrical signals,
		sound waves
Highly versatile	Versatility	Usually purpose-built for one
		function
Performance slows down and		
becomes selective	Overload capacity	Sudden breakdown
Can cope with unforseen	Reactive capabilities	Incapable of reacting, must
		follow logical sequence

Adapted from Strank (1973)[7].

cashier's ability to deal with the customer, to cope with any problems and to handle flexibly different methods of payment.

Design of Work System Layouts

Increasingly the benefits of scientifically arranging foodservice facilities and equipment based on principles similar to those of the modern factory are being appreciated. The greater the distance workers have to move between pieces of equipment in the kitchen or between the kitchen and the customer in a conventionally operated foodservice operation, the greater the staff cost and, probably, the greater the staffing levels required. As discussed in Chapter 4 (see page 63), minimizing the worker flow between equipment, equipment and customers, and between the various other workplaces by the careful design of workplaces, is beneficial. Data can be obtained by analysing worker movements in existing operations through the observation of patterns of worker movement; by recording workers' impressions of various equipment relationships and worker movements; or by trailing workers and charting their every movement.[8] BurgerKing has used a restaurant simulation model based on experience in existing restaurants to aid kitchen design and to project accurately the most effective positioning and division of labour and the number of crew members needed within restaurants.[9]

As a result, substantial labour savings and additional profits have been enjoyed from the moment new restaurants open.

Capacity Management

Managing of capacity on a day-to-day basis is discussed in depth in Chapter 11. But there are a number of factors related to supply aspects of capacity management which will affect staffing levels. These include how able the system is to operate with fewer employees during off-peak periods, whether changes can be made to the organization structure,[10] the make-up of staff and their hours, how reliably sales forecasting methods are used, whether scheduling is adequate, the degree to which capacity such as central food production facilities can be shared with others and the extent to which consumers can get involved with service delivery. If the consumer can be persuaded to do some of the work this reduces the demands on staff. Examples of consumer involvement include buffet service, food bars and cafeteria-style foodservice. Fast food operations encourage consumers to carry food and drink to their own table and to clear their table. In some operations consumers place their own orders and one or two operations have even sold the idea of consumers preparing or finishing their own food, such as the customer use of grill stones in Holiday Inn restaurants or fondue cooking by customers.

Production and Service Processes

Clearly, numerous factors associated with the production and service processes utilized in a foodservice operation will have consequences for staffing levels. Reference has been made to some of these, particularly technology, in earlier sections of this chapter. The production process is concerned with all those activities which a foodservice operation uses to enable the appropriate quality and quantity of food to be produced on time. Four major food-production systems have been identified: conventional; commissary; ready-prepared food systems including cook-freeze, cook-chill and sous-vide; and assembly serve (See Figure 1.1).[11] Each of these has different staffing implications in terms of numbers of staff, staff skills needed, when and where staff work and the extent to which their work is tied to demand. Generally, as the extent of preparation increases and as production becomes more complex, the numbers of job categories, the degrees of specialization and staff inputs are likely to increase. Similarly the type of service will have an effect upon staffing. As the service becomes more complicated, going from self-service to full silver service, more staff will be required to perform the service and the degree of expertise required to perform the service will increase. The use of automatic vending systems requires no staff input apart from that involved with filling and cleaning. Again these service types have been classified.[12] Staffing levels will also be influenced by the abilities and motivations of staff to work with the production and service processes. These will in turn relate to such factors as training and the ability of management to ensure workers achieve quantity and quality performance standards.[13]

PLANNING STAFFING LEVELS

Once the factors that affect the staffing levels of different types of foodservice operation have been established, there are two main aspects in determining the specific level of staffing required for any operation. Some forecast of demand must be made and productivity standards set. Once standards are derived which are accurate, are representative of tasks and can be used reliably, the numbers of people and schedules are calculated by applying the standards to the forecast volume of work, which largely corresponds to the sales forecast.

Demand Forecasting

The forecasting of demand for goods and services is the cornerstone of managerial decision making throughout foodservice operations and is very important to labour cost control and profit management. A food and beverage manager, for example, can use a forecast of covers to optimize staffing for both cost savings and revenue enhancement.[14] It is essential for a foodservice operation to be successful that there should be a close relationship between the expected volume of business and the number of staff employed and the times they work. The determination of staffing numbers and the efficient scheduling of staff are just some of the many areas which can benefit from demand forecast information. Virtually every aspect of foodservice operations from planning and control to day-to-day operational matters can gain from the accurate forecasting of demand.

Forecasts of demand, by their very nature, cannot be completely accurate. The future always has some uncertainties because of such things as consumer attitudes and patterns of buying behaviour, changes in technology and economic and political changes. Consequently, the establishment of staffing levels and the forecasting of future staff requirements are often more subjective than quantitative, although in practice a combination of the two is often used. Operations managers should be involved in the forecasting process to ensure that they appreciate the assumptions and limitations of the figures. They are also probably best placed to appreciate the implications that such characteristics as patterns of demand, the intangibility of service and the simultaneity of demand and supply have upon forecasting and, subsequently, the determination of staffing levels.

Often there are wide fluctuations in demand for foodservice; during the day, between days and between months. Even when patterns are identifiable there is always an inherent unpredictability of the pattern of business in foodservice operations. This is true even in so-called captive market situations such as hospitals where patient demands for foodservice are influenced by patient movements, operations and their desire and ability to eat at any one time. The unpredictability of demand will always generate difficulties for the scheduling of staff and the consequent maximization of labour efficiency.

Forecasting demand for foodservice is aided by having a quantifiable measure of sales volume. Obtaining such a measure can be difficult given the intangible nature of the service element in the foodservice package. In a fast food restaurant, for example, should staffing be based on the amount of food sold or should lost consumers who depart because of queues also be considered? A further complication might be whether any consideration is given to the different attitudes consumers have toward the service package with its many components. Services are normally produced and either consumed in full or in part simultaneously. Consequently staff must be available to provide the service when demand occurs. If they are not, then consumers will either have to queue for the service or will depart without receiving the service. On the other hand, if staff are available to provide a service but there is no demand for it then excess costs will be incurred.

Table 5.2 Forecasting methods.

Class	Examples of methods	Features
1. Qualitative	Managerial judgement, Delphi technique	Subjective, judgemental, based on estimates and opinions, relatively high cost, typically used in small organizations
2. Time series	Trend projections, moving averages	Based on the idea that what happened in the past can be used to predict the future analysis, relatively very low cost
3. Causal	Regression, correlation	Based on relationships between connected variables, relatively moderate cost
4. Simulation models		Dynamic mathematical models, usually computer based, relatively high cost, tend to be used only in large organizations

The need for forecasting which minimizes any potential gaps between staff availability and consumer demand for services is therefore important. Several factors require consideration when selecting a forecasting approach for determining staffing levels. These include:

(a) Costs – the development and operating costs associated with the forecasting approach.
(b) Accuracy – this depends on the circumstances in each operation, and particularly upon the degree of flexibility in staffing the workforce. Precise forecasts are less important where people can be geographically moved from one unit in an organization, such as a restaurant chain, to another, where staff are flexible and where staff can be easily hired.
(c) Quality of data – most forecasting is based upon historical data. Advances in computer technology and the increasing uptake of systems in foodservice operations have vastly improved the quality of past sales data and facilitated easier, cheaper and more accurate staff forecasting.
(d) Duration of the planning period – forecasts tend to deteriorate if the planning period is too long. This may be because past data often become less relevant for the longer term.

Table 5.2 classifies the way of forecasting sales and summarizes their features. A more detailed description of these forecasting methods can be found elsewhere.[15-18]

Productivity Standards

It is essential that staff numbers and schedules are determined by applying work standards to a forecast of customers or covers. Standards for the control of labour costs can be divided in two. *Quality standards* refer to the degree of excellence of work. In some hotels and restaurants, higher degrees of skill are required for the product and service of food and drink than would be required in a motorway service station, a city centre fast food outlet or in a school refectory. Quality standards are determined by the catering policy of each foodservice operation and are thus specific to each operation. *Quantity standards* can be developed once appropriate quality standards have been established. Quantity work standards indicate how long tasks of a given quality should take, for example a dishwasher must process 110 covers/hour.

Work measurement (see Chapter 12) has been successful in setting up standards of performance in a variety of foodservice contexts such as in food production facilities operating on decoupled lines and in some fast food and quick food service operations which have industrialized. However, in many traditional foodservice operations work measurement is less useful in setting standards as production is more closely related to immediate demand. The tasks involved in traditional operations are governed to a great extent by the perishable nature of the product, and by the fluctuating nature of customer demand. Also, workers in traditional operations do not usually undertake repetitive tasks for long periods. Therefore in traditional operations other standard-setting approaches need to be adopted. One approach involves reusing schedules which were deemed appropriate when previously used; in other words, using past experience as a standard. Another approach is to employ standards which are deemed appropriate by other similar operations. Attempts have been made to develop industry-wide quantity standards;[19] while others have revealed the standards of particular companies.[20] The use of such standards must be treated with caution and must be considered in the context of the particular foodservice operation. However, the use of such quantity-based standards for forecasting staffing levels is preferable to the use of labour cost percentage standards based either on an operation's past records or on industry norms. Their value to the establishment of staffing levels has been identified as being inadequate for several reasons.[21,22] Foremost of these is that it is based upon financial measurements.

Matching staffing levels to different levels of demand is particularly sophisticated in the fast food or 'quick service' sector of the industry. Operators in this sector use data from point-of-sale transactions to produce a forecast of hourly activity for any given day from which precise staffing levels are established. Figure 5.1 illustrates one such operation. During peak demand, each of the 20 workstations is filled by a single employee; whilst during quieter periods each employee takes on several roles, so that the restaurant can operate with as few as three on duty.

Job Design

One of the key ways to achieve staffing and other operational efficiencies in foodservice, to realize product and service quality objectives and to satisfy any requirements for productivity is through job design. Besides being of value to the organization, job design is also important to the individual foodservice employee as it normally specifies job content in terms of duties and responsibilities; identifies the methods to be used in carrying out the job; and determines supervisory arrangements and the relationships between different job holders in the organization. Through job design both personal and individual requirements of the jobholder and the needs of the organization can be satisfied. The ideal objective of job design is to aim for a 'best fit' between these different needs, as a trade-off between maximizing the output of staff and satisfying individual worker's needs will reduce overall effectiveness.

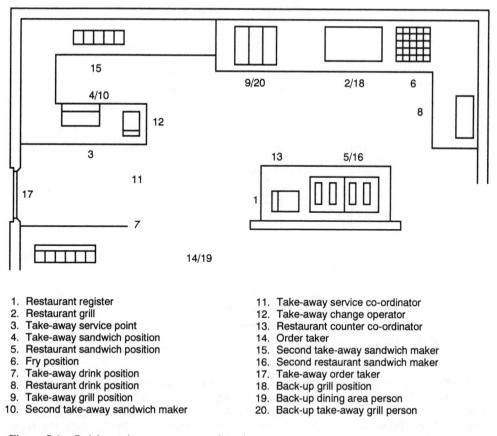

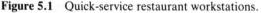

1. Restaurant register
2. Restaurant grill
3. Take-away service point
4. Take-away sandwich position
5. Restaurant sandwich position
6. Fry position
7. Take-away drink position
8. Restaurant drink position
9. Take-away grill position
10. Second take-away sandwich maker

11. Take-away service co-ordinator
12. Take-away change operator
13. Restaurant counter co-ordinator
14. Order taker
15. Second take-away sandwich maker
16. Second restaurant sandwich maker
17. Take-away order taker
18. Back-up grill position
19. Back-up dining area person
20. Back-up take-away grill person

Figure 5.1 Quick-service restaurant workstations.

A variety of approaches to job design have been advocated and practised including job specialization, job rotation, job enlargement and job enrichment. All approaches are potentially useful but the choice of which one(s) to use is largely dependent on the particular organization, employee and working conditions and the expectations of everyone associated or affected by the job.[23,24] In a fast food operation, for example, customers and employers may want fast service but this may lead to lower job satisfaction and higher labour turnover. These may be acceptable if suitable replacement labour is available.

The process of job design must start from an analysis of what work needs to be done and why it should be done. This is where the techniques of work study, process planning and organizational analysis are used. Beyond this, as Figure 5.2 shows, decisions must be made about who is to perform the task and where, when and how it is to be undertaken. Obstacles may exist to the introduction of redesigned jobs. These include the lack of evidence supporting the link between job design and productivity; the lack of management support for enriching operative jobs; trade union resistance; and the conflicting philosophies associated with industrial engineering and quality of work techniques. These obstacles and management's role in implementing job design plans in foodservice and other hospitality operations are explored further by Mill.[25] Merricks

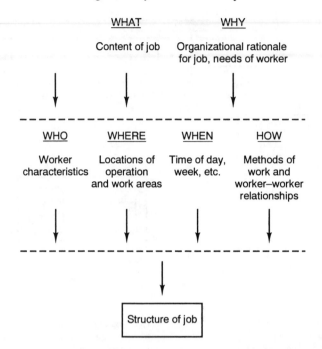

Figure 5.2   The process of job design for foodservice operations.

and Jones[26] question the application of job design theories (which are mostly based on Herzberg's theories of motivation) and concepts to the foodservice industry. They contend that some employees may not have a strong desire for achievement and are happy to accept work-related instructions; many employees, particularly the large number of part-time employees, are motivated by extrinsic factors, such as money, and therefore motivation through intrinsic factors may be unnecessary; many employees do not undertake repetitive tasks; many foodservice employees can see the results of their endeavours; opportunities for promotion and advancement exist owing to the high levels of labour turnover. While there may be some validity in these contentions in certain circumstances, they do not have universal applicability to all employees in the industry, and the factors motivating employees have not been conclusively established.

Job Specialization

The industrial origins of specialization date back to the Industrial Revolution when organizations began to develop and exploit technology as a means of increasing worker efficiency. Adam Smith in *The Wealth of Nations*, as long ago as 1776, demonstrated how pin production could be increased through the division of labour, specialization and the use of improved tools. These ideas, coupled with the proper allocation of work to people and machines, were central pillars of the scientific school of management. F.W. Taylor, the father of scientific management, contributed to specialization and used systematic studies of work to discover the most efficient method of performing a task. Specialization, involving the concentration of both managers and workers upon

Table 5.3 The potential advantages and disadvantages of specialization.

	To management	To operatives	To customers
Advantages	Increased speed of training. Recruitment could be easier. High output owing to simple, repetitive work. Lower labour costs as easier to replace operatives. Greater control of workflow and workers.	Ease in learning job. Develop an expertise. For certain jobs little education required for employment.	Improved goods, services and prices
Disadvantages	Quality control could be difficult owing to fragmentation of work. Hidden costs of worker dissatisfaction, e.g. labour turnover, absenteeism, disruption to system, hostility to customer, etc. Limited perspective of operatives may reduce scope for improvement.	Boredom. Little scope for control over work pace, career progression, showing initiative, communication with other workers.	In some situations, e.g. fast food, may be sold as a mass-produced product.

Adapted and extended from Ball[28].

specific functional activities, has long been used in foodservice operations. Traditionally kitchen and service jobs, whether in hotels, stand-alone restaurants or hospitals, were frequently designed along these lines. As Ball[27] points out, specialization of labour skills has been a feature of modern fast food operations. Many foodservice managers have also found their jobs becoming much more specialized. Whilst specialization has made possible high-speed, low-cost production, taken to extreme, and combined with other technologies, it may have disadvantages. The task for management is to determine the optimum level of specialization or the point at which the disadvantages outweigh the advantages. Table 5.3 summarizes the potential advantages and disadvantages of specialization.

Job Rotation

Job rotation involves the movement of a worker, either voluntarily or compulsorily, from one job or task to another. The rotating of staff from kitchen to service work is an example. This can benefit the foodservice operation by increasing staff flexibility and reducing occupational status while at the same time leaving work processes undisturbed. Job rotation enables rest periods to be staggered and provides cover when staff are missing owing to lateness, medical appointments or illness. Job rotation can overcome some of the disadvantages of specialization. In fast food operations, for example, specialization is increasingly being combined with the use of multi-skilled staff and job rotation. For operatives, rotating jobs can help reduce boredom, add variety to work, enable them to identify more closely with the operation as a whole, and increase skills acquisition. However, job rotation is often resisted by staff. This could be because extra demands are placed upon them or because one boring job is being replaced by another.

Job Enlargement

Job enlargement generally involves increasing the scope of a specialized job horizontally to provide variety and make it more interesting to the job holder. Tasks would be added which are similar to those currently being undertaken by the individual. An example is allowing commis chefs to undertake additional preparatory tasks. Job enlargement may be resisted as it may require greater knowledge, skill and training, some of the problems job simplification sets out to eliminate. As with job rotation, it might be seen simply as increasing the number of routine, boring tasks workers have to undertake.

Job Enrichment

Job enrichment aims to maximize the interest and challenge of work by extending a job through a combination of enlargement, autonomy and responsibility. There are many ways of enriching a job. Essentially it is the technology and the circumstances which determine the most appropriate method(s). Methods include:

1. Increasing responsibility of individuals for the monitoring and control of their own work; for instance, secretarial staff could be encouraged to check any letters they have typed, rather than expect others to spot mistakes.
2. Giving workers more scope to vary methods, the sequence and pace of their work, or their break times.
3. Giving workers increased financial responsibilities; for example, kitchen staff could be made responsible for ordering certain supplies and controlling wastage, whilst certain staff may be given discretion to set work schedules.
4. Allowing workers more influence in setting targets and standards of performance and an opportunity to review results.
5. Allowing workers to undertake a more complete delivery of service, for example by allowing kitchen staff to help with service and vice versa.
6. Require employees to undertake complete 'units of work'; for instance, producing 20 salads is a more meaningful work process and work experience than washing lettuce for 100 salads.
7. Allowing workers who do not normally have contact with customers to do so, as in carvery operations. This can make work more interesting as well as develop new skills and give workers the opportunity of obtaining first-hand feedback from customers.

The addition to a job of discretionary aspects such as planning and control, referred to in the first four points in the list above, is commonly called vertical loading.

One of the outcomes of job design is the job description. These should specify the contribution that each job makes to the objectives of the business by focusing on key result areas and in particular upon outputs and expected standards. Invariably, though, in foodservice operations they comprise a list of component tasks. This and the impact job design has on employee motivation are discussed further in Chapter 10 (see page 163).

STAFFING STRUCTURES

Staffing a foodservice operation can be viewed in terms of different employee classifications which in turn comprise different groups. These classifications include:

    managers and operatives
    fixed- and variable-cost staff
    full-time, part-time and casual staff
    core, opportunist and peripheral staff
    production and service/high contact-low contact staff

Each basically covers the entire workforce, except the first, which may exclude administrative staff, and the last, which may exclude both these and managers. Each of these classifications has been devised for different purposes. Dividing the workforce into managers and operatives enables roles and responsibilities to be defined and reporting relationships established. This is usually captured on the typical organization chart. A feature of the modern foodservice industry has been the so-called 'shake-out' of many managerial staff, reducing the number of levels of management within the organization – the 'flattened hierarchy' – and increasing the number of staff each manager/supervisor is responsible for – their span of control. This shake-out has clear implications for productivity. Thinking in terms of fixed- and variable-cost staff is also one way in which labour costs can be managed. In foodservice operations with wide and unpredictable levels of demand, it is more cost-effective to employ hourly paid employees, whose hours can be adjusted to match demand. In the fast food sector, this enables extremely tight scheduling of employees. The definition of full-time, part-time and casual employment is established by UK legislation, and has implications for national insurance, contracts of employment, and other employer responsibilities. The fourth classification, or core, periphery and opportunist employees, is relatively recent. It stems largely from the fundamental review of business practice that has gone on in the late 1980s which emphasizes that very large, diverse companies may not be the most effective. This has led to the breaking up of firms into smaller business units, the contracting out of some activities, and a focus on the core business, along with the core workforce needed to support it. Finally, the concept of back-of-house and front-of-house employees has been understood in the hospitality industry for many years. But the importance of this, with regards to all kinds of service businesses, was only made apparent in the management literature in 1978. In discussing job design, it was hinted that front-of-house staff, in direct contact with the customer, may need very different skills to those required back-of-house. One of the things that made fast food such a revolutionary concept in the foodservice industry was that it did away with the distinction between these two categories of employee.

The precise numbers of staff to be found in each group, for example the number of managers and operatives, will depend upon a host of variables ranging from company policies to the time of day. Different foodservice operations will be staffed with different mixes of each group. The structural differences between sectors and the implications this has for staffing are discussed in Chapter 12 (see page 192).

CONCLUSION

The establishment of staffing levels in foodservice operations requires management to analyse and understand fully the complexity of factors involved in the production of the foodservice product. Consideration of the foodservice delivery system can facilitate this analysis. The employment of the right number and type of staff at any particular time facilitates the tight control of labour costs which is so vital to the success of most foodservice operations.

The origin of most staff within a foodservice operation is sales. The only exception are those staff who have to be present regardless of the volume of business, the fixed-cost staff. A pattern of sales or forecast of sales is simultaneously a pattern of variable-cost staff requirements. Therefore forecasting sales is fundamental to determining staffing levels.

Demand forecasting is difficult. Whichever method is used, accuracy will be limited. However, despite this it is necessary to forecast business volume when staffing and scheduling, for the alternative is pure guesswork. The establishment of staffing levels and staffing schedules should also be underpinned by productivity standards. These allow sales forecasts to be translated into staffing requirements.

Job design offers a way to structure jobs so that it will raise productivity and provide employee satisfaction. It can affect staffing levels. Foodservice management can use job design to determine whether, for example, it is more appropriate to have fewer, more skilled employees performing more complex tasks for greater productivity or to have more staff doing simpler tasks.

REFERENCES

1. Anon. (1991) 'Operating with fewer employees', *Cornell HRA Quarterly*, pp. 10–11, May.

2. Pickworth, J. (1988) 'Service delivery systems in the food service industry', *International Journal of Hospitality Management*, Vol. 7 No. 1, pp. 43–62.

3. Jones, P. (1988) *Food Service Operations*, Cassell, London.

4. Levitt, T. (1976) 'The industrialization of service', *Harvard Business Review*, September–October.

5. Ball, S. D. (1992) *Fast Food Operations and Their Management*, Stanley Thornes, Cheltenham.

6. Nowlis, M. (1988) *Food Service Personnel of Tomorrow: Robots and Computers*. Paper from International Association of Hotel Management Schools, Autumn Symposium.

7. Strank, H. (1973) *Ergonomics: Functional Design for the Catering Industry*, Edward Arnold, London.

8. Avery, A. C. (1973) 'Equipment arrangement for greater productivity' in Pedderson, R.B. *et al. Increasing Productivity in Food Service*, Cahners.

9. Swart, W. and Donno, L. (1981) 'Simulation modelling improves operations, planning and productivity of fast food restaurants, *Interfaces*, Vol. 11 No. 6, pp. 35–47.

10. Anon., op. cit.

11. Jones, P., op. cit.

12. Jones, P., (1993) *A Taxonomy of Foodservice Operations*, 2nd Annual CHME Research Conference, Manchester, April.

13. Dittmer, P. and Griffin, G. (1980) *Principles of Food, Beverage and Labour Cost Controls for Hotels and Restaurants*, CBI, London.

14. Miller, J. J., McCahon, C. S. and Miller, J. L. (1993) 'Foodservice forecasting: differences in selection of simple mathematical models based on short-term and long-term data sets', *Hospitality Research Journal*, Vol. 15 No. 1, pp. 43– 49.

15. Buttle, F. (1986) *Hotel and Food Service Marketing: A Managerial Approach*, Holt, Rinehart & Winston, Eastbourne.

16. Chase, R. B. and Aquilano, N. J. (1982) *Production and Operations Management*, McGraw-Hill, New York.

17. Fisher, M. (1981) *Controlling Labour Costs*, Kogan Page, London.

18. Fitzsimmons, J. A. and Sullivan, R. S. (1989) *Service Operations Management: A Life Cycle Approach*, Irwin, Homewood, Ill.

19. Mill, R. C. (1989) *Managing for Productivity in the Hospitality Industry*, Van Nostrand Reinhold, New York.

20. Johns, N. and Wheeler, K. (1989) *Productivity and Performance Measurement and Monitoring*. Proceedings of International Association of Hotel Management Schools Conference.

21. Freshwater, J. F. and Bragg, E. R. (1975) 'Improving foodservice productivity', *Cornell HRA Quarterly*, Vol. 15. No. 4, pp. 12–18, February.

22. Pavesic, D. V. (1983) 'The myth of labour-cost percentages', *Cornell HRA Quarterly*, Vol. 24. No. 3, pp. 27–31, November.

23. Boella, M. (1987) *Human Resource Management in the Hotel and Catering Industry*, Hutchinson, London.

24. Torrington, D. and Chapman, J. (1983) *Personnel Management*, Prentice-Hall.

25. Mill, R. C., op. cit.

26. Merricks, P. and Jones, P., op. cit.

27. Ball, S. D., op. cit.

28. Ball, S. D., op. cit.

6

Developing Operating Standards

Andrew Lockwood

INTRODUCTION

When customers enter a food and beverage operation, their main interest is in the food and drink they are about to enjoy, the service they will receive and the surroundings in which they will be staying while they eat. They are not really interested in how the operation managers provide these facilities, but they *are* interested in the standard of what they receive. Their satisfaction with the meal experience will be a measure of whether the outputs of the operation are to a standard that meets their expectations. For the operation, on the other hand, the final delivery of a meal to a customer is the result of a sequence of complex operations that must be co-ordinated correctly to achieve consistent performance. Each step of this sequence must deliver the required standard if the final result is to be as expected. The manager's role is not only to monitor and control the day-to-day operation but to be instrumental in determining and establishing the operating standards.

THE ROLE OF STANDARDS

The important role of operating standards as a central part of any operation is recognized in a number of approaches to quality, including BS 5750.[1] This British Standard for a quality system identifies 'control procedures' and 'work instructions'. Control procedures are detailed statements saying what has to be done, by whom, where and when. The work instructions provide, in greater detail, a specification for exactly how a particular task should be carried out. For example, a standard recipe details the ingredients and their weights as well as the complete preparation and cooking procedures with times and temperatures as required.

Within Heskett's[2] model of the strategic service vision, operating standards provide a key part of the operating strategy. They link the customer promise of the service concept to the capabilities of the service delivery system. We have seen in Chapter 2 how such service concepts are devised. In Heskett's view, 'service vision' has three integrative elements, each of which involves standards. First, operating standards are part of the *positioning* of the operation – what are the standards that this particular customer segment expects? How will these standards differ from those of the competition? What are the standards that will constitute good service? The service concept may be designed to offer an advantage over the competition. For example, in home delivery pizza operations the speed of delivery may be seen as a key customer requirement, so if one firm guarantees delivery within 20 minutes of ordering, a new entrant into the market may guarantee to deliver in 15 minutes. Likewise, if the temperature of the delivered food was a key element then a competitor may set standards to deliver a consistently hotter product. Second, operating standards will have a direct effect on the *value cost leverage* of the operation. Setting very high standards may offer high perceived value to the customer but may also incur high costs. Decisions must be taken about whether the added value can be recouped through higher prices. For example, a standard recipe for beef stroganoff may specify prime fillet steak. Evaluating this standard would have to consider the customer-perceived value of this ingredient versus the cost of supplying it. It would be possible to replace the fillet steak with a cheaper cut of meat and this might have no perceived effect on the customers' satisfaction with the finished dish. Third, operating standards must be considered in the light of the *capabilities of the service delivery system*. There is no point in setting a standard that the operation is not capable of delivering. If the operation cannot meet the standard, either the standard needs to be reviewed to decide whether changes could be made that would bring it within the operations capability, or the service delivery system needs to be changed to cope with that standard. For example, a fast food operation may wish to introduce a new menu item but not be able to produce the dish to an acceptable standard with the existing kitchen equipment. A decision would have to be made about whether the dish could be changed to facilitate production of existing equipment or whether new equipment should be introduced to produce the original dish.

Operating standards therefore present a focal point at the interface of customer requirements and operating performance that will determine, to a large extent, the success of the operation as a whole.

DEVELOPMENT OF OPERATING STANDARDS

Operating standards must be based on customer expectations, but they are determined by management and provide direction for employees in the operation. This requires customer expectations to be translated into standards, the operation to be configured to deliver these, and regular monitoring and control of standards to ensure they are being achieved. Figure 6.1 illustrates these three interlinking stages of operating standards development: the design stage, the configuration stage, and the control stage. This process of establishing standards presents many challenges. It is often thought that poor-quality products or service result from the service provider not performing to standard. However, it is just as likely that poor quality can result from correct performance to an ill-conceived standard. For instance, the operational standard in one large chain of family restaurants was that the menu be given to customers as soon as they were seated at a table, even though during busy periods customers would be asked to

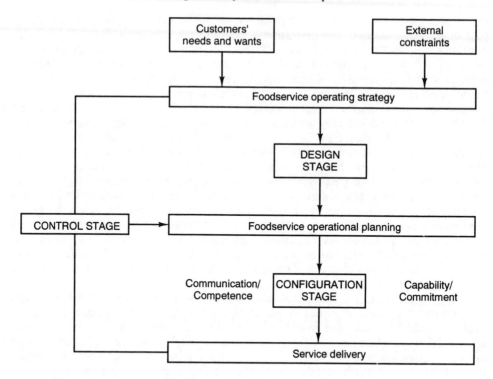

Figure 6.1 Development of operating standards.

wait in the bar area. Customers complained of such waits until the standard was changed, with menus being given to people whilst they were still in the bar.

As each of these stages it is possible for the 'wrong' standards to be established. At the design stage it may be difficult for customers to articulate their expectations and for foodservice operators to discover them. It is also possible for operators to choose to amend standards to meet their requirements to deliver a branded operation. At the competence stage, management may be unable to deliver a standard to meet customers' exact requirements owing to cost constraints, unavailable technology, or some other technical reason. And at the control stage appropriate means of measuring performance to standard need to be utilized. Chain restaurants use mystery shoppers, for instance.

Design Stage

The first stage of operating standards development is design. The objective here is to identify the specific needs of the target customers and translate these into operating strategy. It is important to identify what Nightingale[3] calls 'customer service standards', not simply to rely on established practice. In Chapter 2 the range of options available for market research and market segmentation were discussed as they applied to developing the foodservice concept. But these techniques are also relevant to determining the specific standards within that concept. Once customer requirements have been identified, they must be translated into operational requirements – what does the operation need to do to deliver the expected service and products to the customer? These requirements may be tempered by outside constraints, which may include the organizational constraints of conforming to a brand identity, the legal constraints of complying with such things as licensing, fire, hygiene or safety requirements, or the requirements of an outside body such as the AA or Michelin.

Configuration Stage

The second stage of standards development is configuring the operation to ensure that the operating strategy is achievable. It is no good setting operating standards to meet customer needs if the operation is not capable of delivering them. Effective configuration requires four main things. First, the standards must be *communicated* in a clear and unambiguous form so that they are understood by employees at all levels within the operation. The now common practice of using photographs of how the finished dish should be served on the plate is a good example of making things clear in a simple way. An operating standards manual which sits on a shelf in the manager's office is of no use. Gardner Merchant, for example, has developed an extensive collection of standard recipes to cover all its many different types of catering outlets. These recipes are printed on cards and include full details of ingredients, preparation, cooking and serving procedures. At their training centre in Kenley, their chef managers are trained to use a daily menu board designed to hold the standard recipe cards for that day's dishes so that they are easily accessible to all staff.

Second, simply making the information available is not enough. The organization needs to make sure that all *staff are competent* to deliver to the communicated standard. This must involve a commitment to training. Scott's Hotels, as part of its approach to quality management, developed a set of operating standards for its hotels. It then spent approximately a year training all its staff to meet these standards. Each member of staff was then assessed and certified as competent by the hotel general manager.

The third area for attention is ensuring the *capability of the organization* to support the staff in displaying their competence. The organization needs to provide the necessary equipment, technology, systems, environment and culture to facilitate service delivery. The perennial teaspoon famine comes to mind. Service staff are not going to be able to concentrate on serving the customer if they find that basic service equipment is not available. Hunting high and low for missing teaspoons is not going to put foodservice staff in a particularly positive frame of mind. Installing a computerized ordering and billing system may go a long way to speeding up service and controlling revenue, but if the technology is unreliable or there are not sufficient terminals for the volume of business, this will easily detract from the service standards that staff are competent to deliver.

The final area of competence is one of *commitment*. Standards may be well communicated, staff may be well trained and the operation may be more than capable of supporting operating standards, but unless staff are committed to delivering those standards consistently they will not be achieved. One way of developing this commitment may be to involve staff in setting the standard in the first place and in monitoring their own performance. Indeed, East[4] suggests that the only people who can prepare work instructions or standards effectively are the people who do the job.

Control Stage

The final stage of developing operating standards is control. Control involves the assessment of how well the operation has conformed to the operating standards set and also whether there is still congruence between the standards and customer needs. The operating standards themselves provide simple measures of performance that can be monitored on a periodic basis. Some measures of performance may include tolerance limits – a range of performance deemed to be acceptable. For example, service temperatures may be expressed as a range. As long as the temperature is within this range it will conform to the standard.

These measures can then form the basis for a service audit – a complete review of the operation conducted either internally by members of the management team or externally by consultants or by mystery shoppers. Harvester Restaurants, for example, has developed a sophisticated system of using mystery shoppers to evaluate its service standards from the customer's perspective.[5] More detailed discussion of the use of audits can be found elsewhere.[6,7] Where variations from the operating standards are identified, procedures must be in place to investigate the problem and implement improvements.

The final aspect of control is to check that the operating standards are still congruent with customer requirements. The use of some measure of customer satisfaction, such as comment cards, complaint monitoring or customer surveys, will provide some information on how customers' tastes are changing. More detailed market research will be needed to establish whether the change is sufficient to warrant action to amend the operating standards. In the past, a restaurant concept may have lasted without change for many years; in today's marketplace the pace of change demands amendments, however small, on a much more frequent basis. Consider, for example, the number of new menu items introduced by Pizza Hut or McDonald's over any recent 12-month period.

In summary, operating standards:

- provide a concrete manifestation of customer requirements
- give training and competence guidelines for service employees and allow self-control
- identify control parameters and deviations from standard
- in addition, they prevent loss, waste, inefficiency by providing a comprehensive identification of the necessary components and parameters of the service delivery system.

SELECTING OPERATING STANDARDS

When determining operating standards several key strategic decisions have to be taken. These will include the service level to be offered, the effect of standards on resource productivity, the chain effect of standards and the type of standards that need to be set.

Service Level

The overall level of service will depend on the target market to be catered for, but even within this market a range of price and service level combinations will be possible. There will be a range of acceptable price and service level combinations that meet both

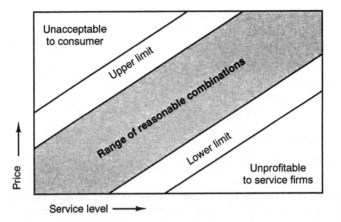

Figure 6.2 Service level–price combinations.
Adapted from Sasser, Olsen and Wyckoff [8].

the customers' and the organization requirements. Combinations above this may be more than any reasonable customer is willing to pay for this service level. Combinations below this, on the other hand, may be too expensive for the operation to produce and still make an adequate return on investment. For example, it might be possible for a fast food operation to add extra service such as tablecloths, flowers on the table, crockery and cutlery. However, the expense of providing these extras would mean that menu prices would have to increase to cover the additional cost. This would be likely to price it out of the customers' level of acceptability for a fast food operation.

Resource Productivity

The highly interrelated nature of the operation, where decisions about operating standards will have a direct influence on the potential resource productivity of the operation, is illustrated in Table 6.1. In selecting operating standards, decisions must consider the possible trade-offs inherent in this table. A decision to increase the level of service offered would have a direct impact on the labour requirements and so cn potential labour productivity. In addition it would influence facilities utilization, if the higher service levels led to longer service times and so lower potential seat turnover in a given period. Decisions about the standards of product to be offered will have a direct influence on materials costs through the use of more expensive ingredients but may also mean longer preparation times and therefore higher labour resource needs. Similarly, increasing the flexibility of the operation is likely to involve lower resource productivity. For example, increasing menu choice is likely to increase material and labour requirements. Providing a range of different restaurant environments in the same premises is going to be more expensive in terms of investment in facilities and equipment and may lead to a lower space utilization. Increasing the reliability of the operation involves narrowing the limits of acceptability within which standards operate. For example, providing the sterile environment within an operating theatre requires a much higher labour and materials input than the normal high standards of cleaning hospital wards. Similarly, improving the guaranteed delivery time of room service will involve a considerable investment of labour and capital to ensure that the new standard can be met consistently. Changing the availability of the product, as for example

Table 6.1 Influence of customer service standards on resource productivity.

Customer service dimensions		Resource productivity
Service Level		Facilities
Standard of Product		
Flexibility	**affect**	Materials
Reliability		
Availability		Labour

altering the opening hours of a restaurant or bar, makes obvious resource demands on the operation.

The argument here is not that improvements in operating standards cannot be made without a commensurate reduction in productivity but that the potential effects must be considered. Improvements in service standards and their higher input needs may be more than offset by higher outputs from the system through increased revenue or guest satisfaction.

The Chain of Standards

If an operation sets a standard that the food delivered to the customer should be within a certain temperature range, this has implications not just for the staff who serve the customer but all the way down the links of the service chain. To ensure that this standard is achieved for the external customer, a number of supporting standards must be developed for the internal customers. At what temperature should the food be cooked? How reliable are the thermostats on the cooking equipment? How long can the food he held in the kitchen before service? At what temperature will the food be held in the kitchen? How long will it take for food being collected in the kitchen to be delivered to the customer? Is there any heating equipment in the restaurant to restore the temperature? Will food be covered when leaving the kitchen? With what? How far does the food have to travel from the kitchen to the service point? Any service delivery standard will have to have a schedule of supporting standards, as shown in Figure 6.3.

The delivery of the service to the external customer is the result of a complex chain of standards linking all the way back to the external suppliers. Setting incorrect or inappropriate standards at the start of the chain will always result in a poor experience for the customer. For example, developing poor purchase specifications will mean that inferior materials will enter the supply chain and eventually reach the customer as a tough steak or a tasteless chicken breast. The important point here is that setting very strict standards of service to the customer is not enough on its own; these must be backed up by equally rigorous standards of delivery to internal customers. The floor service waiter cannot deliver a meal on time if the kitchen is slow in cooking it, however well prepared he is, however fast the lifts, or however easy it is to push the trolley.

Types of Standard

Ouchi and Maguire[9] have identified two different types of operating standards: process or behaviour standards and output standards. Process standards are useful in situations where there is a low degree of uncertainty in the work process. The task here is strictly determined and, given a particular process or certain behaviour, the outcome should be guaranteed. For example, as long as crew members follow the set procedures for

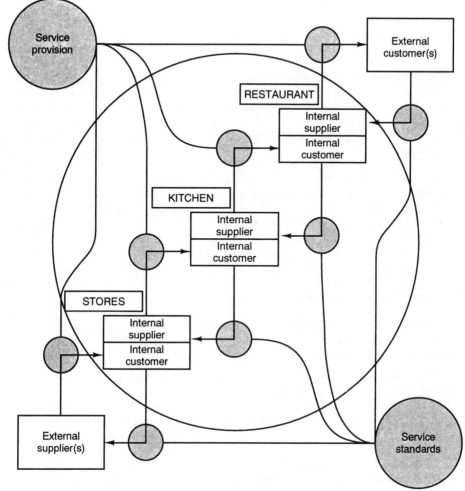

Figure 6.3 The chain of standards.

cooking fries, the standard of the final product is guaranteed. Standards would therefore be set for the process and not for the outcome. Output standards are used where there is high uncertainty in the task and the link between action and outcome is weak. When standards are being established for greeting and seating customers, there can be no one set process that is right for every customer. In this situation it is more useful to set an output standard – a happy customer seated within three minutes, for example – than to specify a detailed scripted procedure.

SCOPE OF OPERATIONAL STANDARDS

In their research into service standards in financial services organizations, Smith and Lewis[10] found that two types of standards were in use: those relating to the procedural aspects of the service and those relating to staff behaviour. They gave examples of procedural aspects as answering the telephone after a certain number of rings, dealing with correspondence and telephone enquiries within a certain period of time and processing customer requests within a time limit. Their examples for staff behaviour included courtesy, greeting or addressing customers by name, the level of staff product knowledge and the standard of cleanliness or tidiness in the unit.

These empirical findings follow almost exactly the framework proposed by Grönroos.[11] He also breaks service down into two dimensions that he calls the technical or outcome dimension and the functional or process-related dimension. He suggests that although *what* customers receive is important to them, (e.g. the hotel room with a bed to sleep on, or the restaurant meal), this technical aspect of the outcome is only one part of the service. In addition, customers pass through a number of more or less successfully handled moments of truth that present the way in which the service is delivered. The customer will obviously be influenced by *how* he or she receives the service, e.g. the accessibility of the restaurant, the appearance and behaviour of wait-staff, how they perform their tasks and what they say. This element he calls the functional quality of the process. Although it may be relatively easy to set objective standards for the technical results of service, it is much more difficult to specify the functional dimension.

Martin[12] has, however, developed a similar scheme which breaks these dimensions down further and applies them directly to restaurant operations. His procedural or technical dimension for food service is divided into service flow, timeliness, customization, anticipation, communication, customer feedback and supervision. His personal or convivial process dimension is broken down into attitude, body language, tone of voice, tact, attentiveness, guidance and selling, and problem solving.

Each area is then represented by a number of separate elements. For example, service flow is further broken down into the following:

- Is each table in a section in a different stage of the service cycle?
- Is the crew working at a steady but comfortable pace?
- Are the kitchen and bar over-extended at any one time?
- Are customers waiting longer than the maximum time designated for service?

On the convivial dimension, tact is looked at under the following headings:

- Is proper etiquette exhibited by all service personnel?
- Are correct language and grammar heard in the restaurant?
- Is slang avoided?
- Is restaurant jargon avoided in front of the customer?
- Is friction avoided amongst fellow employees?

Although these are phrased as questions to form the basis for a service audit, it is easy to see how they could be rephrased as service standards, although they would obviously needed to be added to in order to cover all aspects of the foodservice operation.

However, food and beverage operations do not consist solely of a service element. Standards will need to be set for the product side too. Jones and Lockwood[13] put forward a matrix for hotel operations that is directly applicable to catering operations. They divide the nature of the customers' contact with the operation into social (service) and material (product). Each of these can be seen as having both tangible and intangible characteristics. The food and beverage product has tangible elements such as the food itself, the crockery, cutlery, glassware and furniture that are used, and the menu; but they also have intangible elements to do with the atmosphere that is created. Service is normally seen as consisting of intangible elements such as warmth or courtesy but also includes the tangible elements of speed and effectiveness.

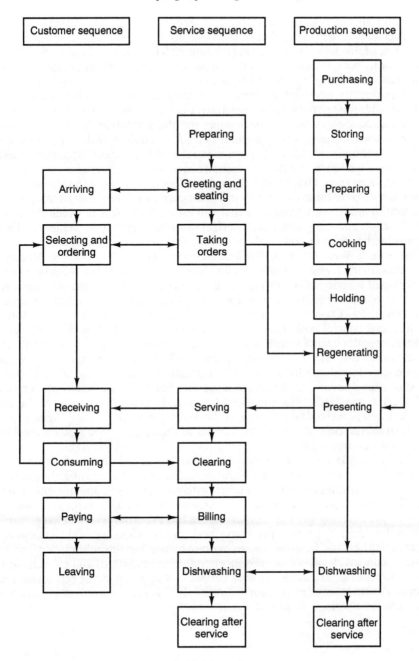

Figure 6.4 Process in food and beverage operations.
Adapted from Lillicrap and Cousins[14].

When establishing operating standards, both the tangible and intangible elements of the product and the service need to be detailed, identifying both the outcomes expected and the style of the delivery process to be adopted. This needs to be done for all areas of the operation, both back-of-house and front-of-house, whether in contact with the external customer or the internal customer. The model shown in Figure 6.4 outlines the procedures directly involved in serving the customer, or providing support for this activity. In addition the back-up administrative services would also need to be detailed.

Using the customers as the focal point for the operation, and determining the operating standards necessary to ensure their satisfaction at each stage of the process identified in the diagram, allows the operation to build a series of supporting standards, for the service sequence and the production sequence, to deliver that satisfaction. The path having been traced backwards through the operation, the standards must then be analysed forwards to ensure that they integrate correctly. The result of this process will be a comprehensive set of standards that will establish the way in which the operation should function and the standards of performance that need to be achieved. They will also form the basis for operational control through service audit.

In the South West Thames Regional Health Authority Catering Management Quality Assurance Review 1990/91, Colin Clark, the Regional Hotel Services Adviser, has developed a series of operating standards which form the basis of such a service audit. The areas covered by the audit include hygiene and food handling, control at the kitchen level, food volume control system, financial control and information about food, financial control and efficiency of catering staff, control of the meal service at ward level, menu content for staff, menu content for patients, flexibility provided by the patients' meal ordering and service system, and customer awareness. It is easy to recognize here the hierarchy of standards operating back through the operation from the customer as described in the previous section. Each of these areas is then split into a set of specific standards. The number of standards in each area shows the relative complexity and perceived significance of the areas. For example, the hygiene and food handling area has some 40 standards, control of the meal service at ward level has 14, and customer awareness has 8.

Another example of a comprehensive set of operating standards is provided by Harvester Restaurants, part of the Forte organization. Its operating standards cover five main areas: administration; restaurant; kitchen; bar/cellar; and hygiene. Each area is further sub-divided into sub-areas. For example, the bar/cellar is split into sections on back-of-house covering stock and orders (stock level v. order level), cellar (cleanliness/hygiene/safety and approved products) and stores (cleanliness/hygiene/safety and product handling), and front-of-house covering behind bar (cleanliness/hygiene/safety, approved products, legal notices/product handling/preparation) and guest areas (front of bar 11 a.m., exterior, and guest area service). A detail from the restaurant area for moments of truth in service is shown in Table 6.2. This extract is only one small part of a comprehensive coverage of all restaurant areas.

CONCLUSION

The discussion above has highlighted the complexity of the task facing managers in establishing operating standards for any foodservice operation. It is obvious that operating standards will differ between sectors of the foodservice industry. The

Table 6.2 Example of restaurant operating standards.

Items		Points	Score	Comments
HOST(ESS)				
Host(ess) at host point		25		
Greeting/smile/eye contact		25		
Correct time given		5		
No smoking offered and operating		5		
Name in full on all bills		10		
Attention to children		5		
	Sub-Total	75		
PHONE ANSWERING				
Answering within three rings		10		
Time of day/Harvester and restaurant name		10		
Booking policy in operation		10		
Offers no smoking		10		
Positive farewell		10		
	Sub-Total	50		

examples given above of standards in the hospital sector and the steak house sector demonstrate the emphasis placed on what each sector considers to be important in delivering service to their particular client group and within their particular environmental constraints. Hygiene and safety are essential parts of the operating standards for any foodservice operation but reach especial importance in a hospital environment. Rewarding contact between foodservice staff and customers is also important in any operation but gains significance in those markets catering primarily for a leisure-orientated customer.

In the design of a new foodservice operation, the task of creating standards for all areas of the business may seem to be an almost insurmountable task. However, if the process of development outlined in the preceding chapters has been followed correctly, the task is not as daunting as it may seem. The market research and concept development stage will have established the service concept to be delivered and should have expressed the customer segment's expectations in terms of the product and service benefits to be provided. The menu planning and design stage will have established most of the standards for food production including purchasing standards and the catering systems to be adopted. The food service layout and design stage will have provided the layout for both the kitchen and restaurant areas and will, along with the production standards, determine the time standards that can be achieved. The establishment of staffing levels will also provide the productivity standards required of staff and systems and the recruitment standards needed to fill the positions created. Once all these standards are in place it should be a relatively simple task to check the integration of the standards to achieve customer requirements and fill in any missing standards especially in the areas of administration and control.

Developing service standards is equally important, if somewhat less complex, in an existing operation. Over time, customer requirements will change and the capabilities of the service system may alter. It is essential that procedures are in place to monitor all deviations from established operating standards so that adjustments can be made as necessary. Monitoring levels of customer satisfaction will give some evidence of changing customer requirements, but more specific market research may be necessary to establish exactly how standards need to be changed.

Operating standards offer the operation a method of ensuring the consistency of the delivery process. They provide a concrete expression of the customers' requirements in operational terms that can be used to communicate these standards to all employees. In this way they provide a framework for establishing, monitoring and controlling the way that the operation should perform. Agreed service standards need to be expressed in terms of the outcomes for the end consumer. Standards also need to be established for ensuring the support of this final delivery through the customer–server chains throughout the organization, so that every employee, and not just those on the front line, is actively involved in ensuring the quality of the delivery process.

REFERENCES

1. East, J. (1993) *Managing Quality in the Catering Industry*, Croner Publications, Kingston upon Thames.
2. Heskett, J. L. (1987) 'Lessons in the service sector'. *Harvard Business Review*, March–April, p. 120.
3. Nightingale, M. (1985) 'The hospitality industry: defining quality for a quality assurance programme – a study of perceptions', *Service Industries Journal*, Vol. 5, No. 1, pp. 9–22.
4. East, J., op. cit.
5. Newton, S. and van de Merwe C. (1992) 'Quality assurance and the mystery guest programme in Harvester Restaurants', in Cooper, C. and Lockwood, A., (eds) *Progress in Tourism, Recreation and Hospitality Management*, Vol.5, pp. 169–174.
6. Cearbhaill, A. O. (1993) 'A quality audit for the catering product'. From the conference on Service Quality held by the International Association of Hospitality Management Schools, University of Göteborg, 13–15 May.
7. Armistead, O. G. (1988) 'Customer service and operations management in service businesses', *Service Industries Journal*, Vol. 9, No. 2, pp. 247–260.
8. Sasser, W. E., Olsen R. P. and Wyckoff, D. D. (1978) *Management of Service Operations*, Allyn & Bacon, Newton, Mass., p. 181.
9. Ouchi and Maguire (1975) 'Organizational control: two functions', *Administrative Science Quarterly*, Vol. 20, pp. 559–569.
10. Smith, A. M. and Lewis, B (1989) 'Customer care in financial service organizations', *International Journal of Bank Marketing*, Vol. 7, No. 5, pp. 13–22.
11. Grönroos, C. (1990) *Service Management and Marketing*, Lexington Books, Lexington, Mass.
12. Martin, W. B. (1986) 'Measuring and improving your service quality', *Cornell Hotel and Restaurant Administration Quarterly*, May, pp. 80–87.
13. Jones, P. and Lockwood, A. J. (1989) *The Management of Hotel Operations*, Cassell, London.
14. Lillicrap, D. and Cousins, J. (1990) *Food and Beverage Service*, Hodder & Stoughton, Sevenoaks.

7

Designing Control Systems

Paul Merricks and Peter Jones

INTRODUCTION

One of the themes of this book is the necessity of adopting a contingent approach to management. Success in any business comes not only from doing things right but from doing the right things. This is particularly true in the area of control systems, because managers with a limited amount of time and resources have to decide where to concentrate the control effort. The control of the costs of paperclips, for example, need not be as rigorous as the control of the costs of whisky. Also, different costs should be controlled in different ways. For instance, the costs of rent and energy might be the same for a year, but the control method should be different because the first is unaffected by management action, whilst the second is manageable. Managers have choices in the emphasis placed on the control of different costs and the control methods which should be used. There is no perfect control system which will meet the needs of all foodservice businesses. Each business will have a preferred control system, depending on its business environment and operational process.

Cost structures in the foodservice industry differ considerably, depending on the type of business, the market situation and the operating methods. Wages may be a largely fixed cost in one operation and a largely variable cost in another. The cost structures within the commercial restaurant sector vary considerably, but normally fall within the range shown in Table 7.1. In the institutional sector, particularly where a catering operation is performed on a subsidized basis, in in-flight and travel catering and many other sectors, the cost structure and cost behaviour will be dramatically different. The ranges for each cost category show that there is no ideal 'template' for business success. The foodservice industry is a diverse industry, and each business will have its own particular cost problems and its own most appropriate system of control. In this chapter we shall look at the overall concept of control as a management function, before considering some of the factors that influence the design of a system. The role that budgets play in the control function is explored, particularly with regard to how these may relate to the foodservice industry's different cost structures.

Table 7.1   Range of restaurant operating costs (as a percentage of sales).

Sales	Percentage range
Cost of sales	34–43
Wages and related costs	19–38
Advertising and promotion	0–4
Other operating expenses	9–11
Rent	4–15
Depreciation	2–5
Insurance	‹1

CONTROL AS A MANAGEMENT PROCESS

Control is *not* concerned with finding more efficient and less expensive ways of providing the same quality; menu engineering achieves this for materials and managing productivity does so for labour costs. Control is the management function which is concerned with keeping costs in line with standards, or performance in line with plans. This concept of control as part of the management process is represented in Figure 7.1. The management process starts with setting objectives. Most foodservice businesses will have a profit objective; all will certainly have some form of financial objective; many will have other business objectives. All employees' activities should be directed towards achieving the objectives of the business. To do this, objectives are translated into detailed plans in the areas of finance, marketing and operations. These plans will cover the target market and the marketing mix, the specifications for the product itself, and the operational methods (each of which have been considered in the preceding chapters). Central to these plans is the primary tool of financial control – the budget – covering how money will be earned and spent. At corporate level, the responsibilities for these three activities – finance, marketing and operations – will probably rest with three different departments. This necessitates the development and co-ordination of three separate plans. Fortunately, at unit level, or in the individual business, this functional division need not occur and managers can get on with planning the business in an integrated way.

The financial control function is concerned with setting a standard (for example, the budgeted wages cost), measuring the actual performance (the wages cost incurred), identifying any variance and if necessary taking corrective action in order to ensure that profit objectives are still achieved. The information needed for planning and control is provided by a management information system. Finally, the nature of control and performance measurement is explored in three main areas: the purchase and storage of stocks, the production process and the labour force.

CONSIDERATIONS IN DESIGNING A CONTROL SYSTEM

Managers have to decide how to design a control system which is appropriate for the needs of a particular business. There are two distinct approaches which can be taken to cost control. The first of these is called *pre-operational control*. Here management

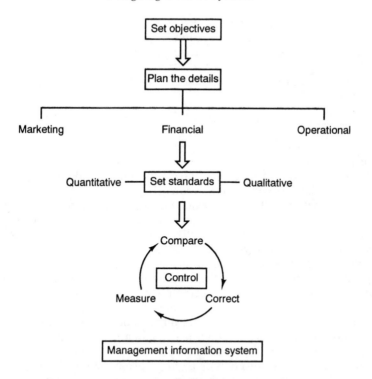

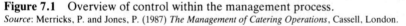

Figure 7.1 Overview of control within the management process.
Source: Merricks, P. and Jones, P. (1987) *The Management of Catering Operations*, Cassell, London.

effort is directed towards limiting the amount available for subordinates to use. For example, Gamble and Kipps[1] describe a hospital catering food costs control system, which in essence releases from stores only the issues required to produce the requested dishes for the day according to standard recipes. The manager has exercised control over the costs which will be incurred before the production takes place. Labour costs are often controlled using pre-operational principles, whereby the manager authorizes the labour utilization in advance (using a schedule or rota), and any subsequent changes to that plan (such as overtime) need the manager's authorization. Pre-operational control is most useful in situations where volume and sales mix can be forecast with a high degree of certainty, for example in banqueting, school and hospital meals catering.

The second approach is called *post-operational control*. Here standards are set, staff are trained and the operation is run in accordance with those standards. The costs are measured after the event. If costs show an adverse variance compared with standard, management action is centred on people problems – finding out who did not comply with standards and preventing the same problem occurring in the future. Post-operational control is necessary where managers cannot plan and control the allocation of resources in detail in advance. For example, food costs in an à la carte restaurant could not be controlled on a pre-operational basis because of the difficulty in accurately predicting sales volume and mix. Post-operational controls require managers to focus on corrective action, which usually involves staff performance.

So a major decision area in the design of control systems is the choice between pre-operational and post-operational controls. The former in our opinion are generally preferable from the point of view of effective resources management and positive employee supervision – but pre-operational control is largely limited to situations where demand is predictable. In practice, both forms of control are often used together, pre-operational controls to limit the use of resources together with post-operational controls to check that the pre-operational control system is working effectively.

Information for Control Purposes

Managers who are involved in designing or reviewing a control system have to specify what information will be required – but weigh this against the costs and benefits of having such information. In specifying the control information needed for a business, managers have to decide on three dimensions of information. They have to decide how specific the information will be – for example, will productivity data be prepared for each employee, or for each shift, or for each department? Secondly, managers have to decide how frequently the information will be prepared. For instance, food costs can be calculated on a daily, weekly or four-weekly basis. Thirdly, the accuracy of the information has to be determined – for instance, beverage costs can be measured to the nearest penny, nearest pound, or the nearest ten pounds. The required accuracy, specificity and frequency of control information will depend on the scope that exists for remedial management action.

There are obvious costs associated with the production of control information, but there are significant hidden costs in management time which is taken up with examining, interpreting, and discussing inappropriate information. Control information should be regularly reviewed, with a critical examination of its costs and benefits. Sometimes control information which was needed some time ago for the improvement of a certain aspect of business performance is still being produced unnecessarily. It is advisable to take a zero-base approach, starting with an assumption of no control information, and justifying the production of each item of data (accuracy, specificity and frequency) in terms of its impact on profit improvement.

The Budget as a Control Tool

Although there may be some advantages in adopting a pre-operational cost control system, most foodservice businesses adopt a budgetary control system, which is an example of post-operational control. The budget is simply a statement of intention in financial terms and is primarily to control the overall profit performance of the business. Budgets can either be fixed or variable. A fixed budget assumes a relatively stable environment with predictable trends. Only one budget is developed and actual performance is compared with this. Variable or flexible budgets are designed to take into account a number of different scenarios, above and below the expected sales level. Performance is measured against that budget that is closest to actual experience.

Different sectors of the foodservice industry have different cost structures owing to the level of capital investment, type of technology, staffing levels and concept. High street restaurants have high fixed costs relative to their variable costs, whilst industrial and welfare catering have relatively low fixed costs as a proportion of total cost. Kotas[2] argues that high-fixed-cost operations must adopt a 'market orientation' as they operate close to their break-even point, and hence need to be sensitive to market trends. High-variable-cost operations are most likely to have a 'cost orientation', focusing largely on cost management rather than customer needs. This is illustrated in Table 7.2.

Table 7.2   Market and cost orientation in the foodservice industry.

	Market orientation	Cost orientation
Cost structure	High proportion fixed cost and low proportion variable cost	Low proportion fixed cost and high proportion variable cost
Investment	High level of capital investment	Low level of capital investment
Product design	Emphasis on service aspects and atmosphere	Emphasis on food and beverage product
Average spend	Relatively high	Relatively low
Gross profit	Relatively high	Relatively low
Sales volume per employee	Low number of transactions	High number of transactions
Number of staff	High in proportion to number of customers	Low in proportion to number of customers
Rates of pay	Relatively high	Relatively low

Adapted from Kotas, R., (1975) *Marketing Orientation in the Hotel and Catering Industry*, Surrey University Press, Guildford.

The cost structure of an operation affects the type of budgetary control system that should be used. Kotas[3] suggests that flexible budgets are more appropriate to market-orientated catering businesses, and fixed budgets more suited to cost-orientated businesses. There is some confusion over the purpose and use of flexible budgets. Some people believe that the budget should be adjusted in the light of actual sales volume. This negates the real purpose of budgetary control: to measure the progress of the business towards its profit and cost control. In our opinion, the budget should form a static plan for profit achievement, which may be revised on a rolling basis depending on the business environment. Budgetary variance analysis can be quite useful for explaining why actual performance does not meet the plan – but the cost of obtaining the data necessary to analyse key variances makes it more suitable to large operations or corporate departments.

The value of a budget as a means of cost control is often limited by the frequency of reporting and the time lag between the period end and the publishing of the data. In market-oriented businesses, there is a need for a shorter reporting period (weekly, or in certain instances daily, for some expenses and revenue categories). In cost-orientated business, however, the reporting period can be less frequent (weekly or four-weekly). Whatever reporting period is selected, a budget will always be a form of post-operational control. There may well be a time lag of four weeks between the time a cost is incurred and the subsequent time at which it is reported. If this results in an adverse variance against a budget, many managers spend time and effort investigating the reasons for the variance (often to report to head office). Meanwhile the day-to-day control of other costs has slipped away and the process repeats itself. It is the classic reactive trap: the manger is caught in a cycle of investigating what has happened, rather than influencing what will happen.

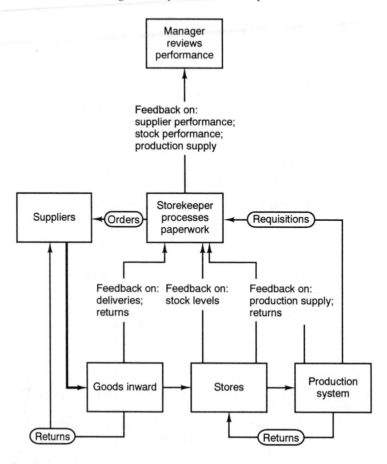

Figure 7.2 Stock control system.

CONTROLLING AND MEASURING STOCK PERFORMANCE

Food and beverage commodities constitute one of the largest single costs in a foodservice business. A variation of 1 per cent in these material costs will have very significant effects on profit. Materials enter the establishment as purchases received, they are stored and issued from the store, they are processed and are either sold or wasted. A foodservice manager who is planning a stock control system has to establish the nature of materials required, a process for obtaining supplies, define how and when purchases are to be made, keep accurate records of stock held, and select a system for valuing stock. The nature of this part of the total control system is illustrated in Figure 7.2. Even with an apparently simple purchasing decision a manager has to appreciate the implications that this purchase may have for the business. First, the item will need to be paid for and this will affect the cash flow of the business. Secondly, the item will need to be stored and storage costs can be considerable. Thirdly, the item becomes an asset of the business and management has a duty to protect and preserve these assets from deterioration and pilferage.

Purchasing Control Systems

In deciding how to control purchases of materials stocks, three standards need to be established: quality standards, quantity standards, and prices. Such decisions are usually influenced by the three Vs: volume, variety and value. Turner[4] describes volume as 'the size of demand for each commodity', variety as 'the range of commodities on offer', and value as 'the relative aspect of the function of the commodity'. In Chapter 3 we looked at menu design and the extent to which these three Vs can vary widely within the industry.

Quality standards derive largely from the decisions made about the menu and the concept. The menu identifies the actual items needed to enable dishes and meals to be prepared. The concept determines the basic cost-price relationship, the technology to be used for production purposes, and the customer expectations about quality. The most basic decision that will be made is whether to 'make or buy'; that is to say, to prepare from fresh on the foodservice premises or buy-in items or dishes prepared elsewhere. Once this decision is made, there are still decisions to be made about grades, brands, degree of freshness, sizes, and method of packaging. Many foodservice operations define each of these factors by preparing standard purchase specifications. The advantages of such specifications are that they eliminate confusion between suppliers and the foodservice operator; they make it easier for suppliers tendering to supply; they provide guidance for storekeepers when receiving goods inwards; and they help in menu planning by enabling variety reduction to occur if need be.

In addition, it is essential to establish the required quantities of items. The ideal stock level for a specific commodity depends on the nature of the business and the characteristics of the commodity, in particular the level of sales, the stability of demand, the terms of supply, the costs of stock-holding, cash flow limitations, the shelf-life of the commodity, the storage space available and market trends in price and availability. Cash flow and storage costs are affected by the extent to which items are purchased in bulk. The advantages of buying in bulk are that items may be cheaper because of bulk discount; there may be protection against sudden increase in demand, protection against sudden shortage in supply, and potentially protection against inflation. Disadvantages of buying in bulk include the fact the cash flow position worsens; stock-holding costs increase; deterioration or pilferage may occur; and future demand may decrease. As far as fresh food is concerned the disadvantages obviously outweigh the advantages. With other products the reverse can hold true. With wine, for example, the product may appreciate in value considerably during the storage period.

In general, unless there is a sound reason to the contrary, stock levels should be kept as low as possible. However, with high-cost, high-usage items, it is often useful to plan the stock levels and reorder methods in more detail. The starting point for planning stock levels is an analysis of the usage rate. Where items are used infrequently (often the case with non-perishable commodities), the *periodic order method* can be used. On a regular basis, for instance once a week or once a month, items will be reordered on the basis of forecast need plus buffer stock to avoid stock-out, less stock in hand. A more sophisticated approach is based around the idea of *economic order quantity* (EOQ). The total cost associated with a purchase is a combination of the invoice cost, plus the administration cost (postage, clerical time, etc) plus the storage cost (running the freezer, etc.). These costs will vary, as shown in Table 7.3. Somewhere between the extremes of one large order and very many small orders lies the point where the total cost will be lowest. The EOQs can be calculated using mathematical formulae or by preparing cost tables. Either method is laborious and time-consuming, and the useful

Table 7.3   Effect of purchase order size on purchase costs.

	Invoice cost	Administration cost	Storage cost
Many small orders	High	High	Low
Few large orders	Low	High	High

application of EOQs is limited to very large-scale purchasing. It should be remembered, however, that there is such a thing as an ideal purchase quantity.

Careful planning and control of stock levels for individual commodities is not in itself completely satisfactory as the only method of stock monitoring. It is useful to have an easily monitored measure of total stock value, the use of *number of days' stock* is to be recommended as a system. It is calculated by dividing the value of current stock multiplied by 365 days by the total value of stock used. Trends in number of days' stock give useful control data on a four-weekly basis – but evaluation of the raw data is more difficult. The norm for foodservice operations is about 15 days' food stock, but this varies with the type of stocks held and volume of business. In addition to being useful for assessing total stock, this measure is helpful for highlighting slow-moving stock.

Selecting Suppliers

There is a wide range of alternative sources of supply for every commodity a foodservice manager may wish to purchase, ranging from growers and manufacturers, through wholesalers, cash and carries, to retail outlets. The three Vs and purchase specification will determine the number and type of different suppliers. Higher fuel and labour costs and scale economies of distribution are making it less likely that single foodservice operations will be able to purchase directly from growers and manufacturers in future. Thus only very large chains are likely to purchase direct; other operations will use a middleman. Large chain operations have two main options with regard to supply. They can either own and operate their own distribution system, like Forte, or they can contract a distributor to make deliveries from the manufacturers to their units on their behalf. Most fast food chains, such as Kentucky Fried Chicken, negotiate a bulk price with the manufacturers and then make delivery arrangements with a distributor. Kentucky Fried Chicken pays the manufacturer directly for the contracted goods. The distributor orders enough goods from the manufacturer to meet the supply requirements of local franchises and is invoiced by Kentucky Fried Chicken at the rates charged to franchises less a fixed percentage as a distribution allowance. Finally, the franchisees pay the distributor. This has several advantages in that the manufacturer only supplies a limited number of locations in bulk and Kentucky Fried Chicken franchisees are assured of weekly deliveries of all commodities in any order size.

For operators who are not part of a chain, commodities must be purchased either from wholesale markets, from wholesale suppliers, from cash and carry outlets or from retail outlets such as supermarkets. The tradition of chefs getting up at 5 a.m. to go to the local market to select fresh meat, fish, fruit and vegetables has become the exception rather than the rule. The growth in availability and use of frozen and irradiated food has resulted in less reliance on truly fresh commodities, and consequently the number, scale and frequency of markets are declining. As markets decline, changes in catering operations, such as the shift from skilled to semi-skilled kitchen personnel, smaller kitchen and store areas and lower profit margins, have meant a consequent move towards what has been called 'one-stop shopping'. This refers to the use of total-supply distributors who can provide the caterers with all their commodity requirements including foodstuffs, disposables and alcoholic beverages. When using total supply only one delivery is made, which cuts down on paperwork, opportunities for pilferage and time spent on receiving goods.

Increased distribution costs now cause many foodservice suppliers to rethink their delivery policy and, especially where order quantities are small, caterers often have to go to the warehouse or cash-and-carry themselves. The main advantage of cash-and-carry to independent operators is that there is no minimum order size. There are, however, significant disadvantages, in particular the lack of credit facilities. Caterers who use cash-and-carry outlets also have to pay for their own distribution costs, which are often comparatively higher than those of a wholesaler.

Whatever the form of supply, effective control requires that there is a systematic approach to placing orders. In most cases, this will be done through a purchase order book, which provides a standard form in duplicate or triplicate, thereby providing a copy for the supplier, purchaser and/or storekeeper. These should be completed even when orders are made by telephone to ensure that only goods ordered are actually delivered. Small operators who purchase direct from cash-and-carries could still use such a procedure in order to provide their 'shopping list', and thereby avoid purchasing items on impulse which they do not really need.

Receiving Control Procedures

Since the prime purpose of purchasing control is to be clear about the quality, quantity and price of purchased items, it is these three things that are checked when goods are received. In the UK supplies will either be accompanied by a delivery note or an invoice. The former is a simple list of items; the latter also provides prices and hence is a bill for the goods. This documentation should be checked against the purchase order. Most large foodservice operations rely on the storekeeper to monitor quality and quantity, and employ a control clerk to reconcile orders, delivery notes and invoices. Quality inspection requires storekeepers to be well trained in the basics of food quality, looking out for split bags, ruptured tins, defrosted frozen items, and so on. In some cases the chef will inspect items, especially high-cost items such as fresh meat and fish. Quantity verification is carried out by weighing or the simple counting of items. Checking on prices may not always be possible at the point of delivery but should always be carried out as soon as the invoice is received. In the event that either quality, quantity or price of items does not match the purchase specification or purchase order, these items should be returned with the driver or the documentation adjusted before the goods are accepted and signed for.

Stock Record-Keeping and Security

One of management's most important tasks is to ensure that the assets of the business are adequately protected from theft, loss or misappropriation. The purchase of food, alcohol and other catering materials presents a particular problem as they are attractive to the petty thief and, because of the large number of small suppliers involved, control is difficult. In addition to purchasing control procedures, it is necessary to assure the security of stock once on the foodservice premises. This sounds simple but when one considers the hundreds of different materials which are used, the dozens of different suppliers, the problems of incomplete orders and returned substandard goods and the opportunities for dishonesty by employees, suppliers and others, then the problem becomes very complex. The design of the goods reception area, the control of keys and the organization of stores are essential to effective control. Details of effective security procedures are discussed in Chapter 9.

There are a number of different ways in which control procedures can be exercised depending on the size of the unit and value of the goods in store. There may be daily records kept of all goods received – called the goods received book in a food store or a cellar inwards book in a wines and spirits store. The stock level of each item held may also be indicated for each item on each shelf by using a bin card system. Such a system assists with control, re-ordering and stock-taking. To ensure effective stock rotation, items that do not have a 'use by' date already stamped on them may be tagged in some way. This is increasingly being done for meat items. Finally, there may be a need to identify and record losses. For instance, in a cellar there will often be a breakages book.

Issuing Control

Figure 7.2 also identifies that there must be control over the issuing of goods from the stores into the production area. In practice some goods may never go to the stores at all, especially highly perishable items such as bread and milk. Such items have been termed 'directs' and get charged to food cost on the assumption that they are used immediately. In small foodservice businesses, all items might be treated in this way. In larger operations, items will normally be requisitioned from the stores by product staff on a daily basis. So all items other than directs get charged to food cost when they are requisitioned from stores. The cost of items will be established by the control office, depending upon the stock valuation method used.

Stock Valuation and Stocktaking

The main technique for measuring food and beverage costs is the valuation of stocks and purchases. The choice of valuation method, particularly in times of rapid inflation, can have significant implications for profit and asset reporting. There are four textbook methods of stock valuation,[5] which can be summarized as:

- FIFO – which tends to give the highest value to stocks and to inflate profits.
- LIFO – which tends to undervalue stocks, with a more realistic profit valuation.
- AVERAGE – which tends to overvalue stocks and consequently overstates profit. It has the advantage of being administratively convenient.
- STANDARD – which is a sophisticated technique forming the basis for a comprehensive cost control system.

These stock valuation methods can all be used for the valuation of issues from stores. The use of any one of these methods facilitates the preparation of a stores reconciliation which will accurately identify any loss (possibly through pilferage) from the stores. Computer-based stock control systems may utilize one or another of these methods. However, if utilized in manual stores issue systems, they present a burdensome administrative task.

There is an alternative method of stock valuation which is administratively far simpler – and is commonly used in many foodservice businesses. This is to value stock using the most recent price paid for a commodity – also known as the current price. There is a significant disadvantage associated with the use of this current stock valuation method, namely that it does not permit an accurate stores reconciliation to be prepared. Managers can choose a more complex method of stock valuation which permits accurate measurement of stores losses, or a simpler (and cheaper) method of valuation and forfeit an accurate control over the stores.

All businesses need to measure the costs of commodities accurately on this basis at least once a year, for the purpose of preparing annual accounts. The most widely used approach is the 'opening stock, plus issues, minus closing stock' model used for the purpose of profit measurement. Physical stocktaking of this type is usually done by a firm of external stocktakers, but this may cost a business up to several hundred pounds for the production of one stocktaking result. Apart from the production of annual accounts, almost all businesses produce a periodic operating statement, usually on a four-weekly basis, and this, of course, requires the measurement of food and beverage costs. Production of accurate consumption figures, based on stocktaking results, has a high cost of control, particularly when external stocktakers are employed. Frequent external stocktaking is usually only considered necessary in chain operations when turnover is very high and the chance of fraud is considerable; for example, in managed pubs and travel catering. An alternative for chain operations, where the possibilities of local fraud are less significant, is to get local management to undertake periodic stocktakes, with an annual or six-monthly validation by external stocktakers. Large single-unit catering operations will often have their own food and beverage control department, which undertakes periodic stocktakes, sometimes with the co-operation of other staff.

CONTROLLING AND MEASURING FOOD AND BEVERAGE COSTS

The second main area in which control is exercised is in the production kitchen. In the stores the goods may be broken down into smaller units, but essentially remain unchanged. In the production kitchen, however, the goods are transformed from raw materials into finished product, from food items into meals. Such transformation is achieved through employing a wide range of different techniques and cookery principles, during which there is always the chance that unnecessary waste will occur. At the same time, these goods are potentially subject to the same level of risk of pilferage and damage as they might be in the stores.

Production Control

Production control is aimed at ensuring that dishes are prepared to conform to a portion size, quality standard and cost consistent with the menu concept. This can be achieved by having a system of standard portioning, standard recipes and standard costing. Standard portions are established by quantifying any item that is to be serviced by weight, by volume, or by count. For instance, UK steakhouse chains have tended to use a 200-gram steak as a standard for steaks; in the licensed trade many items are required

Table 7.4   Comparators for food and beverage control.

Comparator	Focus	Common applications
Cost percentage	Relationship of cost and revenue	Commercial restaurants
Per capita cost	Relationship of cost and volume	Institutional catering
Commodity usage	Correct usage of each ingredient	Fast food Bottle wine sales Retailing High-cost items
Potential sales	Correct sale of each ingredient	Bars Retailing

Source: Merricks, P. and Jones, P. (1987) *The Management of Catering Operations*, Cassell, London.

by law to be served in specific volumes, such as 125 cl for wine by the glass; and particularly for pre-portioned items it is possible to specify portions by the number each customer should receive. In some cases implements are used to establish effective portioning, such as scoops for ice cream or french fries, ladles for soups and sauces, and slotted spoons for vegetables. Once the portion size is established it is possible to define the standard recipe. Such recipes should ensure consistency of appearance, taste and customer satisfaction. The combination of portion size and recipe, along with the known commodity costs, enable the manager to establish a standard portion cost for each item on the menu. The level of complexity of costing will vary widely. Some items may be sold in the same form that they were purchased in, for instance bread rolls or a glass of milk; in such cases the costing is simply the purchase price per unit divided by the number of portions per unit. In other cases, a dish may be very complex, involving the use of many different kinds of commodity, so that the standard recipe will need to be costed very carefully.

Production control also requires that waste is accounted for. There are two possible methods of treating waste food; either an allowance for waste can be built into the overall potential food cost percentage, or waste can be included in the variance allowed on each dish item. Different approaches are taken in industry. If waste is a significant problem worthy of individual control an alternative is to record waste written off, value this at portion cost and itemize the total as a separate variance. The principle is that measuring the nature and level of waste should reflect the current control problems.

Performance Measurement

There are a number of options open to management in measuring food and beverage costs. Stocktaking establishes the actual food cost, which can be expressed as a percentage of sales income. In order for effective control to take place, this actual performance needs to be measured against a standard. There are four types of comparator which can be used for the control of food and beverage costs. The first of these is by using a *target cost percentage* – usually known as a target kitchen percentage or a target food cost percentage. This is widely used in commercial catering operations. Such a target can either be fixed or variable. Fixed targets are established as a constant and worked to over an extended period, whereas variable target food costs take into account variations in commodity costs.

In small businesses, where one person can keep personal control over profits, volume, quality standards and production techniques, a fixed target food cost percentage is an entirely appropriate way to control costs. In businesses with large turnover and division of responsibility, the choice of a constant target food cost percentage (for example, 35 per cent) may affect the optimum balance between quality and cost. Where sales mix and purchase price variations may bring about an increase in food costs, undue pressure on food production staff to attain an arbitrary food cost percentage may result in loss of quality and drop in volume. Instead of adopting an arbitrary target food cost percentage, larger businesses are well advised to calculate a variable, or potential, food cost percentage based on sales mix, current portion costs and selling prices. Depending on the changes in the sales mix and the movements in food prices, the potential food cost percentage may need to be recalculated on a four-weekly basis. With a large sales mix and complex dishes, this is a daunting task if done by hand. However, the selection of a computerized point-of-sale system which stores sales mix data, and the use of an inventory control and dish costing computer package, enable this task to be achieved in a matter of an hour or so.

The second comparator for food and beverage costs is the *per capita cost*. This is appropriate to the institutional sector, where managers have to operate within closely defined subsidy levels. For example, an RAF catering officer will have a set feeding allowance for each airman, each day. This is an ideal situation for the use of pre-operational control, where menus can be pre-costed and only sufficient food requisitioned to meet the requirements of the day's planned production. The army's CATPAC computer catering control system for hospital caterers also works on the pre-operational control system – and is focused on the calculation of per capita food costs as the main control comparator.[6]

The third comparator for food or beverage cost control is the production of *potential commodity usage* data. This type of comparator is most appropriate to businesses with limited product range and a high degree of standardization, as in fast food operations. For example, point-of-sale systems such as the Positran system do much more than analyse a sales mix and control cash. The systems store details of the standard recipes used for each item. Stock levels for each commodity are also stored and updated as deliveries are received. As each item is sold, the system decreases the inventory totals for each ingredient by the amount specified in the standard recipe. On demand, managers can obtain a printout of the potential stock levels of each commodity. A quick check of what is actually in store will reveal exactly where shortages have occurred. Potential commodity usage is also widely used for the control of wine sales by the bottle – using either the traditional cellar ledger, or a computer-based inventory control system. Potential commodity usage is also used selectively to control high-cost items – such as steaks – and this usage is well explained by Kotas and Davis.[7] However, potential commodity usage is not suitable for operations where a wide range of commodities are processed into a wide range of different items for sale.

The fourth comparator for control of food and beverage costs is somewhat different from the previous three, because it focuses on the *potential sales value* of the commodities that have been consumed. It is most useful for ensuring that commodities have been correctly transformed into revenue, and is widely used in bars or retail outlets. The principle is that each commodity is valued at its retail value. After a stocktake, the sum of the potential sales value of all commodities used is compared with the actual sales revenue. Any shortage suggests that either money or stock has been wasted or misappropriated. This method is suitable for sales outlets where items are resold – for example, a kiosk selling prepacked snacks and portion controlled drinks – but not suitable for sales outlets where commodities are processed – for example, a cocktail bar. Some people suggest that mixed items, like cocktails, should be priced according to the potential sales value of their ingredients. This does not seem a sensible approach for businesses in the commercial sector – it is, in effect, the control tail wagging the pricing dog!

Managers can select the comparators which suit their business needs. In practice, several comparators may be used within one cost control system. Within a hotel the food from the main kitchen may be controlled by means of a potential gross profit percentage, and, equally, certain high-cost items – for example, pre-portioned meats – may be controlled by commodity usage. The sandwiches issued to the night porter may be controlled by a potential sales value and staff meals may be controlled on a per capita basis. Similarly, a cocktail bar may be controlled by commodity usage based around a sophisticated point-of-sale system, but a doubles bar in the same establishment may be better controlled using potential sales value.

Cost Allocation

Ascertaining food and beverage costs for the whole business by periodic stocktakes and the preparation of trading accounts is relatively straightforward. However, in a foodservice business which has more than one sales outlet the management is faced with a difficult problem of cost apportionment. In, for example, a large hotel, the hotel kitchen may serve a restaurant outlet, a coffee shop, banqueting, floor service and the hotel lounge. Two very important questions need to be answered in such a situation. First, if departmental operating statements are to be prepared for each of these sales outlets, how can food costs be apportioned? Secondly, how can the managerial effectiveness of the head chef be assessed when the kitchen percentage will vary depending on the sales mix in each of the sales outlets?

The Standard System of Catering Accounting[8] side-steps the first of these problems, by assuming that only two departmental operating statements will be prepared: one for all food operations and one for all beverage operations. Most managers do not accept that this is adequate, as it foregoes any attempt to measure the profitability of individual outlets, each of which may have a turnover of several hundred thousand pounds. This is possibly one of the reasons why the Standard System has not been adopted by many operators in the foodservice industry. Lepard[9] summarizes a method which would seem to be the most effective way of dealing with these problems. In its most sophisticated form, this requires the calculation of a potential gross profit percentage for each outlet, for each meal period. These potential gross profit percentages are applied to the actual sales revenue for each outlet, to give the potential food cost for each outlet, and this is used as the basis for food cost allocation. The difference between the total of the potential food cost for all the outlets and the actual food cost, is a measure of the chef's effectiveness.

Table 7.5   Factors determining total rate of pay.

Basic rate
Employers' National Insurance contributions
Overtime payment rate
Shift allowances
Public and annual holiday pay
Sick pay scheme
Employers' pension scheme contributions
Costs of meals and commission or other bonuses

CONTROL AND MEASUREMENT OF LABOUR COSTS

Many people who buy meals or drinks in a restaurant relate the value of their purchase to the cost of the materials. They compare the restaurant price with what it would have cost to prepare the dish at home – and this ignores labour costs and other overheads. In some foodservice businesses, the largest single item of cost is no longer food but wages, and the control of labour costs is as important as the control of food and beverage costs. A foodservice manager who is planning a labour cost control system has to do similar things to those needed for food and beverage control. In this case, however, the 'supplier' and 'materials being purchased' are identical, i.e. the employees.

Elements of Labour Costs

There are two elements of labour costs which need to be controlled: the time taken and rate of pay. The rate is far more than mere basic pay, as is shown in Table 7.5. These factors are determined by an employee's contract of employment. Many of the factors mentioned above are also fixed either by law, by corporate policy or by agreement with trade unions, so managers' ability to change most of these rate factors is very limited. They can only be controlled when a new employee is recruited or when an existing employee's rates are revised, for example after an annual appraisal. These rate factors are largely uncontrollable, and therefore there is little merit in reporting them in detail in the short term.

Likewise, there is limited discretion over the time factor of labour costs. The scope for varying an employee's hours is limited by the contractual base of employment and mode of employment, such as full-time, part-time or casual. Each mode has different conditions associated with it. Only some jobs, depending on the rostering system and the modes of employment adopted, have a high controllable element. For example, an hourly paid employee in a fast food store can be rostered for a daily minimum period which may or may not be extended depending on the actual sales volume. Classifying jobs as controllable or uncontrollable is a useful prerequisite to cost control.

Cost Allocation

The difficulty in allocating food costs between departments in order to prepare profit centre accounts has already has discussed. This is not such a significant problem with labour costs as the apportionment is normally achieved using either a manual timesheet or a time card control system. In most foodservice businesses, employment costs are reported for the purpose of costs control as a weekly departmental wage bill, often broken down into job categories. This figure usually represents the actual expenditure on wages during the past week, but may include accrued payments for such items as unsettled public sector pay awards. The accounting treatment of certain items of employment costs varies – and in some cases significant items, such as employers' pension fund contributions, may either be reported as a corporate headquarters cost or as an allocated cost at unit level. It is important for managers to understand the basis used for cost allocation. If costs are allocated on the basis of a controllable factor (for example, hours worked) then the canny manager will know how to reduce the apportioned costs. However, if the costs are allocated on the basis of an uncontrollable factor (for example, flooring area) then the costs are to all intents and purposes largely uncontrollable and as such are not a problem worth worrying about.

With businesses which have high daily fluctuations in demand and, consequently, fluctuating staffing requirements, it is advantageous to measure labour costs from a manual wage system, but computerized time card systems, such as those provided by Microtime, can provide the necessary information. A number of foodservice point-of-sale systems can also provide daily payroll control information. Point-of-sale systems allow employees, together with details of their rates of pay and details of hours worked, to be recorded. On request, such systems produce a comprehensive payroll report showing the hours worked and the costs incurred during the day.

However promptly or frequently employment costs are reported, they can rarely give managers all the necessary payroll control information. Most managers prefer to have a regular report of the number of hours worked – often broken down by job category. Four types of manhour data should be separately reported, all of which are easily extracted from either manual or computerized payroll systems. The four categories are: basic hours worked, premium hours worked, sickness and absenteeism hours, and holiday hours. The combination of these items of information permits a manager to evaluate employment costs more usefully. For example, total employment costs may have risen substantially, but the manhours analysis may show that the actual number of hours worked (basic plus overtime) is as normal; however, sickness has occurred and holidays have been taken – both of which incur additional costs. The combination of monetary value and manhours can provide the answers to such questions as why overtime rates had to be incurred.

Measuring Labour Costs

The choice of comparators when designing a cost control system will have great influence on what managers think of as problems and if and when they take control of catering labour costs. The first of these, which emphasizes the relationship of labour costs to revenue, is the *target labour cost percentage*. As discussed in the preceding paragraph, most businesses do not have a cost-effective system for measuring daily labour costs, and therefore actual percentages are calculated on a weekly basis (or even less frequently). It is easy to overlook the fact that a weekly labour cost percentage is an average figure, and it is erroneous to assume that if target labour cost percentage has been achieved in two consecutive weeks, then cost control has been equally effective in those two weeks. The average weekly labour cost percentage may hide missed opportunities to increase productivity through better rostering or more effective control of overtime. The actual labour cost percentage will also fluctuate owing to changes in holiday pay and sick pay. Target labour cost percentages are usually derived by adopting inter-unit norms or by the use of a 'percentage template' which is deemed to lead to maximum profitability. Neither of these methods recognizes the potential cost savings which may (or may not) be possible in a particular unit. In the light of these inherent weaknesses it would seem that a target labour cost percentage alone is not a suitable comparator for food and beverage businesses.

The second comparator is a *target monetary value* of employment costs. This comparator is most appropriate for businesses where labour is largely a fixed cost and/or volume fluctuations are limited – for example, in the institutional sector. The actual figure will also fluctuate owing to changes in sick pay and holiday pay; however, for cost-orientated businesses, this comparator is quite appropriate – but in a situation where the use of labour is relatively fixed.

The third type of comparator is *target personhours*. A static target of, say, 320 manhours per day is appropriate to businesses with no fluctuations in demand or with largely fixed jobs. For businesses where volume fluctuates, targets can be set for different levels of volume dependent on the optimum staffing levels, as described in Chapter 5. Weekly personhours targets may hide possible opportunities for improvement. Planning and measuring personhours on a daily basis is worthwhile in businesses which have fluctuating demand and modes of employment which permit flexible rostering. This, of course, requires a system of volume forecasting.

Rather than set detailed personhours targets for several ranges of volume, in smaller businesses it may be more appropriate to find a less exact method of comparing the utilization of manpower and the volume of business. The most commonly used measure is *target covers per personhour* – the fourth comparator. Actual 'covers per personhour' performance can be assessed on a daily basis without difficulty from payroll or roster data.

The fifth comparator is used to assess how effectively managers have acquired and utilized their manpower: how they have controlled the use of premium rates of pay, how they have used the correct grade of employee for the correct job, and how costs of sickness or absenteeism have been minimized. The best single measure of this is *target average rate per hour*. If measured on a weekly basis, and on moving annual total basis (to smooth out the effects of seasonal holidays, sickness and absenteeism), this will show the short-term and the long-term trends in manpower utilization.

The five choices of comparator for labour costs are shown in Table 7.6. These comparators may be used alone or in combination. In one business different comparators will be more appropriate for different jobs. Most labour-cost control systems work predominantly on pre-operational control principles, by relating staffing levels to forecasted volume. Post-operational control is also necessary to review how effectively the staffing and rostering have been undertaken.

Properly applied variance analysis techniques are useful for highlighting the exact cause of shortfalls in performance, and for directing management's attention to the important problem areas. As a general rule, analysis of the profit effect of rate and manhours variance are useful to all catering businesses. The Standard System of Catering Accounting makes some specific recommendations concerning the control of kitchen wages. The SSCA suggests that the kitchen labour element of each dish should be calculated and that these standard labour costs should be used as a basis for a cost allocation system for distributing kitchen labour costs to sale outlets. Although the SSCA recommendations are theoretically possible, we know of no one who has adopted these ideas. It seems more appropriate to treat a kitchen as a cost centre, responsible for food cost efficiency variance (as previously described) and for kitchen labour costs, fuel

Table 7.6 Comparators for labour cost control.

Comparator	Focus	Common applications
Cost percentage	Variable nature of labour costs	Commercial restaurants
Monetary value	Fixed nature of labour costs	Institutional catering
Manhours	Efficient productivity	'Fixed' jobs
Covers per manhour	Efficient productivity	'Variable' jobs
Average hourly rate	Proper selection and rostering	All sectors

Source: Merricks, P. and Jones, P. (1987) *The Management of Catering Operations*, Cassell, London.

and other direct overheads. Kitchen labour costs should be controlled by setting target manhour levels for different volume ranges, and also by using a covers per manhour measure. Periodic reviews of staffing levels, rostering and work organization should be undertaken with a general view to improving kitchen productivity.

COST CONTROL AND INFORMATION TECHNOLOGY

Until the early 1980s, most information for planning and control in food and beverage businesses came from manual records such as payroll documentation, bin cards, restaurant bill summaries, goods received notes and manual sales mix analyses. Information took a long time to prepare and was often of such dubious reliability that managers' first action was to recheck the data! The advent of cheap computing power has dramatically changed the variety, quantity and quality of information that is available to and expected by food and beverage managers. Indeed, with the advent of bar code readers, it is not only information that can be computerized, but also the physical control of stock. For instance, all in-flight tray equipment at one of British Airways' production units at Heathrow is stored in bar coded bins. Any kind of equipment is then drawn from stock upon request automatically.

The growth in foodservice computer systems has been such that all but the very largest or most specialized businesses will now buy-in a package rather than have a system designed to meet specific criteria. In order to be able to select the best package for their needs managers have to be able to explain clearly the functional requirements of the intended system – or, in other words, what the system should be able to achieve in order to meet the businesses' control requirements. Many people do not find this an easy task as they have been conditioned to think in terms of processes (costing a menu) rather than in terms of result (achievement of potential dish costs). Of course, not all of the functional requirements of a control system discussed above are pertinent to all foodservice businesses. They are only expressed in general terms, and each business will need to specify its exact information needs before deciding how to best meet those needs. In most cases, however, food and beverage software is an integrated system that provides real-time adjustments to purchase requirements and stock records, based on retail sales transactions. For instance, the sale of a hamburger over the counter in a fast food outlet would adjust the stock records of each component of that item, such as the bun and the pattie, and modify the next purchase order if necessary. At the same time, a series of transactions would enable the manager to establish the productivity level of counter staff and enable the measurement of labour cost against the appropriate comparator.

CONCLUSION

Cost controls are powerful behavioural influences and managers need to plan, implement and revise systems carefully to meet current business needs. Off-the-peg control systems seldom provide exactly the right fit for a particular business. Designing a food and beverage control system involves consideration of the accuracy, frequency and specificity of measurement of actual costs. Decisions need to be made regarding pre- or post-operational control techniques. The best comparator or comparators need to be selected – from the available options of cost percentage, per capita cost, commodity usage or potential sales value. If responsibility for cost control is delegated, particularly if profit centres are implemented, the selection of methods for allocating food or beverage costs comes to be of key importance. These decisions are necessary precursors to the selection of computer-based systems. Unless a clear specification of the functional characteristics of a control system is prepared before selection starts, managers end up with the most sophisticated system available rather than the one which fits their business needs.

Control of labour costs cannot be achieved with the same degree of certainty as control of food or beverage costs. An egg is an egg – but, despite efforts to standardize on the calibre of staff, many establishments are faced with employees with widely differing individual abilities. This lack of standardization in many parts of the industry is still a major factor limiting the use of effective labour-cost control techniques. Even so, it seems likely that most businesses do not exercise the degree of control over their labour costs that the situation merits, and we anticipate that most businesses will devote more management attention to this area in the 1990s. Budgetary and cost control systems are powerful behavioural tools. Used insensitively, they can generate distrust and hostility. In the right hands they can produce constructive attitudes and effective action among supervisors and operatives, and are essential tools for managers in any part of the catering industry.

Finally, once established, control systems are not fixed forever. If the business changes, control systems need to change with operational activity. School feeding is an example of how each sector needs to have appropriate systems and how these need to change with the times. In 1983, an investigation[10] of school meals found that reporting systems were usually designed to give three items of information. These were food costs per meal, number of meals produced and income received, and other costs incurred, such as wages and salaries, overheads, etc. The 1983 report highlighted that these control systems were inadequate owing to an 'innovation' in school meals, namely cash cafeterias. Such cafeterias, especially in secondary schools, were gradually replacing the traditional system of a menu cycle over a number of weeks that provided a single main course and sweet item. The report states: 'whilst this (type of information) may be sufficient for control purposes where service consists of a no-choice meal at a fixed price and staffing is based firmly on the old DES scale, such a system does not give a clear overall picture of each kitchen's performance; in accountancy terms, there are no trading accounts. The lack of trading accounts for individual kitchens [was] a serious disadvantage with the introduction of cash cafeterias, when the concept of unit meal cost vanished.' The report advocated the adoption of a budgetary control system based around trading accounts for each school kitchen. Since 1983, a further development has been the introduction of central production kitchens using cook-chill technologies in some education authorities. This too has required control systems to adapt. Finally, in 1983 the control system also identified one other, fairly unusual, item of information: the nutritional content of meals. The information was probably only recorded in this sector and hospital feeding at this time. Since then, the commercial sector has identified a growing market for healthy eating and it too is reviewing nutrition in a systematic way. In school meals nutritional content was controlled because of legislation which identified that education authorities had a responsibility to provide a nutritious main meal. Ironically this legal obligation has now been removed, once again illustrating how systems change over time.

REFERENCES

1. Gamble, P. and Kipps, M. (1983) 'The conception and implementation of a micro-computer based catering information system', *International Journal of Hospitality Management*, Vol. 12, No. 3.

2. Kotas, R. (1975) *Marketing Orientation*, Intertext, Glasgow.

3. Kotas, R. op. cit.

4. Turner, Michael (1991) *Food and Beverage Management*, HCIMA.

5. Sutton, D. (1983) *Financial Management In Hotel and Catering Operations*, Heinemann, London.

6. Gamble, P. (1984) *Small Computers and Hospitality Management*, Hutchinson, London.

7. Kotas, R. and Davis B. (1981) *Food and Beverage Control*, Intertext, Glasgow.

8. HMSO, *A Standard System of Catering Accounting*, HMSO, London.

9. Lepard, N. and Cade, H. (n.d.) *Improving Food and Beverage Control*, Northwood.

10. Department of the Environment Audit Inspectorate (1983) *Education School Meals*, HMSO, London.

8

Designing a Quality Strategy

Dolf Mogendorff

INTRODUCTION

There are a number of definitions of quality. For many years, in the foodservice industry, good quality was mistakenly associated with expensive, upmarket restaurants. Operations that were aimed at mass markets, such as motorway service areas, fast food outlets, and licensed houses were perceived as simple and were, therefore, equated with 'poor quality'. However, this is the wrong way to think about quality. The so-called 'Quality Gurus',[1] who have now spent several decades developing concepts and practice in this area, think about quality in a quite different way. Japanese experts like Shingo, Ishikawa and Taguchi, and Americans like Deming, Crosby and Juran, adopt a relative measure of the quality of something. Juran, for instance, has defined quality as 'fitness for purpose'.[2] The British Standards Institution likewise define it as 'the totality of features and characteristics of a product or service that bear on its ability to meet stated or implied needs'.[3] So any kind of operation can be high or low quality depending on whether or not it serves its customer well or badly. Garvin[4] sums this up succinctly: 'Quality means pleasing customers, not just protecting them from annoyances.' A more detailed definition of quality has been provided by Murdick, Render and Russell et al.[5] when they state that 'quality . . . comprises the degree to which attributes of the service desired by the users are identified and incorporated in the service and the degree to which desired levels of these attributes are perceived by the users to be achieved.' This points to one of management's main problems to be solved in the present decade, namely, constantly changing (that is, increasing) customer expectations. One of the problems of eating-out guides, such as Egon Ronay and the *Good Food Guide*, is that they still tend to measure quality in absolute terms rather than recognize that quality has to meet the expectations of the customers for which the service is offered.

Having established what we mean by quality, this chapter goes on to look how quality can be designed into the organization and operation of foodservice businesses. Four basic strategies are reviewed: quality inspection (QI), quality control (QC), quality assurance (QA), and total quality management (TQM). The whole approach to quality in industry in general and in foodservice in particular has gradually become more sophisticated over the years. The most unsophisticated strategy – quality inspection – was largely the way quality was managed up to and including the 1950s in the UK foodservice industry. During the 1960s, a number of sectors introduced new technologies and created specific food service systems, along with which quality control systems were established. However, as with many service operations, the service worker can directly impact on customer satisfaction so that the control approach, in some cases, was further modified in order to achieve quality assurance. Finally, the 1980s and 1990s are seeing the development of the concept of total quality management.

As well as operational strategies, foodservice firms may also seek external recognition or accreditation of their quality standards. A number of schemes exist aimed at demonstrating good quality. These include the British Standard BS 5750 (with particular reference to Part 8 dedicated to service industries) and its international equivalent, ISO 9000, as well as the later BS 7850; Investors in People; and, in the public sector, various charter schemes, such as the Citizen's Charter. This chapter concludes with a review of these and their relevance to the foodservice industry.

QUALITY INSPECTION

The simplest way to manage quality is to inspect the product before it is sold to the customer. Therefore the goals of a QI system are very simple: set up a specification of the product, cost it, and detect any defects before delivering it or selling it to the end user. It is very much a 'shop-floor' activity, involving only those employees directly concerned with the making of the product or delivery of the service, and their superiors. While it is easy to install, the point at which quality is checked is at the output point of each sub-system. This means QI takes place *after* the product has been produced. A head chef standing at the 'hotplate', for instance, having already checked the raw materials as they came in from suppliers, will inspect prepared food just before it is handed to the service staff – after the dish has been cooked. If it is not according to specification it has to be returned to the chef who prepared it for 'reworking' or, if that is not possible, complete replacement by another dish. After that it is, once more, brought to the head chef for inspection and, hopefully, this time the customer can receive the (delayed) order. Although such inspection could apply to other stages of the operational process, not just the production of food, it is often only at the hotplate that QI is most rigorously and regularly applied.

While this fulfils the systems approach discussed in Chapter 1, including a feedback loop, it does create problems in terms of costs (correcting the dish or providing a replacement, and an essentially non-productive 'inspector') and does little for staff motivation in that it accentuates only negative quality in terms of dishes returned and customer complaints received. The system can only be improved by increased inspection, thus increasing cost; because of this, there is often a trade-off between quality and cost. It is a simple system often found in small foodservice businesses, but does not achieve a great deal in quality terms. Finally, it cannot really cope with the intangible aspects of the total product/service package and therefore provides the foodservice operator with only a partial quality management system.

QUALITY CONTROL

Quality control (QC) goes further than QI because quality is designed into the product specification and quality checks into the production system. The focus switches from a simple inspection of the end product, to a check on the product at stages during the production process, so that if necessary it can be reworked at an early stage. The goals of this strategy therefore include defect detection but also cost reduction. It is still, however, preoccupied with the product rather than with the whole 'meal experience'. Since the goals of QC are more sophisticated, the QC system is more sophisticated too. There will be a greater emphasis on some agreed supplier quality and inspection of supplies, the production process design and operation, and clearly identified points and times when quality is inspected.

Specialists are sometimes employed; for instance, in a large centralized food production unit, quality control staff may be involved in taking food samples at different stages of the process for testing. This may involve the technique of Statistical Process Control (SPC) and other analytical tools as ways of monitoring performance and to identify areas which require attention. SPC, for instance, can involve the application of the normal distribution and the use of simple control charts on which sample results are plotted and interpreted in relation to the overall process. Variances from the standard procedures which are often laid down in manuals can thus be identified and corrective action taken. SPC is not commonly found in the foodservice industry, although large-scale producers, notably in-flight caterers, are adopting this technique as a way of checking quality in areas such as the wash-up, tray lay-up, and dish presentation.

The advantages of Quality Control are mainly that the quality of the final product is improved and that errors in the production process are found and, hopefully, corrected before that product is served. Through the use of specification manuals (for both product and process) more staff can be involved, although the element of control is still a negative motivator. The development of manuals, control techniques and training mean that it may take up to a year for QC to be part of the operation system. QC does not, however, easily address intangible issues related to customer service, and that is probably its main drawback. The customer is still seen as being external to the organization. Some effort is made to elicit feedback from the customer, either orally or through questionnaires, but fundamentally the emphasis is on managing complaints.

QUALITY ASSURANCE

This quality strategy builds on the Quality Control concept but introduces for the first time the idea of 'doing things right the first time'. In order to ensure performance to this level, it involves a focus on the employee. It is therefore focused less on technology and more on behaviour. The aim of a Quality Assurance (QA) programme is to organize quality into organization processes by conformity to specification through continual improvement. This is done by the 'blueprinting' (i.e. detailed design) of operations with quality being a key element. QA focuses on the customer rather than on production processes. The service element now enters the quality arena and thus the concept becomes output oriented rather than merely input driven. In other words, the organization's approach to quality now moves beyond dimensions of product quality as, for instance, proposed by Garvin,[6] such as Performance, Features, Conformance and Perceived Quality to encompass, additionally, service quality, represented by, for example, Schonberger's four dimensions of Quick Response, Quick Change, Humanity and Value;[7] or Berry, Parasuraman and Zeithaml's more developed service attributes of Reliability, Responsiveness, Competence, Access, Courtesy, Communication, Credibility, Security, Understanding the Customer and Tangibles.[8] These have, in turn, been regrouped under four main headings by Armistead and Clark[9] as Product, Support, Service and Process.

The concept of 'right first time' essentially means that staff now become central in the pursuit of quality. Through careful training, based on the system design, staff become keenly aware of their place in an overall process which involves the concept of the quality chain. This recognizes that organizations are not simple systems but, in fact, complex systems made up of numbers of sub-systems. The output from each of these sub-systems becomes the input to the next; the latter sub-system is, therefore, a customer of the former. In the case of a food production and service system in a conventional restaurant such a quality chain can easily be recognized: the store's output of raw materials becomes the input of the same to the kitchen and it is essential that, at that point in the process, both quality and quantity are correct, every time. The examples can be extended throughout the rest of the production and service process, right up to and including the process involved in the customer settling the bill. This was also discussed earlier in Chapter 6 (page 100). Johns,[10] adapting an earlier model developed by Nightingale,[11] stresses not only the customer's central role in the quality process but also that customers' quality standards, coloured by previous service experiences, influences their perceptions of the level of satisfaction they gain from the current meal experience. These, in turn, will influence the service system and its standards, while organizations will need to constantly adjust their quality standards in order to survive – normally upwards, in line with changing customer expectations.

Just as the chain moves forward through the process to involve the customer, so the suppliers also become part of the quality chain. Going far beyond production specifications, the supplier now gets actively involved in product and service design through reciprocal visits with the caterer, thus creating better understanding of each other's needs and capabilities. The 'right first time' idea now incorporates such issues as on-time delivery, guaranteed quality of all related processes, and clear procedures devised for when things go wrong, as they, inevitably, will do at some time. Sometimes, bonus agreements are involved which only come into play where agreed, very high, targets of reliability have been achieved, e.g. 97 per cent.

While techniques such as SPC still have a role to play in QA, employees now become a vital part of the quality system. They are not just trained to understand and manage their part of the overall system, but are indeed encouraged to get involved in problem solving since, as was noted above, the accent is on continual improvement; such techniques are discussed in Chapter 16.

A further feature of QA is the idea of teamwork in problem solving performed by progress groups, often known as quality circles. One source defines such groups as 'including a small number of individuals from within one department, who carry out similar work. The group meets regularly (in normal working time) to identify, implement and monitor the progress of actions taken to resolve problems arising within their work area.'[12] Some authors prescribe the working of such groups in great detail, suggesting, for instance, that the optimum number of individuals should be nine and that it should be led by a supervisor, while others have stressed that the group should have no superiors in it and that the group should choose its own leader. What is important, however, is that the team includes employees with specific expertise rather than those chosen on the basis of seniority. Another important feature is that an additional person can join the circle in order to add specific expertise for limited periods.

A 'mega' quality circle may also be in place which co-ordinates the working of the individual, departmental ones in cases where the problem to be solved concerns more than one department. In all cases, thorough training, and the authority to act (albeit within certain limits such as budgetary controls), are essential if employees are to be able to participate to full effect and especially if they are to implement solutions themselves.

As with previously discussed quality systems, QA has costs attached to it in terms of procedures and equipment as well as training and time; these quality costs are discussed in Chapter 16. Such costs should be more than outweighed by the savings gained by operating more effectively (reducing the 'dissatisfiers' and increasing the 'satisfiers'); while profit rises steeply where the 'satisfiers' can be turned into 'delighters' resulting in brand loyalty.

Quality assurance is typically found in such operations in the foodservice industry as fast food organizations, especially such as McDonald's and BurgerKing where, because of their standardized product and their ability to develop highly detailed blueprints, QA is readily and effectively implemented. Because quality assurance is central to the continued well-being and indeed survival of the foodservice organization it is vital that the introduction of such a system is managed as a major organizational change. Therefore it can often take up to three years for it to be fully embedded into the foodservice system.

TOTAL QUALITY MANAGEMENT

A significant development of the 1980s has been the emergence of the concept of Total Quality Management (TQM). The strategy is entirely customer driven and its holistic approach is adopted with an almost missionary zeal. Oakland[13] defines TQM as 'a way of organizing and involving the whole organization; every department, every activity, every single person at every level'.

Jones[14] has proposed that a TQM strategy in the hospitality industry involves a number of key steps, as illustrated in Figure 8.1. Whilst this includes some of the features of the QC and QA strategies, TQM differs from these in a number of ways. First, it is holistic and involves the whole organization, in line with Oakland's definition above; secondly, senior executives play a key role in leading the quality drive and communicating the quality message. Together this adds up to a definition of quality as 'performance leadership in meeting customer requirements habitually and competitively by doing the right things right first time'.

A further key aspect is employee empowerment which involves staff more actively in the decision-making process. While it has been described by some authors as, for instance, allowing employees 'to do something about quality defects as they notice them'[15] so that organizations can continuously correct their performance, it should encompass more than that. Employees at all organization levels should be allowed to make decisions (which should be monitored) within clearly defined parameters in order to free up their superiors for their tasks. This issue is discussed more fully in Chapter 10.

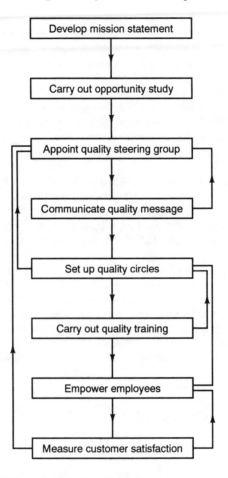

Figure 8.1   A model of TQM in hospitality organizations.

In order to achieve guaranteed quality in an organizational environment where everyone is a customer, Continuous Quality Improvement (CQI) is central to effective TQM. The term reinforces the cyclical, never-ending idea which underpins TQM, and should be considered in relation to such issues as: improving external customer satisfaction, improving the quality of external suppliers, improving internal supplier–customer effectiveness, reducing waste, improving internal communications and improving flexibility and adaptability.[16] Teamwork techniques, such as Quality Circles (discussed above), are essential tools when applying CQI.

Developing the appropriate organizational culture (see also Chapter 10) and a concomitant leadership style are fundamental to the development of TQM in line with the requirements of the effective introduction and reinforcement of any major organizational change. Because of this it can take up to five years to get the system up and running, and many organizations give up before they have achieved their goal. These are some of the reasons why very few foodservice system have, as yet, fully introduced TQM. Lascelles and Dale[17] suggest that there are six kinds of organizations that claim to be working towards TQM. They define these as Uncommitted (those organizations which have not yet started the formal process of quality improvement); Drifters (those which will probably have been engaged in a process of quality improvement for between 18 and 36 months and, in general, have followed the available advice on TQM); Tool Pushers (those with more operating experience of TQM than a Drifter, say 3-5 years); Improvers (involved for five to eight years and made important advances in terms of cultural change and recognition of continuous quality improvement); Award Winners (winning, say, British, Scottish, Irish, European Quality Awards which allows companies to use recognition as a competitive tool); and World Class, 'characterized by the total integration of quality improvement and business strategy to creatively delight the customer.[18]

Sadly, many foodservice firms are still in the first two categories; a few may be Tool Pushers, just one or two are Improvers. None, as yet, are Award Winners, let along World Class! One example of a foodservice organization that has introduced fully fledged TQM systems is Quadrant, the in-house foodservice operation for the Post Office.[19]

EXTERNAL RECOGNITION OF QUALITY

Whichever of the quality strategies a firm adopts, it may also seek to gain recognition or accreditation of quality through any one of a number of schemes. In many cases, firms use these schemes as one of the ways to upgrade and improve their approach to quality, since they provide a specific objective for management and employees to work towards. Some of the major standards being currently used in the UK are briefly described, comprising BS 5750 (ISO 9000); Investors in People; the Citizen's Charter and Charter Mark Scheme; and the European Foundation for Quality Management Scheme. All the schemes have formal accreditation routes available in the UK and are generally recognized as marks of quality.

BS 5750 (ISO 9000)

The British Standard BS 5750 was initially published in 1979 to define to suppliers and manufacturers what is required for a quality-orientated system. The standard was originally devised for manufacturing industry where it was first implemented. However, the standard has now been successfully adopted and implemented in service sector organizations, including financial services, catering, health care and educational establishments. The standard is very process orientated, relying heavily on fully documenting and controlling all aspects of 'production' processes. The standard covers the definition and description of a wide range of operational activity, as illustrated in Table 8.1. Contract foodservice firms particularly are adopting the British Standard. This is partly because their clients specify that suppliers should be so accredited. For instance, Gardner Merchant's Royal Insurance contract in Peterborough gained BS 5750 recognition in 1992.

Investors in People

The 'Investors in People' quality award was developed as an initiative by the Department of Employment designed to encourage employers to improve their performance by linking the training and development of all their employees to their

Table 8.1   BS 5750 specifications.

1. Management responsibility.
2. Quality system principles.
3. Internal quality auditing.
4. Quality-related cost considerations.
5. Quality in marketing including contract review.
6. Quality in specification and design (design control).
7. Quality in procurement (purchasing control).
8. Quality in production (production process control).
9. Control of production.
10. Material control and traceability (product identification and traceability).
11. Control of verification status (inspection and testing status).
12. Product verification (inspection and testing).
13. Control of measuring and testing.
14. Control of non-conformity of product.
15. Corrective action.
16. Handling of post-production functions (handling, storage, packaging and delivery).
17. After-sales servicing.
18. Quality documentation and records (document control).
19. Quality records.
20. Personnel (training).
21. Product safety and liability.
22. Use of statistical methods.
23. Purchaser supplied products.

business objectives. The quality standard issued in 1991 focuses on improving an organization by fully developing the skills of the employees. It is not specifically aimed at service organizations, but a number of service firms, such as De Vere Hotels, have successfully been accredited. The scheme does not address all the issues required for an organization to meet its goals but focuses mainly on using four main principles:

- Making a public commitment from the top of the organization to develop all employees to achieve the organization's business objectives.
- Regularly reviewing the training and development needs of all employees.
- Acting to train and develop individuals on recruitment and throughout their employment.
- Evaluating the investment in training to assess achievement and improve future effectiveness.

The main issues to be addressed and defined are listed in Table 8.2

Citizen's Charter and Charter Mark Scheme

The Citizen's Charter was launched in 1991 by the government to raise the standard of public sector services. The Citizen's Charter focuses mainly on customer service delivery and customer consultation. The majority of the mechanisms required to achieve business goals, including customer satisfaction, are not addressed. The criteria for qualifying for a Charter Mark are sub-divided into nine sections, as illustrated in

Table 8.2 'Investors in People' specifications.

1. Written business plans.
2. Identification of employees' contribution.
3. Means of assessing employees' development needs.
4. Communication of the 'Vision'.
5. Identifying resources for employee development.
6. Managers to set targets for individuals.
7. Managers to agree individual development needs.
8. Standards linked to NVQ/SVQs.
9. Plans and actions for the induction of new recruits.
10. Continual development of existing employees.
11. Employee responsibility for their own development.
12. Review benefits against business goals.
13. Evaluation and continued commitment from the top.
14. Target revision through evaluation.

Table 8.3. This approach to quality is most likely to be adopted by those caterers operating in the public sector, such as local authority school meals or hospitals.

European Foundation for Quality Management Scheme

The European Foundation for Quality Management (EFQM) was formed in 1988. A total quality management (TQM) model for self-appraisal was issued in 1992. The scheme allows institutions to introduce a TQM scheme which is self-assessed for the purposes of obtaining a quality award. However, a representative of the Foundation may request a site visit to validate the information given in the self-assessment. The scheme is not focused on products, customers or services but is a total quality scheme which attempts to address all aspects of quality within an organization including:

- Leadership
- Policy and strategy
- People management
- Resources
- Processes
- Customer satisfaction
- People satisfaction
- Impact on society
- Business results

Each of the categories can be further split down, describing the major issues to be addressed as listed in Table 8.4.

The various quality schemes outlined all have their shortcomings when applied to services in general and particular sectors. The aims of introducing quality into an organization need to be defined first and then appropriate schemes to achieve the aims must be identified. If the primary requirement is to introduce TQM then a combination of schemes, the most appropriate one being chosen for the task under consideration, may be a suitable approach. For example, certain operations may be identified as being

Table 8.3 Charter Mark specifications.

- **Standards**
  - (1) Service standards are set which are appropriate to the service delivered.
  - (2) Service standards are published in a variety of ways and are readily accessible by customers.
  - (3) Management information systems are in place and performance information is published.
- **Information and Openness**
  - (1) Information must be readily available and meet the needs of its customers.
  - (2) Customer surveys are carried out to check if information is full and comprehensible.
- **Choice and Consultation**
  - (1) A formal programme of customer consultation must be in place.
  - (2) Service standards must be set in consultation with customers and reviewed regularly.
- **Courtesy and Helpfulness**
  - (1) A customer service policy must be in place and widely publicised in offices.
  - (2) Formal training in customer service must be given to all members of staff.
  - (3) Name badges are usually worn and names are given over the phone and in correspondence.
  - (4) Customer needs are assessed and the service is tailored to customer needs.
- **Putting things right**
  - (1) Procedures are defined and published for formal and informal complaints.
  - (2) Complaint procedures are easy to access and use with named individuals to complain to.
  - (3) Customers' views on complaint procedures must be sought.
  - (4) Procedures specify time limits for investigating complaints.
  - (5) The availability of an independent review is publicized.
- **Value for money**
  - (1) Clear commitment must be given to improving value for money with evidence of specific examples.
  - (2) Quality, measures of value for money and performance must be incorporated into the planning process.
  - (3) Evidence of efficiency improvements must be made showing money savings. Commitment to improve efficiency must be made.
  - (4) Claims and achievements must be validated by external audit or survey data.
- **Customer satisfaction**
  - (1) Levels of satisfaction must be determined and key customer satisfaction measurements must be in place to identify quantitative and qualitative improvements.
- **Measurable improvements in the quality of service over the last two years**
  - (1) Measurable improvements in the quality of service must have been achieved in the last two or more years. Specific examples must be given.
- **Plans to introduce innovative enhancement to services with no costs**
  - (1) A plan to produce an innovative enhancement to services to the customer must be in hand or have been carried out which involves no additional costs to the customer or taxpayer.

suitable for use of the BS 5750 standard in order to introduce quality. For other areas it may be more suitable to use the concepts of 'Investors in People', whilst specific service areas may have their goals set by the goals expressed in the charter approach.

The cost of introducing such quality standards is hard to quantify. Quality systems generally result in considerable savings in staff time and wastage. The cost of running a quality programme in monetary terms has been shown, for instance, to be typically of the order of £50,000 to £60,000 per annum for organizations introducing BS 5750. There is usually an ongoing requirement of at least one high-level full-time quality manager with administrative support, and time will have to be allocated by many other staff to

Table 8.4 European Foundation for Quality Management Schemes.

Leadership
The behaviour of all managers in driving the organization towards total quality.
(1) Visible involvement in leading quality management.
(2) A consistent total quality culture.
(3) Recognition and appreciation of the efforts and successes of individuals and teams.
(4) Support of total quality by the provision of appropriate resources and assistance.
(5) Involvement with customers and suppliers.
(6) Active promotion of quality management outside the organization.

Policy and strategy
The organization's values, visions and strategic direction and the ways in which the organization achieves them.
(1) Policy and strategy's incorporation with total quality.
(2) Definition of policy and strategy using information.
(3) Business plans and policy and strategy.
(4) The communication of policy and strategy.
(5) The regular reviewing of policy and strategy.

People management
(1) The continuous improvement of people management.
(2) Skill development through recruitment, training and career progression of its people.
(3) Performance target setting, reviewing with staff.
(4) The promotion and involvement of all people in quality and continuous improvement.

Resources
The management, utilization and preservation of resources.
(1) Control and development of financial resources.
(2) Control and development of information resources.
(3) Control and development of material resources.
(4) The application of technology to improve quality and performance.

Processes
The management of all the value-adding activities within the organization.
(1) Identifying and defining key processes.
(2) Systematic management of key and support processes.
(3) Reviewing of processes based on performance parameters to improve them.
(4) The stimulation of innovation and creativity in process improvement.
(5) The implementation of process changes and evaluation of benefits.

Customer satisfaction
The perception of external customers, direct and indirect, of the organization and of its products and services.
(1) Product and service quality.
(2) Indirect methods of measuring customer satisfaction.

Table 8.4 European Foundation for Quality Management Schemes – *cont'd.*

People satisfaction
(1) Working environment.
(2) Work quality.
(3) Recognition and rewards.
(4) Job security.
(5) Communication and management.
(6) Training and development.

Impact on society
Society's perception of the organization including the approach to quality of life, the environment and preservation of global resources.
(1) Involvement in the community.
(2) Reduction of nuisance and harm to neighbours as a result of operations.
(3) Policy on resource usage.
(4) Indirect measures of impact on society: complaints, awards, legal battles.

Business results
The achievements in relation to the organization's planned business performance.
(1) Financial results.
(2) Non-financial measures.

---

operate the system. In general, in the long term the benefits would outweigh the costs. The implementation of a quality scheme is best carried out by initially briefing senior managers on what is involved in introducing quality systems and then launching the scheme as a pilot scheme focusing on a particular area of operations. The pilot scheme should have clearly definable goals and should maintain a high profile with regular reports being issued so that all members of the institution are aware of what progress is being made. Regular briefing sessions will be required in order to maintain the high profile of the project so that staff realize the importance of the introduction of quality. When the initial project has been completed other areas can be targeted and the programme rolled out.

CONCLUSION

This chapter has reviewed four main ways in which quality can be managed in foodservice operations. Moving from QI, through QC and QA, to TQM, these strategies increase in complexity and sophistication. We have also seen how organizations can seek external recognition of their quality through the British Standard, Investors in People, Charter Mark Scheme and European Foundation for Quality Management. BS 5750 illustrates the complexity of quality by identifying the relationship between customer needs, marketing, design of the service operation, actual service delivery and customer evaluation. This is illustrated in Figure 8.2.

However, the adoption of a specific quality strategy does not of itself guarantee success. These strategies need to match or fit with the nature of the operation and be implemented correctly. In Chapter 16 we explore some of the day-to-day issues that arise from managing quality and ways these issues may be resolved.

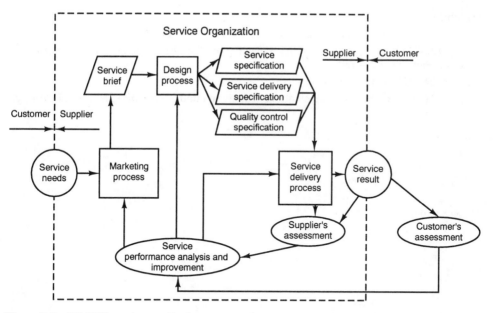

Figure 8.2   BS 5750 service quality loop.

REFERENCES

1. Bendell, A. (1989) *The Quality Gurus*: What Can They Do For Your Company? DTI, Managing into the 90's, London.
2. Juran, J. (1979) *Quality Control Handbook*, 3rd edn, McGraw-Hill, New York.
3. British Standards Institute, (1987) *BS4778, Quality Vocabulary*, BSI, London.
4. Garvin, D. (1990) *Managing Quality: The Strategic and Competitive Edge*, The Free Press, New York.
5. Murdick, R. G., Render, B. and Russell, R. S. (1990) *Service Operations Management*, Allyn & Bacon, Newton, Mass.
6. Garvin, D. op. cit.
7. Schonberger, R. (1990) *Building a Chain of Customers*, Hutchinson, London.
8. Berry, L. L., Parasuraman, A and Zeithaml, V.A. (1985) 'Quality counts in services, too,' *Business Horizons*, Vol. 28, May-June.
9. Armistead, C. G. and Clark, G. (1992) *Customer Service and Support: Implementing Effective Strategies*, Pitman, London.
10. Johns, N. 'Quality management in the hospitality industry,' Parts 1–3, *International Journal of Contemporary Hospitality Management*, Vol. 4, Nos. 3 and 4 (1992); Vol. 5, No. 1 (1993).
11. Nightingale, M. (1985) 'The hospitality industry: defining quality for a quality assurance programme – a study of perceptions,' *Service Industries Journal*, Vol. 5, No. 1.
12. Munro-Faure, L. and M., (1992) *Implementing Total Quality Management*, Pitman, London.
13. Oakland, J. S. (1989) *Total Quality Management*, Butterworth-Heinemann, Oxford.
14. Jones, Peter and Riggott, Guy (1992) 'TQM in five star hotels: old style hospitality or modern day operations management?' International Operations Management Conference, University of Manchester.

15. Johns, N. op. cit.

16. Thomas, B. (1992) *Total Quality Training*, McGraw-Hill, London.

17. Lascelles, D. and Dale, B.G. (1991) 'Levelling out the future', *Total Quality Management*, December, pp. 325 – 330.

18. Lascelles, C. and Dale, B. G. op. cit.

19. Anon. (1994) 'Quadrant – It's all about attitude of mind', *Hospitality*, No. 142, February.

PART B
MANAGING THE OPERATIONS

9

Protecting Assets

Peter Jones

INTRODUCTION

Until recently, for many foodservice operations the protection of the company's assets seems to have been a fairly low priority for managers. The only exception to this has been the licensed trade, which has always been highly security conscious. There were all sorts of reasons for this: other aspects of management such as marketing, customer service, and quality were more challenging; there were few explicit performance targets set; sales turnover and profit were derived largely from managing food and labour cost rather than capital assets and overheads. However, this perception has significantly changed during the early 1990s. High-profile cases, reported widely in the media, highlight some of the issues. A report in *The Times* in 1989[1] estimated that simple frauds by employees engaged in public service travel catering – mainly British Rail and British Airways – were costing £3 million per year. In the USA it is estimated that 35 per cent of all restaurants go out of business because of theft.[2] The CBI News in 1991 reported on conference security and the instance of a bomb discovered at a London hotel. In New York, the restaurateurs on 46th Street have hired so-called Guardian Angels to discourage drug peddling and improve the image of the area, paying their unofficial security force by providing free restaurant meals. And one of the in-flight caterers at Manchester airport paid £183,000 in compensation to two customers in July 1993, following a food poisoning outbreak caused not by their foodhandling but by contaminated supply of eggs.[3] These and other cases have changed foodservice managers' perceptions and made them more aware of their responsibility for security and safety.

There are basically five main types of 'asset' that need to be managed: the built environment or property itself; the plant and equipment in the environment; the materials handled, processed and consumed, in this instance mainly food and drink; people using the outlet, whether employees, customers, or others; and finally money or cash. Each of these presents specific problems and requires particular policies, procedures and systems for their effective management. They need to be 'protected' from an equally diverse range of possible threats. Such threats can be natural phenomena, such as storm damage, flood, earthquake, and so on; they can be due to human error, such as a gas explosion, fat fire, chemical spillage; or due to deliberate acts, which include vandalism, arson, robbery and terrorism.

GENERAL APPROACH TO PROTECTING ASSETS

The whole focus of protecting assets is on prevention. The operation should be designed to avoid as many potential risks as possible. Where risks cannot be totally avoided, action should be taken to ensure the impact is minimized. The need to prevent incidents from occurring is fairly obvious. First, it is ethically correct that managers should be concerned about the health and safety of their employees and customers and care for the environment in which they operate. As we shall see, many of the innovations in restaurant design, sanitation, energy use and waste management derive from the growing awareness of so-called green issues. Secondly, failure to protect assets is expensive. The cost of a fire or vandalism to a building is not simply the replacement cost, but those costs associated with loss of business during reconstruction – and thereafter, if customers start to use a competitor. Even though such expenses may be covered by insurance, the long-term impact on operational success can be great. Thirdly, the effective management of assets may also reduce ongoing overhead costs, such as repairs and insurance, as well as reducing capital investments by extending the working life of equipment. Fourthly, customers may be deterred by incidents allied to negative media publicity. Press reports about food poisoning, drunkenness, aggressive behaviour and so on, are not generally regarded as the best way to promote a business. For the restaurant business, the old adage 'there is no such thing as bad publicity' is definitely not true. Finally, foodservice operators have a large number of legal obligations which if not complied with can lead to criminal prosecution, as well as any civil action that might be brought as a result of negligence. One of the most significant recent pieces of legislation in the UK has been the 1991 Food Safety Act, which has required managers radically to rethink their whole strategy for handling foodstuffs and training staff.

Within the broad strategy of prevention, policies and systems are generally designed with five main functions in mind. These are to deter, delay, alert, inform, and react. Deterrence can be achieved either by removing the risk altogether or by putting in place systems that greatly reduce the risk. For instance, the risk of payroll theft is removed if all staff are paid by direct bank transfer, or reduced if a security firm is employed to deliver cash. If attempts to deter fail, there should be systems and procedures in place that delay. For instance, internal doors should be locked to prevent the free movement of intruders within a building. The third function of any system should be to alert the appropriate person should an incident occur; burglar alarms, smoke detectors and video surveillance are examples of this. Effective alert systems can also deter criminals from completing their crime. The system should also provide information. The increased use of video is aimed at providing much more information about the incident and the people involved with it so that action can be taken immediately or at a later time. Likewise, computerized fire systems provide a detailed analysis of where a fire has broken out within the building. Finally, there should be an appropriate level of reaction to the incident. Employees should respond effectively, and if necessary the relevant emergency services should be contacted.

SECURITY OF THE BUILT ENVIRONMENT

The built environment refers to the building in which the foodservice outlet is located, all the ground on which it is located, and the space that surrounds it. Looking after this starts at the point from which the manager is legally responsible for anyone. This certainly includes car parks attached to restaurants, but may also include public spaces not owned by the operator such as pavements. For instance, planning permission for some fast food outlets such as McDonald's has been granted only if the operator has agreed to erect additional litter bins along the street and staff additional refuse collection of disposable waste in the area. As well as ensuring the management of the perimeter and any exterior areas, consideration must also be given to the building construction itself, with a special focus on means of entry such as doors, windows, and even air ducting. However secure the building might be, there will also be the need for security systems, communications and alarms, and routine and emergency procedures, all designed to enable the assests to be as protected from possible threats.

It is not possible to be entirely prescriptive about how security should be implemented. The number of sectors of the foodservice industry creates a huge range of different contexts in which catering is carried out. Each type of outlet and location presents special problems. Roadside diners and motorway service areas are often located outside built-up areas, whereas fast food restaurants are located in high streets. A small rural pub may employ one or two part-time staff in addition to the landlord, whereas one of British Airways' in-flight kitchens at Heathrow is 24 hours a day operation staffed by 1,200 employees. The number of customers serviced can range from 30 or so in a small restaurant, up to 5,000 a day in a university, and 25,000 a day for an in-flight kitchen. Some operators own the property in which foodservice is carried out; others, such as industrial contract caterers or university caterers, operate on premises managed entirely by others. Each manager therefore needs to adopt a level of security that matches the location of the outlet, level of perceived risk, and financial viability of the operation.

As far as exteriors are concerned, looking after fences, gateways, car parks, gardens, walls, windows and roofs is important if only from an aesthetic point of view. Customers will not be encouraged to patronize the business if the exterior is soiled, dirty or poorly maintained. Such areas should be designed to ensure that customers, employees and suppliers can safety enter and exit from the building, whilst at the same time prevent unauthorized access. This may entail establishing a perimeter around the property that is walled or fenced, with only one or two gateways. If necessary, these gateways can then be subject to surveillance by video camera or be manned by security personnel. Such tight security is rare in the foodservice industry, except for one specific sector. In-flight catering production units typically have secure perimeters owing to the threat of terrorism and because they are bonded warehouses dealing with materials exempt from both excise duty and VAT. Other action that can be taken to ensure that exteriors are safe and secure include adequate lighting, effective signage, speed bumps or other traffic calming measures, proper drainage, and the use of non-slip building materials for pathways. Once installed these need to be regularly cleaned and maintained to the best standard. At least one national restaurant chain carries out a monthly inspection of all of these things to ensure they are correctly maintained. In addition they provide a play area outside for children which is also subject to strict design considerations and regular monthly checks.

Of major concern are points of entry into buildings. Most break-ins will occur through doors and windows, and employees acting dishonestly will also use these to remove stolen items from the premises. These points of entry therefore need to have the best quality of frames, openings and locks that is affordable. There is no point in having an expensive lock in a door that can be smashed down with a sledge-hammer. In the USA, restaurant operators are installing computerized locking systems. Such systems deny access, even to key-holders, except during approved opening times and record every time someone attempts to open a locked door, authorized or not.[4] Once they are installed, management must also establish a policy for monitoring these access points. Like the perimeter, they could be subject to continuous physical surveillance by security employees or electronic surveillance by video. Free access to buildings can also be prevented by requiring some kind of pass system for employees to use or restricted access codes on doors. Many large hotels have a single back employee entrance, continually manned during opening hours, for instance. Outside opening hours, a security firm can be employed to carry out routine, random checks to ensure the building is secure.

A common approach to building security is an alarm system of some kind. Alarm systems can be linked to a security firm or the local police force, and often ring a warning bell on the premises themselves. In 1989 there was great concern about such alarms when it was estimated £125 million was spent on wasted police time investigating alarms that had gone off by accident.[5] Foodservice operators need to be very clear about the status of such alarms with regards to police policies in their area for answering alarm calls and the attitude of insurance companies to their effectiveness. In addition to there being effective prevention and monitoring, emergency plans need to be established to cope with any possible contingency. The most usual of this type is a fire emergency plan, which will provide a detailed outline of what employees should do in the event of a fire. Evacuation procedures may also be needed in the event of other kinds of emergency such as a chemical spillage, electrical blackout, or gas leak. Increasingly, foodservice operators also develop plans to deal with bomb alerts and armed robberies. For instance, BurgerKing provides guidelines and training for its staff on 'what to do in the event of a hold-up'.

The foodservice manager is also likely to be the person responsible for opening up and closing down the property. These are particularly vulnerable points as often opening and closing take place early in the morning or late at night, when there are not many other people around. Such procedures are mainly needed for operations where cash is handled and valuable stocks are held which make robbery worthwhile. Typical opening procedures might include recommendations that the restaurant be opened by more than one person, visual check of the car park or vicinity to check on suspicious persons or vehicles, checking all points of entry before unlocking the entrance, using the main entrance, locking after entry, and routinely checking all areas within the restaurant before starting other duties. Closing procedures are similar, involving a thorough check of the premises to ensure no one is left inside the building, locking and checking of all windows and doors, and leaving the restaurant as a group, not alone. Finally, key security is vital. Only authorized staff should be issued with keys and only authorized managers should take keys off the premises. If a key is lost it is common practice to change all the locks. It is also common practice in at least one restaurant chain in the UK to change all the locks to all its restaurant doors when a manager leaves or transfers, even if he or she has handed over the keys to their replacement. The licensed trade does similarly.

EQUIPMENT SAFETY, MAINTENANCE AND CLEANING

The cleaning and maintenance of equipment has several implications for foodservice managers. First, there is a clear impact on quality. Poorly cleaned equipment can cause contamination of foodstuffs or, if observed by customers, deter them from returning. Poorly maintained equipment is likely to break down, which may delay or slow down service times or prevent service altogether. Cleaning and maintenance are also significant elements of cost. There are the obvious direct costs of labour, materials and replacement parts. For maintenance these are relatively easy to establish; but for cleaning, the number of operative staff involved may make this area less easy to monitor. Some staff are employed solely as cleaners, but many others engage in cleaning activities: for instance, waiting staff clean and polish table equipment. In the fast food sector, all employees have a cleaning role as well as performing service tasks. Finally, poorly cleaned and maintained equipment can have an adverse effect on employee morale. This can lead to a disinclination to clean and hence a spiral of worsening circumstances. This kind of task is perceived as very routine and low status by many employees, which makes if difficult to encourage 'clean as you go' policies. Research tends to suggest that keeping good standards of cleanliness is one of the most taxing and persistent problems facing direct line supervisors.

To achieve the right balance in cleaning and maintenance costs, the foodservice manager needs to consider the trade-off between spending too little and spending too much. If the level of maintenance is so high that no breakdowns occur, maintenance costs will also be high but there will be none of the costs associated with breakdown. On the other hand, too little maintenance leads to breakdowns, with the cost of service time, replacement parts, lost productivity, shorter working life of the equipment. This trade-off is illustrated in Figure 9.1. There is a similar trade-off with regards to cleaning activity. The manager needs to be aware of the significance of keeping equipment and areas clean in order to ensure the frequency of action taken matches the need. Even after roadside diners had been operating successfully for many years, little market research had been carried out. When the first major survey investigated why motorists stopped, the principal reason was to use the toilet facilities. This finding significantly changed the thinking of operators. In their new-build operations the toilets were redesigned to be more spacious and better equipped; and the frequency of the cleaning schedule was altered to ensure they were checked and cleaned once an hour.

Much of the plant and equipment used in foodservice operations is taken for granted. In particular the main services – electricity, gas, water and sewage – are so routinely used both at the place of work and in the home that they tend to be ignored. All four of these services need to be routinely monitored, but checking and maintenance should be carried out by authorized and specialist personnel. The sort of monitoring that can be carried out by the manager is regular physical inspection of the building to ensure pipes and cables have not been damaged and that shut-off valves are readily accessible. In all kinds of emergency situations it may be necessary to shut off the water, gas or electricity supply at the mains as quickly as possible. It is also essential to check that materials are stored safely so that combustible materials do not catch fire or water supplies and waste are contaminated. In some cases, equipment can be used to monitor these services. For instance, computerized energy management systems aimed at minimizing energy costs can also check the continuity of the supply.

Statutory regulations also require foodservice managers to maintain certain items of plant and equipment in good working order. Some of this legislation is quite specific and

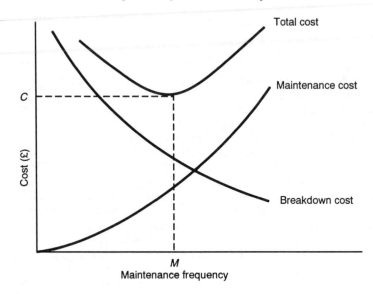

Figure 9.1   Optimum maintenance frequency.
Adapted from Hughes, C. (1985) *Production and Operations Management.*

identifies exactly what the manager must do. Increasingly, however, performance standards are not specific in the regulations; operators are expected to show 'due diligence' and are left to interpret what this means. Major areas of concern are lighting, especially emergency lighting, temperature controls, exhaust systems, chemical storage and fire control equipment. All of these just relate to the premises themselves, before we even start to consider the plant and equipment used to prepare foodstuffs, cook meals, serve customers.

Most foodservice operations will be subject to the Fire Precautions Act 1971 and other related legislation. This requires the fire authority to issue a fire certificate, based on satisfaction about adequacy of means of escape, fire-fighting equipment and fire warning systems. The basic principle of satisfactory means of escape is that persons should be able to walk unaided to a place of safety, regardless of where the fire might break out in the building. This requires staff training, effective signing and emergency lighting if there is power loss. Fire fighting equipment varies widely according to which type of fire is to be tackled. The British Standard BS 5306 provides details of these, along with a code of practice. Portable extinguishers should be sited close to fire risks, exit doorways, and at the same location on each floor or at each place in uniform buildings. The method of operation should also be the same irrespective of the extinguisher types. There are four types of fire, classified as follows:

Class A   fires involving solid materials – typically extinguished by cooling water or powder extinguishers;
Class B   fire involving liquids such as oil or fat – typically extinguished by excluding oxygen by smothering in a blanket or foam;
Class C   gas fires such as butane or propane – fire fighting should be left to experts, but shutting off the gas supply is essential;
Class D   chemical fires – should only be tackled by fire specialists.

FOOD SAFETY

Just as the Health and Safety at Work Act is a major influence on management action with respect to the built environment and equipment, the Food Safety Act has dramatically affected foodservice managers' approach to food handling and sanitation. Broadly speaking this legislation requires operators to demonstrate a duty of care towards their customers.

Food spoilage is a natural process, although the length of time it takes for different kinds of food to deteriorate varies widely. The food manufacturer or caterer interferes in this process by transforming the food in some way, often with the objective of extending the life of the foodstuff. Likewise the process can be accelerated if the food is contaminated in some way. There are basically four kinds of food spoilage. *Microbiological spoilage* is the most common. There are three basic types of microorganism: bacteria, moulds and yeasts. These can have both beneficial impacts, as in the fermentation of alcohol or development of cheese, or undesirable effects, as in the case of food contamination that leads to food poisoning outbreaks or moulds on foods such as bread. *Biochemical spoilage* is caused by natural food enzymes. These frequently react with air to produce off-odours, off-flavours and off-colours. For instance, when apples are peeled they go brown due to enzymic action. *Physical spoilage* is a result of the breakdown of the cell structure of the foodstuff due to excessive temperature changes, dryness or moisture. Finally, *chemical spoilage* can arise from the contamination of foods or drinks by the interaction with the air, light, or other things in contact with the items. For example, carbonated drinks usually need purified water to avoid the chemical spoilage that would arise from using typical tap water, which is frequently highly akaline. Fast food chains have a least one, and usually two, water purifiers linked to their soft drink dispensing units.

Food contamination can occur at source with the supplier, whilst in storage in the foodservice outlet, or during the process of preparing or serving the food. Most contamination is caused through physical contact between the food or drink item with the contaminant. Such contact can be made by employees handling items, unclean containers and utensils, work surfaces, insects and rodents, and airborne sources. There are a number of ways of preventing such contamination. These include the setting up of a rigorous, systematic approach to food handling, such as HACCP (see below); the adoption of correct sanitation procedures; the prevention of infestation; and effective staff training.

Some sectors of the catering industry have always adopted a systematic and rigorous approach to food safety, especially if preparing a large number of meals in bulk for vulnerable groups, as in hospitals or in-flight catering. These operations adopt the Hazard Analysis and Critical Control Points (HACCP) approach. For instance, in 1988, the DHSS published new guidelines on pre-cooked chilled foods that included HACCP as a central proposal, and in 1991 the Department of Health published a leaflet entitled *HACCP: Practical Food Safety For Businesses*. There is a suggestion in the USA, partly as a result of the US National Advisory Committee on Microbiological Criteria for Food developing a standardized HACCP system, that HACCP programmes may become mandatory.[6]   There are seven basic steps in HACCP implementation. These are:

1. Perform a hazards assessment.
2. Select critical control points.
3. Establish critical limits.

4. Establish monitoring requirements.
5. Establish corrective action to be taken when deviations at control points occur.
6. Establish record keeping systems on the plan.
7. Establish a verification system.

A relatively simple example of HACCP[7] is illustrated in Table 9.1, showing the critical points for control in a hotel restaurant. Critical limits relate to the temperatures at each stage in the food production and food service process. Critical points are usually those where foodstuffs are being stored, with attention placed on refrigerated and freezer storage and heated holding cabinets and serving counters; or handled, with an emphasis on good personal hygiene and equipment sanitization; or processed, wherein thawing of frozen foods, reheating and cooling of cooked foods are particularly hazardous.

East[8] suggests that the successful planning and implementation of HACCP may be carried out in three ways, depending on the size and expertise of the foodservice operator. The first option is to employ a specialist consultant to carry out each of the seven implementation steps and follow up with regular visits to check on the system. The second approach is to use specialist external expertise to set up the system and then take over responsibility for managing HACCP within the foodservice operation. Alternatively, the HACCP system can be set up by the foodservice firm, with only step 7, the verification of the system, being carried out by a specialist.

Sanitation encompasses more than just cleaning. As Thorner and Manning state,[9] 'cleaning means the removal of residues of food, dirt, dust, foreign material or other soiling ingredients or materials. Sanitizing means the effective bacterial treatment of clean surfaces and equipment.' Some detergents are only effective as cleaning agents, others include chemicals that act as sanitizers. Heat also kills microbiological organisms, at a temperature above 70°C. Hand dishwashing of utensils is typically carried out at less than 50°C, and even good mechanical dishwashing only at around 60°C. Thus effective sanitization requires both high-temperature washing and bactericidal treatment, usually by chlorine. Effective sanitation procedures and schedules should be established for four main areas: warewashing, large equipment, interiors and exteriors. Warewashing refers to all items of kitchen and foodservice equipment that can be handled through a dishwash process. Usually back-of-house equipment is treated separately from front-of-house equipment. Most hotels, for instance, have a kitchen pot wash and a restaurant wash-up facility, and in-flight catering kitchens employ very large plant using conveyor belts that have come to be known as flight wash-up machines. Large equipment sanitation focuses very much on ensuring the users of the equipment apply strict and routine procedures for cleaning their work areas. Fast food operators apply extremely rigorous standards to this. There is some evidence to suggest that the effective working life of equipment may be significantly increased if such routines are employed, extending its life from around four years up to seven or eight. Both interior and exterior sanitation is usually carried out by cleaning staff employed for that purpose, either directly by the operator or on a contract basis. Contractors may often be needed to carry out specialist work, for instance with regard to preventing contamination of water supplies or air pollution. Most kitchens have extractor hoods over the main cooking areas to remove heat, fumes and odours, and these require both daily cleaning to remove solid particle build-up and more thorough routine cleaning to prevent contamination.

Another area that may require specialist expertise is infestation. There are a number of pests that typically endanger health and safety in foodservice operations. Operators have legal duties not only under the Food Safety Act and the Health and Safety at Work

Table 9.1 Critical points of quality control for a hotel restaurant.

Critical point	Controls/ documentation	Control/ procedures	Corrective action	Personnel responsible
Menu design and specification stage	1. In accordance with management objectives 2. Precise documentation	1. Cost parameters 2. Staff skills 3. Equipment availability	1. Test 2. Review and evaluate	1. General manager 2. Food and beverage manager 3. Chef
Food purchasing	Purchase specifications	1. Receiving inspection 2. Lot by lot sampling	Acceptance/ rejection	1. Supplier 2. Storeperson 3. Chef
Storage	1. Storage procedures 2. Inventory control 3. Storage conditions	1. FIFO 2. Sampling checks 3. Stock control checks	Write-offs/ issues	Storeperson
Preparation	1. Standard recipes 2. Controlled issues	1. Sampling 2. Assessment against standards	1. Remedial/ corrective action 2. Training 3. Motivation	1. Commis 2. Sous Chef 3. Chef
Cooking	1. Standard recipes 2. Temperature setting 3. Cooking instructions 4. Cooking times	as above	as above	as above
Cooked/cold food storage	1. Hot plate settings 2. Production times 3. Government regulations: hot food storage $\geq 62.7°C$ cold food storage $\leq 10°C$	1. Thermostatic controls 2. Check on times 3. Sampling 4. Correct use of equipment	1. Regular maintenance of equipment 2. Rapid repair of equipment in event of failure	1. Engineer 2. Chef
Assembly/ portioning	1. Standard yields 2. Dish layout 3. Garnishes 4. Temperature of service dishes 5. Colour photos	1. Comparing 2. Screening	1. Corrective action 2. Training 3. Demonstration	1. Aboyeur 2. Chef 3. Waiter
Distribution	1. Standard methods, i.e. dishes covered 2. Time taken in distribution	Sampling check	1. Return to reheat	1. Chef 2. Restaurant manager
Service	1. Standards of performance 2. Standard service methods	1. Management supervision 2. Screening by restaurant manager	1. Demonstration 2. OJT	1. Restaurant manager 2. Chef de Rang 3. Training officer
Consumption	Menu	1. Customer's satisfaction 2. Sensory attributes	1. Acceptance/ rejection 2. Complaints	Customer

Source: Jones [7].

Act etc., but also Public Health Acts and the Prevention of Damage by Pests Act to control such pests. A control strategy has three main elements: prevention through sound design and construction of premises and equipment; discouragement by effective cleaning, storage, and hygiene; and destruction if infestation occurs. Some pests do threaten not only food safety through contamination by their droppings or contact with materials, but also the building itself. Rats, and even mice, have been known to gnaw through electrical wiring thereby causing fires. Insects such as wasps and fleas may be less likely to contaminate food, but may injure employees working in the operation. Flies and cockroaches are particularly prevalent in catering and are a serious cause of contamination. Operators must take care that steps taken to discourage or destroy pests are in themselves not dangerous. Electrical devices for attracting and killing flies must be sited over areas of floor where falling insects cannot enter the food chain. Poisons should not be used for controlling birds, and only by specialists in the control of rodents.

Food safety also depends on employees being properly trained and adopting safe practices. Such training is mandatory under the Food Safety Act, but no specific recognized qualifications are specified. Many employers are, however, adopting the Institution of Environmental Health Officers (IEHO) hygiene certification as a means of demonstrating their due diligence. Employees can contaminate food if they are infected with pathogens or suffering from diseases that promote the spread of pathogens, such as diarrhoea, sore throats, colds, jaundice; or if they have infected lesions such as boils or cuts; or if they fail to maintain their personal hygiene by smoking, sneezing, not washing hands after visiting the toilet. The UK's Food Hygiene Regulations 1990 state that food handlers should keep clean all parts of their person or clothing liable to come into contact with food. Likewise they list notifiable diseases that must be reported to employers, including typhoid, dysentery, salmonella infections, and staphylococcal infections. In practice, employees should be encouraged to report any illness that involves diarrhoea or vomiting.

CREATING A SAFE ENVIRONMENT FOR PEOPLE

In discussing the security and safety of the building, equipment and food handling processes, we have already been concerned with the health and safety of the people on foodservice premises. Many of the features designed into the physical environment adopt the philosophy of prevention that underpins this key result area. Nonetheless, despite the good design and maintenance of the property and equipment, it is possible that accidents will still occur. Both employees and customers need to be 'trained' in an effort to reduce this likelihood.

Employee training encompasses the area of hygiene discussed above, along with that of safe working practices. Risk assessments have shown that some work tasks have the potential for accidents or injuries to staff if proper safety procedures are not followed. Most foodservice operators will have policies and procedures covering main 'danger' areas such as the prevention of slips and falls, pushing or pulling loads, handling hot foods or equipment, handling chemicals and detergents, slicing, and electrical equipment. There are general policies that apply to all such situations. In the case of handling chemicals this would include avoidance of contact with eyes, fume inhalation, use of protective clothing, and so on. More detailed assessment and procedures may then be needed for each specific task. Chemical usage is subject to COSHH (Control Of Substances Hazardous to Health) Regulations 1988, which require a written programme for each task. An example of this is shown in Figure 9.2. All substances are coded as either an irritant, harmful, corrosive or toxic. Each category of hazardous substance requires different kinds of safety precaution.

It is also possible to 'train' customers to behave in ways that increase their safety and the safety of others. Signs both outside and inside can inform them of how the system operates and remind them of safe practices. For instance, restaurant customers are often asked to wait near the entrance before being sat at a table. It may also be required or advisable to state rules or regulations that customers must comply with. Pubs and licensed premises have a number of such statutory notices relating to who may be served and drinking-up times. They, and roadside diners, may also post non-statutory signs relating to the use of children's play areas with regards to parental responsibility for their children.

In the event that incidents or accidents do occur, it is essential that effective reporting procedures are in place. Some injuries or dangerous occurrences must be reported to the Environmental Health Office, namely fatalities, major injury, four days' or more lost time, and dangerous occurrences. Major injuries include fractures, amputations, loss of eye sight, loss of consciousness, illness due to infection at work, or more than 24-hour hospitalization cases. Lost time injuries are those that take place at work and result in an employee being absent from work. Dangerous occurrences include 14 different events, such as lifting-machine failure, explosions, electrical short circuits, building collapse, and so on. In addition to these events, foodservice operators may also wish to record near-miss incidents and first-aid cases in an on-site accident book.

SECURITY OF CASH AND OTHER ASSETS

Most foodservice operations have assets that are worth stealing. The most obvious target is cash, but other items, especially liquor stocks, are also valuable. It has even been known for thieves to steal artefacts such as carpets, paintings and equipment from hotels and restaurants. Although armed robbery and burglary have been mentioned above, when discussing the security of buildings and opening/closing procedures, most losses from foodservice businesses derive from employee theft. It is estimated in the USA that the foodservice industry loses $20 billion a year to theft and cash mishandling.[10] Regrettably, this same report in 1992 suggests that 'one out of every three employees will steal if given the opportunity'. In the UK, a similar report in *Caterer and Hotelkeeper* in 1992 states that one in four employees 'will always steal, given the opportunity'.[11] A number of reasons are put forward why the hospitality industry in general is so prone to dishonest workers. These include the low status of jobs in the industry, low skill requirements and low pay. There is also some suggestion that 'perks' and 'fiddles' in some sectors have been institutionalized over the years. Some might say that all of these 'causes' are within the remit of foodservice managers to put right.

Efforts can be made to hire responsible employees in the first place. For security reasons, workers employed by British Airways and caterers in central and local government may be security vetted before employment. But even this does not ensure complete security. Some agencies also exist to provide employment records of reliable and experienced staff. However, if it is not possible to hire only honest employees, advice is available on how to spot the dishonest ones! A presentation to the British

JOB/TASK:	**RESTAURANT:**
Cleaning and Sanitizing Walk In Refrigerators/ Freezers	**REF. No:** BK 015
	ISSUE DATE: 8.3.93

JOB/TASK DESCRIPTION:
Cleaning and sanitizing above

SUBSTANCES/CHEMICALS USED:
CAPITAL Multipurpose Concentrate, KAY-5 Sanitizer, KADET Quarry Tile Floor Cleaner

BY-PRODUCTS/FUMES PRODUCED BY PROCESS:
None

RELEVANT OES/MEL AND RESULTS OF ENVIRONMENTAL MONITORING:
KADET Quarry Tile Floor Cleaner contains Phosphoric Acid   1mg m^3 O.E.S.

CONTROL MEASURES USED:
CAPITAL pre-measured Concentrate, written procedures, training, Manufacturer's Data Sheets, Cleaning and Sanitation Guide, colour coded containers

MAINTENANCE OF CONTROL MEASURES:
Supervision

FACTORS THAT MAY AFFECT EXPOSURE (i.e. FAILURE OF CONTROL MEASURES/SPILLAGE):
Spillage

INFORMATION/TRAINING/INSTRUCTION AND SUPERVISION REQUIREMENTS:
Cleaning and Sanitation Guide, training, Manufacturer's Data Sheets

DURATION OF EXPOSURE:
Dependant on size

FREQUENCY OF TASK: **NO. OF PEOPLE EXPOSED:**
As and when required   1

OTHER PERSONS THAT MAY BE EXPOSED (INCLUDING CONTRACTORS/PASSERS BY):
Kitchen Staff

ASSESSMENT RECOMMENDATIONS:
None

INITIAL ASSESSMENT CONCLUSIONS: SATISFACTORY [✓] NOT SATISFACTORY [ ]

ACTION RESULTING:
None

COMPLETION:	**ACTION COMPLETE BY:**
MANAGER:	**REVIEWED:**
	DATE BY:
ASSESSOR: *Barry C. ...* **DATE:** 8/3/93	
MANAGER: **DATE:**	

Figure 9.2   BurgerKing COSHH assessment.

Association of Hotel Accountants in 1987 identified eight 'symptoms' of unreliable employees. Things to look out for include staff declining to take promotions into other areas of work or reluctance to take holidays, frequent visits to the cloakroom possibly to hide stolen cash or items, misuse of tills, life-styles that do not match the pay packet, close social or personal contacts with suppliers or customers, and lack of company loyalty as displayed by sarcasm or cynicism about the employing organization.

Cash remains the most likely temptation to the dishonest employee. Most foodservice operations that handle cash – and not all do – have very clear procedures laid down for cash handling. These include the operation of tills and cash draws, on-site security of cash in safes, payroll procedures, and banking. Till procedures are largely designed to ensure that employees do not commit theft or fraud. When cash drawers are set up, the amount in each should be checked and noted; all voids or no sales should be approved by management and the reason noted; where possible only one employee should be allocated to each cash drawer; change should not be exchanged between cash drawers; and refunds given only with management approval. Operations with high-volume sales also typically 'skim' cash drawers, i.e. remove money, especially large-denomination notes, during peak periods to avoid a build-up of cash. At the end of the operating period, cash should be counted in a secure location and reconciled with the till record; cash overs and shorts dealt with according to the specific policy of that operation; and cash either banked immediately or secured on site in a safe.

Some sectors of the industry have equally rigorous control over liquor stocks because of their high value. In pubs and clubs the traditional approach to control has been frequent physical stock takes to reconcile stock usage with case receipts. An operation in the licensed trade with poor stock reconciliation may have random stock-takes made as frequently as once a week in an effort to identify how stock is being lost. Modern systems use controlled-measure dispensing of spirits and beers, along with bar code computerization aimed at producing a real-time reconciliation of stock usage and cash received.

INSURANCE

Whilst the main thrust of management in this key result is on prevention, protecting assets is also about assessing risk and judging what action should be taken. Risk assessment is the essence of the insurance industry. The foodservice manager must therefore use this industry's expertise to insure the property, its contents, and the people using the building in the most appropriate way. There are many different kinds of insurance. These are summarized in Table 9.2.

Just as with health, safety and food hygiene, there is legislation that requires businesses to take out a minimum of insurance cover as indemnity. Insurance is also an overhead cost that has to be managed. The effective implementation of policies and procedures designed to protect assets from the range of threats discussed can lead to significant savings in insurance premiums. One fast food chain has achieved such savings in its high street restaurants by developing a specialist head office function called 'loss control management' and introducing a programme aimed at improving security and safety on their premises.

Table 9.2 Type of insurance.

Fire Insurance and Consequential Loss Insurance may cover loss of profit arising from closure following fire flood or explosion.

Fidelity Guarantee Insurance covers possible loss caused by employee theft.

Cash in Transit Insurance covers cash robbery between the catering premises and the bank.

Employer's Liability Insurance covers injuries to employees that may occur due to employer's negligence.

Public Liability Insurance covers injuries to the public caused by employer or employee negligence. This usually includes food poisoning.

Burglary Insurance and Engineering Insurance covers damage to plant.

Credit Insurance covers bad debts, usually to 75% of the full amount.

Adapted from Batty, J. (1970) *Management Accounting*, London: Macdonald & Evans.

ENVIRONMENTAL AND ENERGY MANAGEMENT

So far in this chapter, we have considered routine ways of dealing with issues of security, safety and sanitation. Such policies and procedures need to be placed in a wider context, however. A current major trend affecting management performance in the foodservice industry is the environment. There are a number of 'green' issues in foodservice. These include the use of disposables in fast food, menus and healthy eating, the use of cleaning agents and detergents, recycling of waste, and energy efficiency. In this key result area of protecting assets we shall examine two of these issues: waste management and energy efficiency.

The amount of waste a foodservice outlet produces varies widely. In the fast food sector much of this waste is paper and compactors are used to reduce its volume by 20 per cent prior to collection. Operators are considering a new technology that shreds such waste down to 5 per cent of its volume, thereby reducing the need to have waste collected daily from each restaurant. On a much larger scale is the food waste produced by an in-flight production unit, estimated to be 70 tons per day for the larger operations. Managers have always put a great deal of effort into minimizing waste; in the 1990s as much effort is now put into ensuring that waste is 'clean' and where possible recycled. In the past, much food waste was 'recycled' by selling it to the pig man, who used to collect it for feeding to farm stock. Ironically this has now stopped owing to the unhygienic and potentially hazardous nature of this practice. Modern recycling takes different forms. Many large-scale foodservice outlets now treat effluent waste water in order to remove grease and fat. Some chains, and even independent restaurateurs, have instituted recycling policies with regards to aluminium cans.

The use of efficient energy is also environmentally friendly, but fortunately feeds directly into bottom-line profit. Fast food chains for a number of years have utilized computer-based panels for switching on and off their equipment. Such panels control the 'fire-up cycle' so that equipment is switched on in sequence rather than all at once. This keeps the current surge or KVA as low as possible thereby reducing the cost of electricity. Other approaches to energy efficiency include the use of energy-efficient lighting and computerized thermostats for heating control and air-conditioning of buildings. During the early 1990s the biggest impact on energy costs has been derived not from using less of it, but from buying it more cheaply. Following the privatization of

Restaurant Loss Control Evaluation

Score two point for a "Yes", one point for a "Part", and no point for a "No"

Restaurant:....................................
Duty Manager:..............................
Evaluating Manager:.......................
Date/Time:...................................

	Yes	Part	No
A. Notices.			
Health & Safety (EHO contact details) ____			
Employers Liability Insurance ____			
Fire & Police contact ____			
UPR Wages Council order ____			
Management aware of loss reporting procedure___			
Site Incident Report Forms available & used ___			
Fire & Security Log up to date___			
Schedules posted ___			
Emergency procedures posted ____			
Cash policy posted ____			
Meals policy posted & followed ___			
H & S policy posted ___			
B. First Aid.			
First Aid/Aids kit available/stocked/location marked			
Medical aid procedures posted ____			
Treatment card in first aid available & used___			
Accident book up to date ___			
First aider on duty ___			
Sharps bin available ___			
C. Training.			
Name of restaurant safety co-ordinator? ___			
Staff trained on safety & security (video & test) ___			
Staff can state correct use of fire extinguishers___			
Staff lift correctly ___			
Manager has latest Loss Control Manual ___			
Staff have suitable shoes ___			
D. Chemicals.			
All chemicals approved ___			
Cleaning & maintenance log up to date ___			
All chemicals labelled___			
COSHH data displayed ___			
Chemicals stored correctly___			
Chemicals handled correctly ___			
Staff have seen chemical training video & know safe system of work ___			
E. Security & Cash Control.			
Safe properly locked (combination spun) ___			
Safe comb, changed monthly/manager change___			
Warning procedure followed for cash shortages___			
All bank deposit information current & recorded ___			
Minimum of 3 deposits/day ___			
POS down kit available/current ___			
Safe key locked away from office overnight ___			
Void/Coupon/Cheque procedure followed ___			
Open/close procedures follow loss control manual___			
All managers signed Cash Policy ___			
All cashiers signed Cash Policy ___			
Money not left unattended in office ___			
Office door locked when safe unlocked ___			
Safe key with manager who has signed for safe___			
Current safe control record in safe ___			
All cash/cheque deposit books in safe ___			
Restaurant team trained in loss control security ___			
Intruder alarm fitted & working & used ___			
Police have correct keyholder information ___			

	Yes	Part	No
F. Kitchen equipment.			
Condition of gas service line, electrical lead & plug			
Baskets in good condition ___			
Correct heat lamps in use/working/covered___			
Ansul fusible links clean/nozzles capped ___			
All equipment properly mounted (restraint chains)__			
Cleanliness under equipment ___			
Approved containers with covers for old oil ___			
Protective equipment readily available (apron/ face shield/goggles/gloves/boots/evidence of use) _			
Spare personal protective equipment available ___			
Shortening filter machine in good working order ___			
(hoses/insulators/electrical leads) ___			
Fry skimmer/vat brush/drain hook available ___			
Unused shortening stored in a sanitary manner ___			
Equipment casing in good & safe condition ___			
Microwaves secure ———————			
G. Rubbish Area.			
Compactor in good repair & guarded against unauthorised use (min. 18 yrs.) ___			
Check compactor interlock operation ___			
Refuse area clean and free of hazards ___			
H. Slicing Equipment.			
Two Whizard gloves available & used ___			
Knives with blunt ends & finger guards ___			
Tomato slicer has proper mounting & guard ___			
Corer in good condition ___			
Correct/clean chopping boards ___			
I. Water heater.			
No combustibles within 3 ft. of boiler ___			
Gas line in good condition & labelled (yellow)___			
Hot water temperature 50° to 62°C ___			
Cold water temperature less than 20°C___			
J. Compressed Gas.			
Caps on full cylinders not in use ___			
All cylinders adequately restrained ___			
Condition of CO_2 pipes ___			
CO_2 meter in operation ___			
K. Physical Plant/Building.			
Gas shut off valve accessible ___			
Water shut off valve accessible ___			
Electric shut off accessible ___			
All exits properly signed/lit/unlocked & clear ___			
Wet floor signs/caution cones available & used ___			
Mats in place at entrance doors ___			
Undercounter lighting protected where fitted ___			
Dining room furniture in sound condition ___			
All lights working in dining area ___			
All lights working in staff areas ___			
All staircases have secure handrails ___			
All unused power sockets to be covered___			
Water treatment log current ___			
Door closers function properly ___			
High chairs & booster seats in good condition ___			
Baby changing unit in good condition ___			

Top copy – Keep in restuarant. Pink copy – District. Page 1 of 3

Figure 9.3 BurgerKing's restaurant loss control evaluation. Reproduced with permission.

the gas and electricity supply industries in the UK, large-scale operators are now able to purchase both energy sources in bulk from a single supplier. For instance, in 1993 Burger King signed a contract with a single supplier, Allied Gas, that will considerably reduce its gas bills in all of its company-owned UK restaurants.

CONCLUSION

Protecting the assets of the foodservice operation is at first sight not the most exciting or challenging of the many activities a manager must engage in.

This chapter has reviewed all the different things that must be considered. It has highlighted the concept of 'deter, delay, alert, inform and react'. In doing so, it illustrates just how important this key result area is and what the implications are of failing to do so. Protecting assets demands increasingly sophisticated approaches to security, safety and sanitation. This sophistication includes the need to reward the manager for taking effective action in this area. And whilst the focus of policy and procedure is on prevention, in the event of an emergency there are equally sophisticated ways of dealing with emergencies and potential crises.

A relatively new idea, developed in the USA, is the concept of 'loss control management'. BurgerKing has adopted this approach, which encompasses many of the policies, systems and procedures outlined so far in this chapter. In effect it has recognized the importance of this key result area and appointed a manager with the responsibility of improving performance in this area. BK's loss control manager has six district co-ordinators reporting to him. Together they develop policies and guidelines, act as advisers to restaurant managers, and carry out inspections.

One of the new procedures BK has developed for this chain is a monthly loss control evaluation to be carried out. This is illustrated in Figure 9.3. This checklist has 21 different sections covering all aspects of safety, security and sanitation. Each outlet is scored against a possible total of 326 points and managers must develop an action plan to deal with any area in which the restaurant has scored badly. More importantly, this evaluation is part of the overall assessment and appraisal system of each manager and influences his or her bonus.

This chain, along with many others in the industry, has also developed the final aspect of management in this area, namely incident and communications management. This refers to how emergencies are dealt with to reduce adverse publicity and long-term losses. Effective communication can prevent emergencies becoming crises – but, if a crisis, then resolve it promptly. BurgerKing therefore has an incident alert hotline that is used to report any potential crisis situations, which includes multiple food poisoning or contamination, product tampering, sabotage, fire, robbery, hostage taking, boycotts or terrorism. In response to each of these events a specific team with the necessary skills and expertise will move into action. This team will liaise closely with the relevant services such as the police or fire brigade and in particular deal with all media enquiries.

REFERENCES

1. 'Perks of the job become £3m fiddle', (1989) *The Times*, 25 August.
2. Lorenzini, Beth (1992) 'The secure restaurant', *Restaurants and Institutions*, 21 October, pp. 85–102.

3. 'Salmonella costs SAS £183,000 (1993) *Caterer and Hotelkeeper*, 15 July.

4. Lorenzini, Beth, op. cit.

5. Sall, Bally (1989) 'Cry wolf at your peril', *Caterer and Hotelkeeper*, 23 November.

6. O'Donnell, Claudia D. (1991) 'Implementation of HACCP at Orval Kent Food Company Inc.', *Journal of Foodservice Systems*, No. 6, pp. 197–207.

7. Jones, Peter (1983) 'The restaurant: a place for quality control and product maintenance'. *International Journal of Hospitality Management*, Vol. 2, No. 2, pp. 93–100.

8. East, Janet. (1993) 'HACCP – The concept, development and application', *Managing Quality in the Catering Industry*, Croner Publications, pp. 81–125.

9. Thorner, M. E. and Manning P. B. (1983) *Quality Control in Foodservice*, Westport, Conn. AVI Publishing.

10. Lorenzini, Beth, op. cit.

11. Goymour, David (1992) 'Thieves behind bars' *Caterer and Hotelkeeping*, 24 September, pp. 39–42.

10

Improving Employee Performance

Peter Jones

INTRODUCTION

The foodservice industry in the UK employs over 1 million people on a full-time or part-time basis. Labour cost is typically between 25 and 35 per cent of total operating costs. Making sure that this workforce is well motivated and performs to high standards is a major task for the foodservice manager. In this chapter we focus on employee behaviour and what a manager can do to ensure that this behaviour matches the needs and goals of the organization and that operational standards are achieved. We examine different approaches to motivating employees and ways of reducing those things that inhibit effective performance, notably boundary role stress. The importance of teams is recognized and ways of enhancing their effectiveness are proposed. Finally we review the role that organizational culture can play in achieving high levels of employee performance.

Strategies and management action aimed at improving employee performance may also lead to a number of other beneficial spin-offs. For instance, staff turnover may be reduced. Well-motivated high performers are more likely to stay with the organization. One estimate of staff turnover costs in the industry[1] identifies that for an hourly paid employee in the USA, direct costs of turnover (advertising, recruiting, management/clerical time, training) were around $2,000 plus another $4,100 in indirect costs (loss of productivity, overtime to others, low morale, loss of goodwill). For managerial staff the estimated cost was nearer $20,000. Secondly, high-performing employees are likely to achieve high levels of productivity. This key result area is further discussed in Chapter 12. Thirdly, levels of customer satisfaction may be improved if the workforce are performing to high standards. All of those – lower turnover, increased productivity, improved customer satisfaction – also have a direct impact on profitability.

NATURE OF MOTIVATION AND MODELS OF EMPLOYEE PERFORMANCE

There are a number of motivational theories that may explain why people work well. All of them are inconclusive and subject to criticism. Mullins[2] explains that such theories are of two main types: *content theories* such as Maslow's hierarchy of needs model, Aldefer's continuum of needs model, Herzberg's two-factor theory, and McClelland's theory of achievement motivation; and *process theories*, such as Vroom's expectancy theory and the Porter and Lawler expectancy model. Content theories focus on what motivates people and attempt to explain the specific things that lead to better motivated individuals. Such theories tend to emphasize psychological rewards, personal growth and achievement. They ignore money as a motivational force, regarding it, if at all, as a means to an end rather than an end in itself. This is contrary to the perspective of most employers and managers, who place great stress on remuneration policies, bonus payments as incentives, and so on. Weaver[3] supports the view that money can be an important motivational force, especially with regards to hourly paid employees.

Process theories, on the other hand, are based on how people are motivated, emphasizing the dynamic variables which make up motivation. These models do include the role that monetary reward has in motivating individuals, although the exact relationship between reward, performance, job satisfaction and motivation is not always clear. Despite the difficulty of understanding these complex models, some clear guidelines emerge for management action. These include:

(1) Individual employee performance needs to be monitored and evaluated clearly through effective procedures.
(2) Employees should be trained or developed to have the necessary knowledge and skills needed to perform their tasks.
(3) Rewards should relate to individual performance.
(4) Other factors, such as policies, systems, and technology should be designed to enhance individual performance.
(5) Inhibiting outcomes of high performance, such as stress, co-worker grievance, or accidents, should be minimized.

Managers also need to be aware of the need to treat employees fairly. Arguably, equity theory is another process theory of motivation, based on the concept that inequity causes tension which reduces motivation. Adams[4] identifies six employee behaviours that result from their perception of inequity in the workplace. These are changing their 'inputs' at work, for instance by working less hard or poorly; seeking to change the 'outputs' at works, such as asking for higher pay, benefits, or promotion for no extra work; distorting their perception of inputs or outputs, such as how hard they are really working; 'leaving the field', through absenteeism, transfers, or resignation; influencing other employees to perform differently; and comparing themselves with a new group of co-workers.

Few, if any, foodservice managers adopt one of these theories and apply it exclusively. Whether they have knowledge of them or not, they will probably develop their own individual model of what motivates others, based on personal values and experience, similar to the guidelines above. The danger of managers' internalizing their own unique theory of motivation is that it may not always match employees' views.

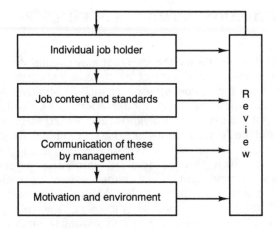
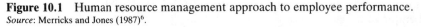

Figure 10.1 Human resource management approach to employee performance.
Source: Merricks and Jones (1987)[6].

Research suggests that there may be a mismatch between what managers think their staff want and vice versa. One study[5] found that managers ranked higher wages, job security and promotion as the most important factors for employees; whereas the employees ranked full appreciation of work done, a feeling of being in on things, and help with personal problems as their three most important.

TRAINING, DEVELOPMENT AND MOTIVATION

Merricks and Jones[6] adopt a straightforward approach to improving employee performance based on the approach developed by industry training boards during the 1970s. In their view, 'performance is influenced by the individual job holder, design of the job content, and the approach adopted by management to communication and review of performance, in order to ensure the achievement of business goals'. In other words, it is necessary to have the 'right' person, in the 'right' job, being told to do the 'right' things in the 'right' way. Only then may it be necessary to motivate employees. This is illustrated in Figure 10.1.

The overall approach to managing in this key result emphasizes the importance of effective human resource management (HRM) policies and procedures. It is clear that in order to employ an appropriate person to fill a job position in foodservice, HRM procedures relating to person specifications, recruitment and selection are essential. The aim of these is to ensure three things. The intellectual capabilities of recruits should match the job requirements. Over-qualified people can perform just as badly as under-qualified, albeit for different reasons. Secondly, employees must be physically able to carry out the tasks required by their job. Such concerns might include their physical strength or manual dexterity, as well as concerns about alcohol or drug dependency. Finally, recruits should display the appropriate emotional or interpersonal characteristics needed for the job. This is especially true of staff employed in front-of-house positions who come into contact with customers. The development of person specifications should include a detailed match of the above three characteristics –

mental, physical and emotional – with the job, along with an analysis of the relevance of previous experience. It should then become evident as to where and how job advertisements should be applied. For instance, if no previous experience is necessary then there is no point in advertising in the catering press. Likewise the selection process can be designed to ensure a match between the person and the process. Merricks and Jones cite the example of an Italian restaurant that asked prospective employees to telephone rather than complete an application form, as telephone skills were more important than writing skills for the post advertised. The applicants were screened at this telephone stage to ensure that they had all the key attributes the restaurant was seeking.

With regard to the job itself, HRM procedures relating to the concept of job design, job descriptions and job specifications play an important role. In Chapter 5 we examined influences on staffing levels and the importance of job design. Foodservice employees can be expected to engage in a simple range of routine tasks as in an in-flight production unit; be multi-skilled to carry out a number of different roles and tasks as in fast food; or carry out quite complex activities as in an à la carte restaurant kitchen. Merricks and Jones identify five principles of job design that 'enrich' the positions for the benefit of employees. First, the grouping of work should be natural; what a person is asked to do is clearly placed in the context of what other people are doing. Secondly, employees or the teams they work in should have responsibility for completing a unit of work. Thirdly, employees should be encouraged to have contact with the 'consumer' or the output – this may be another employee, and not the 'paying customer'. Fourthly, employees should be encouraged to plan and control their work, rather than have it controlled by others. Finally, there should be open and effective ways of receiving feedback on performance. The job having been designed and enriched, it is necessary to ensure that each person has a job description identifying the tasks he or she must perform and the responsibilities the job carries. A typical job description is illustrated in Figure 10.2. Merricks and Jones identified that a major problem with job descriptions is that they tend to focus on tasks rather than performance aimed at meeting business goals. They advocated that job descriptions should be written to focus on outputs and standards of performance rather than tasks. For instance, wine waiting staff job descriptions might include reference to target spend per head on wine, volume of sales per customer, or percentage of total customers who purchase drinks before their meal. There is some evidence that this idea is being adopted, but confined largely to the fast food sector.

Having specified the right kind of employee and designed the job, the next stage focuses on communicating effectively to the employee. This involves effective staff induction and training, the development of standards of performance or operating manuals, and appropriate staff appraisal systems. Training is required when new staff are employed; when change occurs due to new technology, legislation or redeveloped menus or concept; when employees do not perform to the required standard; or when it is part of a staff development process aimed at moving an employee from their current position into another one. Large organizations with standard, sometimes, branded, products place great emphasis on detailed manuals of performance. These include specifications for the product and presentation of food items, completion of documentation, interpersonal behaviour standards, and personnel practice and procedures. As well as written materials, many multi-site operators make extensive use of video materials for induction and training purposes. Smaller organizations may rely on face-to-face communication. Standards are not written down and communicated verbally by managers who coach new employees on the standards expected of them. Kreck[7]

JOB PROFILE: FOOD AND BEVERAGE MANAGER

The Food and Beverage Manager will concentrate on the short-term and long-term needs of the operation in the confines of the corporation's needs and objectives. Therefore, he is the principal agent of proactive change.

He will personally supervise the daily food and beverage operation in its entirety, including:

– Quality and consistency of service and product.
– All cost factors.
– Cleanliness of all food and beverage areas.
– Final selections and training of staff.
– Production of departmental profit.
– The implementation and exercise of all policies and
  procedures.

The Food and Beverage Manager will be actively involved in financial planning, including:

– Preparation of monthly and annual forecasts and budgets.
– Development of recommended concept changes.
– Development of profit potential.

Figure 10.2   Job description of a hotel food and beverage manager.
Source: Merricks and Jones (1987)[6].

suggests that standards should be 'practical, reliable, relevant, observable, explicitly defined and measurable'. Finally, employees need effective feedback. In the food-service industry there is usually a high degree of contact between the workforce and management during a typical working day. This provides many opportunities for informal, ongoing feedback. In addition there are many formal systems for providing feedback such as weekly staff meetings, probationary period reviews, annual staff appraisal interviews, monthly budget reviews, and so on. Within these formal systems it is essential that the criteria for judging performance should be as objective as possible, thereby avoiding influences such as favouritism, halo effects, sexual prejudice and racial bias.

Finally, if, and only if, it appears that employees are failing to meet the required standards of performance then management need to consider the motivation of their workforce. Whilst motivation theorists such as Maslow and Herzberg have had major impact on management thinking, Merricks and Jones believe 'many managers find it very difficult to relate theory to practice'. They suggest a number of practical ways in which employees may be motivated, consistent with the guidelines discussed above. These include acting as a role model, praising employees when they do good work, providing a sense of achievement, increasing the level of responsibility of employees, and taking a proactive view of the organizational climate.

A summary of this approach to this key result area is provided in Table 10.1. Mill[8] suggests that 'a different strategy is required to correct poor performance' according to the cause of the problem. Merricks and Jones adapt this into the context of their approach and illustrate how different solutions may be appropriate for the range of problems that might occur in foodservice.

BurgerKing (Europe, Middle East and Africa) is a good example of a foodservice operation that takes this systematic approach to employee performance. Each Burger-King (BK) restaurant has a staff development manager, supported by operations trainers at area level and eight training executives covering the whole of Europe. Every

Table 10.1 Resolution of poor employee performance.

Process	Symptoms	Action plan
Individual	Poor attitude	Redeploy/dismiss
	Poor skills	Improve selection
Job content	Good skills	Job enrichment
	No inclination to work	
	High conformity	Job enlargement
	Low responsibility	Job enrichment
Communication	Low organizational clarity	Management by objectives
	Low standards	
Motivation	Good skills	Job enlargement
and environment	No inclination to work	Job enrichment
	Low team spirit	Climate of trust
	Few rewards	Positive reinforcement

Source: Merricks, P and Jones P. (1987) *The Management Catering Operations*, Cassell, London.

employee receives a systematic induction and training based in the workplace. For induction the manager has available video, text and flip-chart aids covering an introduction to the company, safety and security, food hygiene and safety, and customer service. Thereafter there is training in each of the eight workstations within the operation: broiler/steamer, whopper board, burger board, fry station, speciality, counter, drinks, and drive through. The standard process for each station comprises the trainee watching the appropriate video, a short test on the video, on-the-job instruction, practice of the task, a written test, and review by the trainer. The trainer records the level of performance of each employee on a training proficiency chart and records these in individual employee training record books. BK makes extensive use of video, with voice-overs in several languages. Video ensures that exactly the same corporate standards are delivered throughout the world and it enables training to be carried out speedily, in groups, and away from the shop floor. Each video is accompanied by the relevant trainee test. The next likely development is interactive video.[9] In the USA, Pizza Hut and McDonald's are developing touch-screen interactive video training that quizzes employees on subjects such as product knowledge, company philosophy and sanitization. It is estimated that interactive video production costs have fallen tenfold since the mid-1980s.

REWARDING EMPLOYEES

In discussing motivational theories above, the role that rewards have in encouraging employee performance is not entirely clear. In particular, money or pay can be viewed as a means to an end rather than an end in itself. Nonetheless, understanding how staff are paid is an important aspect of the foodservice manager's job. Reward systems for different categories of staff in different sectors need to be considered. In Chapter 5, it was stated that one of the ways in which the industry workforce can be divided is into three major categories of employee: full-time, part-time and casual. Decisions about the proportion of each kind of employee are made on the basis of understanding the aggregate patterns of demand within the sector and the operational characteristics of the particular operation. Some sectors employ mainly full-time staff, notably welfare and in-flight catering; others, such as fast food, have a high proportion of part-time employees; whilst the outdoor catering and banqueting sectors of the industry rely heavily on casual staff.

Foodservice employees may be paid in a number of ways: hourly rate, weekly wage, bonus payments, 'commission'. Until fairly recently it was common practice in the hotel sector especially to pay restaurant employees out of the 'tronc', which in effect was a percentage of turnover. In the fast food sector nearly all employees are paid hourly. In the public sector, foodservice workers will generally be paid a weekly wage, although in the schools sector annual contracts may only be for 40 weeks of the year.

Perks and bonuses are also a feature of the industry. In the previous chapter (see p.153) the extent to which employees are likely to behave dishonestly was discussed. Much of this dishonesty derives from industry practices related to so-called 'perks'. In the past it was common to pay staff in kind by allowing them to remove food and drink items from the premises, either openly or with the connivance of management. Employees also came to expect their wages to be supplemented by direct cash payments, or tips, from customers. In the modern industry, where cost control procedures have tightened up stock security and service is included in restaurant prices, employees continue to expect perks and tips but resort to dishonest practice in order to obtain them. As perks have declined, there has been an increase in the use of employee bonuses, often tied to high performance. For instance, any employee identified by the mystery shopper of one fast food chain as providing outstanding service will be given a £25 bonus bond.

EMPOWERING EMPLOYEES

'Empowerment, so far the leading management buzzword of the '90s, will still be the hottest labor topic in 1993. Operators will continue to ask their front-line employees to take control of those moments of truth that help build customer loyalty' – so wrote Jeff Weinstein[10] in the first 1993 edition of *Restaurants and Institutions*. Empowerment strategies appear to have been adopted most widely in hotel chains, especially in the USA, such as Omni Hotels, Marriotts and Westin. It is a process of decentralizing decision making that leads to a flattened organizational structure. This can be relatively structured by providing specific guidelines to employees with regards to the limits on their decision making; or flexible empowerment, which enables employees to make on-the-spot decisions in order to achieve customer satisfaction. Brymer[11] believes three conditions must be in place before it is possible to empower employees: strong management support at all levels; clear outcomes established for an empowerment programme; and specific goals and dates set. The benefits and outcomes of this strategy also need to be conveyed to middle managers, as it is they who will largely implement the programme. He lists seven potential benefits. These are fewer and lower adjustments to customer bills, greater rapport and team work with employees, fewer interruptions of managers' time, less blame shifting, personal and professional development of employees, greater customer satisfaction, and greater co-operation between sections or departments.

Brymer proposes a 14-step programme for implementing empowerment. The first five steps cover the organization of an initial meeting between management and employees. First, ensure all employees attend meetings aimed at 'improving customer satisfaction'; secondly, ensure that these employees are briefed on empowerment and its relationship to customer satisfaction; thirdly, ensure that the commitment of management is demonstrated; explain how empowerment will improve employees' jobs; and fifthly, be clear about the type of empowerment being introduced. The next three steps may also be covered in the first series of employee meetings or in subsequent sessions. These are to introduce the skills needed to support the empowerment programme; develop a list of 'guest satisfiers'; and reinforce top management's commitment. Step 9 is to prepare a written document that clearly identifies the framework, skills, satisfiers and 'ownership'. This is followed by more meetings aimed at establishing guidelines for operations and appropriate motivational support. The final three steps relate to a progress review; positive reinforcement of employees; and regular updates and feedback of performance.

Research indicates that empowerment does lead to some of the benefits claimed. Fulford[12] studied 257 city and country club employees. Three major findings emerged: empowerment does have an effect on satisfaction, loyalty, performance, service delivery and concern for others; the most important variable of empowerment is the sense of value it gives employees, so that jobs designed to be meaningful have the most positive outcomes; and thirdly, full-time and part-time workers differed in their perceptions. These results were supported by Sparrowe.[13] His study of 199 hospitality workers in 36 different organizations in one major US city investigated the importance of psychological constructs of empowerment. He found that the higher the level of empowerment, the greater the organizational commitment and the less the likelihood of staff turnover.

REDUCING BOUNDARY ROLE STRESS

A feature of work in service organizations is the large number of employees who meet with and directly serve the general public. Some kinds of foodservice operation have very low levels of contact, notably vending and to a certain extent takeaway restaurants and home delivery. Others, such as theme and gourmet restaurants, deliver high-contact service encounters. The employees who work in customer contact positions are said to occupy 'boundary spanning roles'.[14] Although all work can be stressful, boundary role workers have been identified as being subject to particular stresses that result from their meeting and dealing with the public on a regular basis. Jones and Lockwood[15] summarise such stress as five main types.

Role conflict arises when the organization and customer have different expectations about what the employee will do. For instance, the operational standard may be that all drinks have to be paid for when ordered in the bar, but the customer may wish the drinks to be added to their restaurant bill. *Role overload* is caused by employees having too many things to do at once, especially if these tasks are quite different in nature. This is most obviously seen amongst inexperienced staff. For instance, newly employed table service employees often find it difficult to serve or clear the table and answer customer questions at the same time. On the other hand, experienced employees are very good at coping with a number of roles and identifying what role is expected of them. For example, the archetype hotel barman plays, and is expected to play, the role of expert (knowledge of drinks and cocktails), skilled practitioner (dispensing drinks), entertainer (mixing cocktails, telling jokes), agony aunt (listening to customers), accountant (billing for sales), and so on. Such overload may be manageable if each role is kept relatively separate from each other. If not, *multiple role conflict* can arise as employees are forced to switch from one kind of behaviour to another very quickly. Stress is caused by confusion and uncertainty about which behaviour to adopt. Stress also arises from *inter-client conflict*. This occurs when two or more customers expect or demand different things of the employee. Some customers may seek fast service with little interpersonal contact with the employee, others may be more relaxed and like to chat. Finally, there may be *role incompatibility* when a person is expected to perform a role for which he or she is unsuited. Lockwood and Jones suggest that the introduction of carvery and buffet service in restaurants has increased the frequency of contact between kitchen personnel and customers, and these employees may be stressed by this owing to their lack of training or experience of customer contact. On the other hand, some foodservice organizations, notably hospitals, have deliberately encouraged back-of-house staff to meet with customers as part of their quality improvement strategy. For instance, British Airways initiated their 'chefs in the air' scheme for first-class travel with very positive feedback from both customers and employees.

No employee works well if they are stressed. Boundary role workers, however, adopt a number of strategies for reducing their stress levels by controlling interactions with customers that are not always compatible with the aims of the organization. Weatherly and Tansik[16] identify four different strategies. Employees may make an *effort* to satisfy all the demands placed upon them. They do this largely by becoming proficient in all their tasks and becoming so familiar with routine ones that they can simultaneously cope with others, such as serving food and talking to the customer. Secondly, employees may *negotiate*, or do things to alter the role demands upon them. They may do this by delegating tasks to others, including co-workers, supervisors and customers; explaining that customer expectations cannot be fulfilled for whatever reason; rewarding customers by providing 'extra' service on a tacit understanding that the customer does not cause hassle; and by punishing others who cause stress, for instance by deliberately spilling food on a customer or serving slowly.

Thirdly, employees may be *pre-emptive* and engage in activities aimed at preventing role stress. They can do this by ingratiating themselves with supervisors or customers so that not too many demands are placed on them, or by distracting others so that they do not get round to making requests. Finally, there is the *avoiding* strategy. This manifests itself in two main ways: ignoring the customer and avoiding eye contact, or reinterpreting a request or demand so that it is less stressful. Such stress-reduction strategies have been clearly identified by one study of restaurant employees.[17]

Foodservice managers will clearly want to avoid employees resorting to the four strategies outlined above. To do so they have to cure the cause of the problem – role stress – rather than try to treat the symptoms. To a certain extent, the adoption of the HRM approach illustrated in Figure 10.1 will assist in this, making sure that the right person is doing the right job to the right standard. But there are two additional approaches that can be adopted to tackle boundary role problems. The first of these is to simplify the complexity of the service encounter by 'scripting'. Most if not all interactions between customers and employees involve verbal communication. In many cases the nature and sequence of this verbal exchange will follow a similar pattern. This means that employees can be trained to follow a script that shapes and controls the interaction, thereby reducing stress. The extent to which the script is prescribed and detailed will depend on the nature and context of the operation. Detailed scripts are most appropriate when speed is an important element of service provision, employees may not be socially skilled, accuracy is needed, and customers are seeking a secure and reliable interaction. This would apply in the foodservice industry to fast food restaurants, home-delivery order taking, and very large self-service cafeteria service. The problem with this highly scripted approach is that the encounter between employee and customer may lack warmth and spontaneity, and employees may be ill-prepared for customers who do not follow the script!

The second approach to managing boundary role stress is to make employees aware of the problem and train them to cope with it. This can be done in two ways. First, they can become more skilled in dealing with the roles and problems that cause them stress, in particular interpersonal relationships with customers. A sound approach to human resource management provides a good base. For instance, Boella[18] cites four factors that contribute to social skills development of foodservice employees: job design; physical aspects of the job; conditions of employment; and training. In addition, employees may be trained in a number of different ways to be more socially and interpersonally skilled. Lockwood and Jones[19] identify transactional analysis, profile training, role play, sensitivity training, and T-groups as being used at some time or another in the industry for this purpose.

DEVELOPING TEAMS IN FOODSERVICE

Effective performance in the foodservice industry does not depend solely on individual employees, but also on how well each one works as a member of a team. As discussed in Chapter 1, most foodservice operations are complex systems in which customer service depends on the contribution of a number of people. Even in a fast food restaurant, where the customer usually only comes into contact with the counter hand, the performance of crew members at six or seven other workstations has a direct impact on the customer's experience. In an à la carte restaurant, the customer may have direct contact with several staff, such as the head waiter, waiter, commis, wine waiter, cashier, and so on, whilst the meal is prepared by a complex brigade of chefs.

A team has a definable membership, shared consciousness, sense of shared purpose, interdependence, interaction and an ability to act to achieve a single outcome. They are the inevitable consequence of allocating tasks to people within an operation. For instance, a hotel may have a kitchen brigade, restaurant team, banqueting team, and floor service team. Effective groups or teams of any kind will develop shared objectives, strong commitment to the group, high levels of trust and dependency on the rest of the team, often decision-making and conflict resolution by consensus, and effective flow of information between group members. But organizations have not only formal groups, but informal ones that result from interactions not necessarily work related. Such informal groups may be based on shared religious, ethnic, or racial values, or just an interest in the same activity. Strong teams, either formal or informal, that collaborate together achieve high performance; however, strong teams may be at variance with each other resulting in inter-departmental conflict with disastrous results for performance.

There are four main factors that contribute to group performance that the foodservice manager can influence. *Group membership* is most positive when the team is not too large, not more than ten or so members; group members share the same background, attitudes and interests; the team has all the necessary skills between them to complete the task set; and the group is together for a relatively long period of time. The *work environment* supports teams by providing common tasks and problems for people to tackle; ensuring there is a suitable time-frame in which to perform; and enabling employees to work together in physically suitable surroundings. The *organizational context* is also important with regards to the style of management; provision of objectives or standards of performance; nature of success and reward offered; provision of appropriate personnel policies and procedures; and the level of external threat. Finally, management can ensure that *group development* is carried out effectively. Groups typically go through stages known as forming, storming, norming and performing.

Forming takes place in the initial stages during which time individuals get to know each other within the group. Storming refers to a period during which time the group is unsettled, until it has established a clear role and identity. Norming is the period during which conflict is resolved and group norms of behaviour and action are established. Performing is the most constructive phase, when the team gets on with the task it has been set. Whilst these four stages are not inevitable, foodservice managers need to be aware that this behaviour can occur every time a group is assembled to carry out work. Some workforces are very stable and change rarely. This is especially true in industry sectors with low labour turnover and traditional staffing practices, such as school meals services, institutional production kitchens, and the licensed trade. Other sectors have deliberately adopted, or are forced to operate on the basis of, part-time or casual staffing. In these operations, notably outdoor catering, in almost every service period there is a unique team working together for the first time. And in operations where staff are multi-skilled, even if the team is made up of individuals who have worked together before, the team performance can be affected by the particular job each person has at the time. A fast food crew may be highly effective with employees working in one way, but highly ineffective with the same employees scheduled at other workstations.

DEVELOPING THE ORGANIZATIONAL CULTURE

If empowerment is the buzzword of the 1900s, corporate culture was the fad of the 1980s. Sometimes called organizational culture or organizational climate, this concept is related to the underpinning values and assumptions on which any organization is based. The culture can be strong and overt, as with the Disney Corporation or TGI Fridays, or weak and almost non-existent. But all organizations will have some kind of culture. Culture can also have a positive effect on performance or a negative effect. And the culture of an organization can change, either because it is directed by senior management to do so or because it drifts along within the context of social, economic and political change that is a feature of modern living. In this chapter we focus on how this concept can help to get the best out of each employee, whereas in Chapter 14, we explore how culture can be used to support effective customer service.

Culture has been variously described but is generally accepted to provide a number of things. It represents the identity of the organization and thereby the identity of the organization's members. Employees who work for an organization with a strong culture do not say 'I work for a restaurant chain', they say 'I work for McDonald's' or 'I work for the Hard Rock'. Culture is also the source of 'organizational meaning', which provides a fund of existing solutions to ongoing and recurring tasks and issues. Culture also influences employees' behaviour and attitudes, or rather it is expressed by these. It is a common frame of reference that is largely taken for granted. Although the important elements of culture are the fundamental ideologies, values and attitudes shared within the organization, these are not easy to identify. Culture is most obviously seen, or manifested, at the operational level through the adoption of symbols, use of specific language or jargon, retelling of stories about events or people in the organization, the taking part in so-called 'rituals', and working to norms and conventions. TGI Fridays is a good example of a restaurant chain with many manifestations of a strong culture. There is a TGI Fridays mode of dress for restaurant employees that enables and encourages individualism with regards to badges and headgear, along with corporate standards in other aspects of dress. There is frequent use of organizational jargon exclusive to the company such as 'hot button'. Within the restaurants a daily ritual is the pre-service briefing.

There is evidence to suggest that organizational performance does influence employee performance favourably. Tidball states, 'the results of this study suggest that culture is a force that affects both employee behaviour and the success of the company'.[20] Her study was conducted in 15 restaurants belonging to the same chain in one large US city. On the basis of this she proposes three essentials of an effective culture: a clear philosophy espoused by top management, turning the philosophy into a living reality, and staying in touch with employees' perceptions. Likewise Fintel[21] identifies four common factors of successful restaurant cultures. These are a bottom-up style of management, having fun, efficient ways of communicating within the organization, and a sense of mission.

In order to make culture more effective, managers may need to modify it in one of three main ways. First, the culture may need to be strengthened or enhanced to have a greater impact, or reduced because it is interfering with effective action. Secondly, the influence or emergence of sub-cultures within the organization may need to be encouraged or discouraged. Thirdly, the culture may need to be transformed completely in order to take into account entirely new circumstances or a new strategic direction. The main way in which managers can achieve any of the above is to ensure that there is a high level of congruence between the strategic aims of the organization, the underpinning values, and the overt manifestations of culture. There are three roles for managers to adopt:[22] 'cultural spokesperson, cultural assessor, and facilitator of cultural modification'.

The *spokesperson* role can be taken by a person within the organization who is recognized as the embodiment of the culture, often because of that person's length of service with the company. More often this role is fulfilled not by a person but by some written statement and regular reference to this in employee communications and newsletters. For instance, in the early 1990s, Pizza Hut produced a brochure called *The Pizza Hut Story* that devoted one page to its culture. It began: 'Our culture reflects our values – the essence of what we believe as a people and as a system. It includes a shared vision of who we are and where we're headed...' Often, an organization may adopt a statement that is meant to enshrine the culture and make it easier to convey the message. For instance, the founder of Domino's Pizzas invented his so-called golden rule: 'Do unto others as you would have them do unto you.' These and other more complex messages can also be reinforced through the induction and training of employees and by the regular reinforcement of rituals. In a number of organizations, senior executives regularly visit outlets in order to meet with employees and directly promote cultural identity and ideas. One US restaurant chain recruited graduate managers by having their recruiters visit campuses dressed in Hawaiian shirts and give a presentation of over 100 slides, most of which showed managers and employees enjoying themselves or participating in sport. The two founders of the company had set up their first restaurant in Aspen, Colorado because they liked skiing in the winter, and their second in Malibu because they surfed in the summer. Seventy-odd restaurants later, sport, recreation and fun were still central tenets of their culture.

In the *cultural assessment role*, managers are expected both to receive and review the culture. In some cases this can be very informal, but in others it may involve managers in advising on what research is needed within the organization, who to recruit into the organization in terms of 'cultural fit', and acting as internal consultants about the culture. A number of specialists within organizations need to be particularly sensitive to the culture. For instance, the Head of Internal Communication or equivalent, with responsibility for the employee newsletter, has a key role to play; likewise, those human resource specialists dealing with employee rewards and awards. So Domino's has a department dedicated to handling employee awards that are designed to reflect and reinforce the culture of that company.

In their third role, managers may also be called upon to facilitate *cultural modification*. Transformation and change within organizations is extremely complex and is largely carried out at strategic level. Operations managers can assist the process by counselling employees who feel threatened by change and providing energy to support the development.

CONCLUSION

This chapter identifies that managing employee performance is very complex. In reviewing alternative theories of motivation this complexity is recognized and the practice of managers 'inventing' their own theory is accepted. The chapter then goes on to look at five main ways in which the foodservice industry tackles this key result area. The human resource approach focuses very much on effective personnel practices. In addition, employees must be paid and rewarded in some way. Reward, job satisfaction and hence performance may also result from adopting the recently developed strategy of employee empowerment. Such approaches to employee performance will not be successful if the employee is suffering from boundary role stress. The different types of stress and how this affects employee behaviour were reviewed, along with ways of preventing or reducing stress.

It is also recognized that employees frequently work as members of a team and the influence of this on employee performance is reviewed. Finally, the overall organizational culture is looked at with regard to its influence on employees. Each of these five will be evident to a greater or lesser extent within any organization, but the extent to which each is significant or appropriate will vary widely.

REFERENCES

1. Jogan, J. H. (1992) 'Turnover and what to do about it', *Cornell HRA Quarterly*, February, pp. 40–45.

2. Mullins, Laurie J. (1992) *Hospitality Management*, Pitman, London.

3. Weaver, T. (1988) 'Theory M: motivating with money', *Cornell HRA Quarterly*, November, pp. 40–45.

4. Adams, J. S. (1979) 'Injustice in social exchange', abridged in Steers, R. M. and Porter, L. W., *Motivation and Work Behaviour*, McGraw-Hill, New York, pp. 107–124.

5. Zacarelli, H. E. (1985) 'Is the hospitality industry turning its employees on – or off?' *International Journal of Hospitality Management*, Vol. 4 No. 3.

6. Merricks, P. and Jones, P. (1987) *The Management of Catering Operations*, Cassell, London.

7. Kreck, L. A. (1985) 'Evaluating training through work performance standards', *International Journal of Hospitality Management*, Vol. 4. No. 1.

8. Mill, R. C. (1985) 'Upping the organization', *Cornell HRA Quarterly*, February.

9. Weinstein, J. (1993) 'Power to the employees', *Restaurants and Institutions*, pp. 99–100.

10. Weinstein, J. op. cit.

11. Brymer, R. A. (1991) 'Employee empowerment: a guest driven leadership strategy', *Cornell HRA Quarterly*, May, pp. 58–68.

12. Fulford, Mark (1993) *Power to the People: The Effects of Empowerment on Employee Attitudes and Behaviours*, CHRIE Annual Conference, Chicago, USA.

13. Sparrowe, Raymond (1993) *Empowerment in the Hospitality Industry: An Exploration of Antecedents and Outcome*, CHRIE Annual Conference, Chicago, USA.

14. Bowen, D. E. and Schneider, B. (1985) 'Boundary spanning role employees and the service encounter: some guidelines for management and research', in Czepiel, J. A., Solomon, M. R. and Suprenant, C. F., eds, *The Service Encounter*, Lexington Books, Lexington, Mass., pp. 127–147.

15. Jones, P. and Lockwood, A. (1989) *The Management of Hotel Operations*, Cassell, London.

16. Weatherly, K. A. and Tansik, D. A. (1993) 'Tactics used by customer-contact workers: effects of role stress, boundary spanning and control', *International Journal of Service Industry Management*, Vol. 4, No. 3, pp. 4–17.

17. Shamir, B. (1980) 'Between service and servility: role conflict in subordinate service roles', *Human Relations*, Vol. 33, pp. 461–487.

18. Boella, M. (1980) 'Are social skills unteachable?' *Hospitality*, No. 17.

19. Lockwood, A. and Jones, P. (1984) *People and the Hotel and Catering Industry*, Cassell, London.

20. Tidball, K. H. (1988) 'Creating a culture that builds your bottom line', *Cornell HRA Quarterly*, May, pp. 63–69.

21. Fintel, J. (1988) 'Restaurant cultures: positive culture can keep companies healthy', *Restaurants USA*, NRA.

22. Lundberg, C. C. and Woods R. H. (1990) 'Modifying restaurant culture: managers as cultural leaders', *International Journal of Contemporary Hospitality Management*, Vol. 2, No. 4, pp. 4–12.

11

Managing Capacity

John Cousins

INTRODUCTION

One of the key characteristics of services that is often identified as differentiating the sale of services from the sale of goods is that the product cannot be stored. The food and beverage product exemplifies this characteristic. For instance, seats in a restaurant which are not sold at one mealtime cannot be compensated for by additional sales at another time. In other words, the sale of food and beverage is limited by the capacity of the operation. Therefore, in foodservice operations it is necessary to consider how the capacity of the operation for customer sales can be managed in order that the goals of the business may be achieved.

The ideal operation is one in which 'a single kind of product [is produced] at a continuous rate and as if inputs flowed continuously at a steady rate and with specified quality'.[1] In reality, most operations are not able to operate in this way. Customer demand will create four kinds of capacity management problems. First, the total *volume* of demand may not match the operational resources, so there will be spare capacity if demand is lower than expected and a shortage of capacity if demand is higher. Secondly, demand may be *variable* over time, with peak periods at different times of the day, week, month or years. In foodservice there are obvious daily peaks relating to breakfast, lunch and dinner mealtimes. Thirdly, customers are likely to expect *variety*, especially in the foodservice industry. In Chapter 3 we saw how different kinds of menu can offer such variety. And finally, within the product range made available to customers, there will be *variation* in what will be chosen, that is to say the sales mix will not remain constant. Customers' eating habits are often affected by the weather for instance, so hot soup is selected more in the winter than in the summer.

In managing capacity in foodservice operations, strategic decisions have to be made about the volume of business that can be taken and the variety of offerings made to the customer. Once these decisions are made, the operations manager has to adopt procedures for dealing with both variability and variation.

174

STRATEGIC CAPABILITY OF OPERATIONS

Capacity in a foodservice operation is measured not only by considering the maximum capacity of customers at a given time but also the capacity that can be achieved over time. For example, a restaurant operation with a maximum seating of 80 covers can achieve a much higher actual capacity for a given meal period if the seats can be used more than once during the period. The potential for this will, however, vary according to the type of operation. A banqueting room, for example, can usually be filled only once during a meal period and thus the size of the function in terms of covers served will determine the capacity achieved at that time. The management of capacity is therefore not a simple issue concerned solely with the volume of customers. It will depend on a variety of factors, not least of which is the type of operation.

Within foodservice operations there are two main systems operating and being managed. These are the food production process and the foodservice process. These can be seen as two distinct systems.[2] One of the key differences though is that as the capacity of the operation increases it requires alterations in the production process, whereas the service process may simply be multiplied. For instance, a restaurant for 40 covers can operate a conventional food production system, with, say, a chef and two assistants. If the restaurant was intended to operate for 400 covers this would fundamentally alter the way the production would be organized. A system could be introduced with the production process separated into various parts of the menu required. This is the basis of the 'partie' system. If the same example was used for the foodservice process the restaurant of 40 covers could be, say, two stations and the restaurant of 400 would be split into 20 stations. This service example is comparable to the opening of additional checkouts in a supermarket or increasing the number of tellers available in a bank as the level of demand increases. The service example is also true for bar operations. Modular bay systems, where a bar was duplicated every 15 feet with the number of open sections being increased or decreased according to the business level, were operating at holiday camps in the 1950s. Likewise in hospitals, conventional food production systems have been replaced by cook-chill production, whilst the service of food continues to be a trolley-serve system.

It has been argued[3] that there are quite clear trends in service operations that have enabled, amongst other things, capacity to be managed more effectively. These three trends are 'production-lining', decoupling and self-service. Production-lining refers to the redesign of the system to improve operational efficiency, or the increased use of technology and automation. The development of fast food and cook-chill systems are examples of this. Decoupling is the separation of front-of-house and back-of-house activities. This has been clearly seen with the setting up of central production facilities supplying meals to a number of outlets. And self-service is evident in the industry, not only in cafeterias but also in restaurants with self-help salad bars. However, even the cafeteria has seen a number of developments designed to improve operational performance with the introduction of free-flow counter arrangements.

Capacity in Food Production

The food production process may be seen in the general model for food production as illustrated in Figure 11.1(a). This model[4] identifies seven stages in the general food production process. These are:

Foods in
Storage
Preparation
Cooking
Holding
Regeneration
Presentation

Each of these operational stages has a separate effect on the capacity of food able to be processed at any time. To take each of the processes in turn:

Foods in. The availability of food and the frequency of delivery clearly have an impact on the maximum food capacity of the operation. Greater and more frequent delivery opportunities increase the potential capacity. In addition, the variety of foods being bought, in terms of either food type or supplier source, will also affect food capacity.

Storage. The storage space and type of storage available determine the type of food that can be bought and the quantities that can be available at a given time. Capacity can be increased by altering the nature of foods being bought, for instance from fresh to convenience and or by increasing the delivery frequency.

Preparation. The extent to which food has to be prepared also impacts on capacity. High preparation requirements increase the space needed and affect the layout required. This stage can be greatly affected by increasing the use of part-prepared or ready-prepared foods and by the use of equipment for bulk preparation activities.

Cooking. The availability of cooking space and the time cooking takes can limit capacity. Again this can be affected by variations in the needs for cooking and the type of cooking required. In addition, the type of equipment used for the cooking processes can be altered to increase the volume of cooking that can be done at a given time.

Holding. Food capacity is limited by the type and availability of holding space. Variations in the need for holding in a given operation can vary the potential food capacity.

Regeneration. This stage follows from holding and has similar characteristics. However, the regeneration potential can be less than the full holding potential, depending on the nature of demand required at a given time.

Presentation. The food capacity at this stage is usually determined by the speed of the service process. This assumes, though, that a critical path analysis approach has been used to ensure that the full range of foods required at a given time are available at the same time. Overall, the need to meet the demands of the presentation stage is determined by the expected volume of business at a given time. Each of the previous stages through the application of careful critical path analysis approaches should be able to be planned and operated to meet the presentation demands.

To ensure operational efficiency and effectiveness it is essential that the capacity of each of these seven stages is balanced. There is no point in having six of the stages able to deliver meals for 1,000 customers a day if one of the stages can only deal with 500. It is also the case that the specific technology employed at each stage can limit the variety that can be offered. For instance, if the regeneration stage is based around cook-chill technology, some dishes such as deep-fried foods may not be accommodated within this system.

In Chapter 1 we saw that differing operations will route foods in different ways. Thus, for instance, a fast food process will flow from foods into store to preparation or cooking, then to holding and then to presentation. A cook-chill process will flow from foods into store to preparation to holding or cooking, then to regeneration and then to presentation. This can be seen diagrammatically in Figures 11.1(b) and 11.1(c). In effect, each of these alternative configurations is designed to operate in the context of different levels of volume and variety. Thus the traditional food production kitchen based on the partie system can offer wide variety but at low levels of demand; cook-chill enables both high volume production along with an extensive product range; whilst fast food also results in high volume output, but with a limited variety (see also Table 1.1).

Capacity in Meal Service

Just as the stages in the production system can be configured to deliver meals at alternative volume levels with alternative variety, so is the service system made up of an operational sequence aimed to provide alternative customer experiences. The operational sequence consists of seven stages.[5] These are:

Preparation for service
Taking orders
The service of food and drink
Billing
Clearing
Dishwashing
Clearing following service

Similarly to the food production stages considered above, it is difficult to determine any stage of the service sequence as being a key stage in the limitation of capacity. Taking each of the stages in turn:

Preparation for service. Within the service areas there are a variety of tasks and duties which need to be carried out in order to ensure that adequate preparation has been made for the expected volume of business and the type of service which is to be provided. The time taken for this preparatory stage can limit the potential availability of service. In addition, the time for preparation is part of the cost of providing the service. One of the preparatory tasks is the taking of bookings. Systems need to be developed so that bookings are taken in a way that ensures the efficiency of the operation.

Taking orders. Taking orders from customers for the food and drink they wish to have takes time. Limiting the choice can reduce this time but this possibility depends on the particular operation. The order-taking process though is part of a longer process which feeds information to the production or bar areas and provides information for the billing system. There are a variety of methods for achieving this all of which are based on the principles of the duplicate or triplicate checking methods.

The service of food and drink. Differing service methods affect the speed and therefore the throughput of customers. In addition, the service method can also affect the time the customer takes to consume the meal.

Billing. In table service operations the billing system is a small part of the operation and therefore the significance of this part of the process on throughput is limited. However, in operations such as cafeteria systems the billing system tends to be the main determinant of throughput. Increasing or decreasing the number of till points ensures that the throughput is maintained.

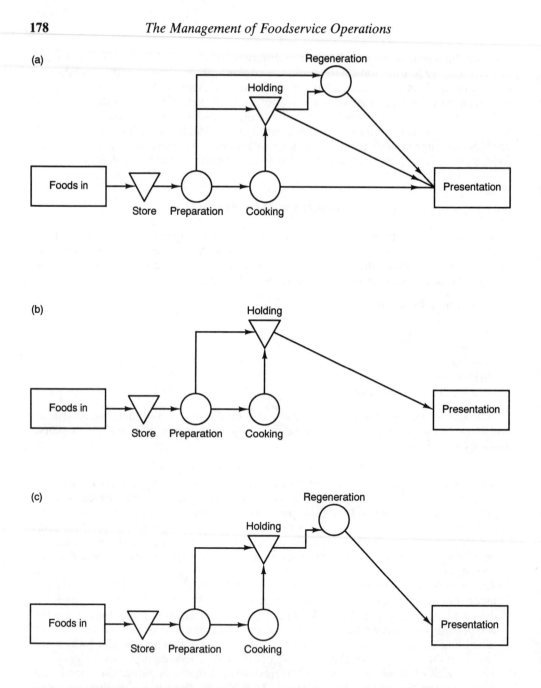

Figure 11.1 Alternative food production systems. (a) General food production process; (b) fast food production process; (c) cook-chill production process.

Clearing. Clearing systems, whether manual by staff or involving customers, affect the overall potential for throughput. The time taken to clear affects the service speed and the potential reuse of the service area.

Table 11.1 Simple categorization of the foodservice process.

Service method	Food and beverage service area	Ordering selection	Service	Dining/ Consumption	Clearing
A. Table service	Customer enters area and is seated	From menu	By staff to customer	At laid cover	By staff
B. Assisted service	Customer enters area and is usually seated	From menu, buffet or passed trays	Combination of both staff and customer	Usually at laid cover	By staff
C. Self-service	Customer enters	Customer selects own tray	Customer carries	Dining area or take away	Various
D. Single-point service	Customer enters	Ordered at single point	Customer carries	Dining area or take away	Various
E. Specialized or *in situ* service	*In situ*	From menu or predetermined	Brought to customer	Where served	By staff or customer clearing

Dishwashing. The capacity of the dishwashing system should always be greater than the operational maximum required. This is because slow dishwashing increases the amount of equipment required to be in use at a particular time and increases the storage space required in service areas.

Clearing following service. After the service periods there are a variety of tasks and duties needed to be carried out, partly to clear from the previous service and partly to prepare for the next. This stage is similar to the preparation stage as above.

The customer's behaviour is shaped by the particular service methods adopted when considering food service from a customer's perspective. There are five basic customer processes in food service, namely service at a laid cover, part service at a laid cover and part self-service, self-service, service at a single point (ordering, receipt of order and payment), and service *in situ*. In the first four types, the customer comes to where the food and beverage service is offered and the service is provided in areas primarily designed for the purpose. In the last type, the customer receives the service in another location and where the area is not primarily designed for the purpose. A summary of the five customer processes is illustrated in Table 11.1. All food and beverage service methods can be categorized within these five customer processes. Service at a laid cover includes waiter service and its variations and bar counter service. Part service at a laid cover and part self-service comprises assisted service where some parts of the meal are served and other parts are collected by the customer from a buffet or salad bar. Self-service is obviously cafeteria service and its variations. Service at a single point (ordering, receipt of order and payment) includes take-away service, vending, kiosks, food courts and bar service. And service *in situ* comprises tray service, trolley service, home delivery, lounge service, room service and drive-ins.

The customer process in all groups other than service *in situ* is similar within the service methods found in each group, whilst the skills, knowledge, tasks and duties required are similar within each group. Service at a laid cover is the most complex and service at a single point the least complex. *In situ* service has a special set of requirements, some of which are different from those found in the other groups. Such systems accommodate different levels of volume and variety. Service at a laid cover makes wide variety possible but to a limited volume of customers; part service at laid cover makes higher volumes possible; self-service enables even higher volumes with some reduction in variety; and service at a single point facilitates the highest volumes usually with reduced variety.

It is possible to alter the delivery of service without essentially changing the customer process by moving between service methods within each group. Thus the change from full silver service to a plate service delivery system does not essentially alter the customer process. It will, however, have effects on the way the service sequence is organized and possibly the production system. In a similar way, moving between the various cafeteria layouts such as going from a straight-line counter to a free-flow system allows customers to select the food and drink at random and from greater throughput because customers are not waiting in line behind others who are choosing foods which require longer time. In addition, the capacity of cafeterias can be determined by calculating the throughput of customers. On the other hand, changing between service method groups substantially changes the customer process.

OPERATIONAL CAPACITY MANAGEMENT

Assuming the food production system and service system match customer demand in volume terms and expectations in variety terms, and that all stages of both systems are in balance, the operations manager is still faced with managing variability in demand and variation in expectations. The extent to which this is a problem is largely dependent on time. In some cases provision is totally planned in advance, as in banqueting, whereas in others it is entirely unpredictable, as in many small restaurants or pubs. The manager would prefer to be able to plan with certainty what the provision will be. If certainty is not possible, then predictions need to be used.

Limited Variability and Variation

Banquet or function catering is an example of foodservice in which both the numbers to be served and the exact meal are known in advance. Nonetheless, the organization of banquet/function catering does have some special considerations in respect of capacity issues. Clearly the capacity of the function rooms will determine the maximum numbers that can be accommodated. However, variations in the service methods and the dining layouts can alter both the maximum numbers which can be served and the volume which can be achieved over time. Selling functions, which are similar in service method and layout for instance, can reduce the preparation for service and the clearing after service periods. In addition, the capacity of function rooms is affected by the combination of the bookings taken. The taking of certain types of functions will reduce or preclude the taking of others. Noisy presentations will, for instance, limit the use of adjoining rooms. If the intention of the operations is to be flexible then this is inevitable. However, if the operation wants to specialize (and therefore reduce the flexibility), it is possible to increase the volume throughput. This is supposing, though, that the volume of business requiring more standardization is available.

Coping with Variability

A further dimension of the capacity issue is the way in which changes in the volume of demand are managed. Where the actual demand is higher or lower than the capacity of the operation, consideration must be given to methods of smoothing this demand. This may be achieved in a number of ways, such as pricing, queuing and reservations.

Modifications to demand can be achieved through pricing policies. In city centre hotels, for instance, the demand for full breakfast is limited in this way through disproportionately higher pricing for a full breakfast compared to other alternatives. Likewise the adoption of a 'happy hour' in the early evening is aimed at encouraging restaurant patronage at this relatively quiet time.

Secondly, there is the use of queues to ensure that the operation is working at full capacity. Examples of this approach are found in fast food operations where, although the queue is controlled by a time limit for the customers to queue, it does provide constant demand at the service point. Another example is TGI Fridays, where the queue for food service is the central bar area. In this operation the queue becomes part of the meal experience and also provides revenue from the queue, through drink sales, whilst customers wait for meal service.

Thirdly, a foodservice operation may adopt a reservations policy, typically in the restaurant sector. Not only does this reduce the uncertainty about how many customers may be expected at any given meal period, it also enables operational activity to be smoothed and occupancy to be improved. This is achieved by having a pattern of table bookings that matches the operation. Since the foodservice business operates around two main peaks – at lunchtime and dinner – restaurants offering service at a laid cover would hope to have a seat occupancy of at least one at lunchtime and two in the evening. With each table occupied only once at lunchtime, reservations can be spread over an hour or two so as to avoid operational bottlenecks in order taking, serving drinks, and so on. In the evening, the operator may have be more proactive in taking bookings only at certain times, such as around 7 pm and 9.30 pm in order to achieve the required level of seat occupancy.

If it is not possible to adopt these approaches because they are unacceptable to customers, the foodservice manager must ensure that the supply of meals is made as flexible as possible and demand be forecast as accurately as possible. This requires the adoption of those tactics for managing productivity proposed in Chapter 12.

Coping with Variation

Even though it is possible to take reservations or establish queues, it will remain the case that customers' selection from the menu may show wide variation. This variation may be due to the time of day or year, customer mix, weather, or special occasions, such as Shrove Tuesday (pancake day). Approaches to managing this are based around early order taking, sales and promotion, and menu engineering.

The most preferable approach to managing uncertain variation in choice is to get the customers to make their choice as far ahead as possible. But it is only in function catering that selection tends to be made weeks if not months ahead of time. However, a number of foodservice sectors have introduced order-taking procedures that do give them enough time to prepare more or less exactly the quantities requested. In hospitals, customers are served *in situ*. Most hospitals provide a daily menu and require patients to make their selection for the following day. Hotels, especially large ones, have encouraged customers to select their breakfast the night before by enabling them to have a continental breakfast in their room.

Customer choice can be significantly influenced by promotions or direct selling by service staff. Promotions such as two for one, discount for specific market segments, and so on are usually part of a wider marketing campaign aimed at attracting new market segments or increasing usage of existing segments. For instance, the AJs roadside restaurant chain has a promotion aimed at attracting the over-60s to their outlets through a discount card. This does affect the sales mix of the outlets as this segment tends to be more conservative in the choices it makes. But the promotion was not devised for this purpose. Other campaigns do have the specific intention of promoting specific items and influencing choice. These include special promotions such as for Beaujolais Nouveau, regular promotions such as the dish of the day, and discounted combinations of dishes sold as a complete meal, such as happy meals in fast food. However, direct selling by service staff is more likely to shape customer choice than promotional materials displayed in the outlet. Many customers, because they are buying an intangible product, tend to be happy to rely on the advice or suggestion of an 'expert', in this case a server. Not only can customers be influenced to select certain items from a menu, they can also be influenced to purchase more than they intended. In fast food, for instance, customers are persuaded to 'trade up' by servers who ask a question in a positive way about a further item, such as 'Would you like french fries with that?' It has also been suggested that products or services with low contribution can be 'demarketed',[6] that is to say, customers encouraged not to purchase some items, often by not proactively mentioning them. For instance, this may be especially desirable if customers share a dessert or only one person from a large party seems likely to order dessert.

Finally, variation can be managed by understanding customer preferences in order to predict the likely level of sales of individual items. The adoption of menu analysis techniques, especially menu engineering, provides a detailed picture of consumer purchasing habits (as discussed in Chapter 13). These data, if coupled with information about factors affecting choice, such as the weather, can provide a remarkably accurate prediction of the sales mix on any given day.

ISSUES IN CAPACITY MANAGEMENT

The management of capacity may involve trade-offs. Such trade-offs include the balance between an objective of profit maximization and operational cost efficiency; between the provision of customer service and achieving resource productivity; and the impact of capacity management approaches on customer satisfaction.

Maximization versus Efficiency

The management of capacity could superficially be seen as simply the maximization of gross profit contribution through the maximum usage of the facilities. However, this view presupposes that the maximum profit contribution comes solely from high volume

Customer service			Resource productivity
Level			Labour
Availability			
Standards	>	<	Facility
Reliability			
Flexibility			Materials

Figure 11.2 Relationship between customer service and resource productivity.

which has been achieved by operating at maximum capacity. Whilst this may be true in some circumstances, a business which aims at simply maximizing the gross profit contribution may run into some difficulty as the costs of labour and the facilities are not taken into account in such contribution calculations.

Business volume inevitably varies throughout any trading period, whether this be a year, a month, a week or even an hour. Operating at under full capacity for any period can lead to a disproportionate increase in costs and thus a reduction in the overall profit (not simply gross profit) contribution. The management of capacity is therefore also about matching the ability of the operations to provide services to the expected volume of business. This does not necessarily always mean operating at maximum capacity. The management of capacity therefore must take into account all the costs of providing the service and matching as far as possible the costs with the volume of business.

Customer Service versus Resource Productivity

On the one hand a foodservice operation is designed to provide customer services, and on the other hand the achievement of profit is largely determined by the efficient use of resources, one of which is the facilities. Customer service can be defined as being a combination of five characteristics. These are:

- Service style: e.g. self-service, tray service, silver service, etc.
- Availability of service: e.g. the opening times, variations in the menus and drinks lists on offer.
- Level of standards: e.g. food quality, decor, equipment cost, staffing professionalism.
- Reliability of the service: the extent to which the product is intended to be consistent in practice.
- Flexibility of the service: the provision of alternatives, variations in the standard product on offer.

The resources used in the provision of food and beverage services are materials such as commodities and equipment; labour; and facilities, basically the premises and the volume of business which the premises are able to support. This can be seen as a model of the kind in Figure 11.2. The management of capacity must therefore take account of the effect that the level of business has on the ability of the operation to maintain the service whilst at the same time ensuring a high productivity in all the resources being used. Thus the achievement of maximum profit contribution does not solely come from a maximization of the use of the facilities. This is because the cost of providing the facilities is only one of the costs involved and the customer service specification may require less efficiency in the use of facilities in order for the specification to be maintained.

The effects of modification to the five customer service characteristics can be seen as follows:

1. *Service level*. As the service level increases the labour costs will increase and as meal times will become longer the capacity of the operation will reduce. In addition, in higher level of service the equipment usage increases.
2. *Availability of service*. Increasing the availability of the service will potentially increase labour costs and material costs and will reduce the efficiency of the facilities usage. In these cases it is necessary to endeavour to match the labour and materials being used to the expected volume of business which will vary over a given period.
3. *Level of standards*. Increasing the level of standards in the food and beverage operation will increase the cost of materials as better grade materials are used and will increase the cost of labour as the level of staffing and the staffing professionalism will need to be higher. In addition, the provision of the facilities will also have a higher cost, again because of the higher grade of finishes being used.
4. *Reliability of the service*. In order to ensure a high reliability in the provision of the service again the labour costs and materials costs will increase as, in order to protect the reliability of the product, it will be necessary to have a higher proportion of labour and materials available.
5. *Flexibility of the service*. Moving away from a limited standard range of product and service will increase material costs and labour costs and will reduce the efficiency of the facilities being used.

In all cases the opposite of the examples given above will potentially increase the efficiency of the resources being used. However, the customer service specification, which should take account of the five characteristics above, will primarily determine the level of resource utilization and therefore the level of efficiency possible.

Impact of Approaches to Capacity Management on Customer Satisfaction

There are two specific approaches that assist in managing capacity but which may have a detrimental effect on customer satisfaction, namely adopting a reservations system to establish planned arrivals or a queuing system for chance arrivals. The extent to which customers are happy to be required to book in advance, in some cases at a time specified by the operator, or line up in a queue may be affected by Maister's 'psychology of waiting lines'.[7] Maister makes eight propositions as follows:

1. Unoccupied time feels longer than occupied time.
2. Pre-process waits feel longer than in-process waits.
3. Anxiety makes waits feel longer.
4. Uncertain waits are longer than certain waits.
5. Unexplained waits are longer than explained waits.
6. Unfair waits are longer than equitable waits.
7. The more valuable the service, the longer people will wait.
8. Solo waiting feels longer than group waiting.

One study[8] has looked at how these may apply to foodservice customers, based on a national chain of family restaurants. Over 70 per cent of customers expressed concern about waiting times. Results of this survey indicated that waiting does affect the mood of customers and their propensity to spend. Results also suggest that whilst customers believe both quality and value are worth waiting for, there comes a point where an unacceptable wait begins to affect their perception of quality. Significant principles identified from the survey were the need to let customers 'see things happening', tell customers how long the wait will be, occupy the customers' time, and ensure there is a smiling face and apology 'at the end of the queue'. An existing 'myth' held by managers, that customers do not mind queuing at weekends, was accepted by restaurant customers.

Having established that response times appear to directly affect customer satisfaction and spending behaviour and that operational understanding of this was limited, the same study reported a number of recommendations for consideration by managers. These included:

1. *Awareness raising*. Managers should be made aware of the impact waiting time has on customer attitudes and behaviour. Critical incidents in the service provision should be highlighted and action taken systematically to address those areas most in need of attention.
2. *Improve data collection*. Response times should be more specifically incorporated into 'mystery guest' reports.
3. *Redesign*. In some cases, the service delivery systems should be redesigned for all operations in order to reduce slow response times.
4. *Occupy time*. Attention should be given to providing distractions to customers who have to wait.
5. *Fairness*. Specific attention must be given to the style of queuing systems employed for different types of service incident.
6. *Uncertainty*. Remove uncertainty by telling customers what is happening.
7. *Out-of-line*. Encourage customers to seek the service off-peak.
8. *Selling*. Use the waiting time for selling to customers by the provision of ancillary products.
9. *Sensitivity training*. Service employees should be sensitized to the different needs of waiting customers. *Ad hoc* observations suggest three types of customers: 'watchers' enjoy the bustle and do not mind waiting too much; 'neutrals' display neither enjoyment nor frustration; 'impatients' hate waiting, will try queue jumping and are likely to complain.

Within the company in which the study was undertaken, these recommendations have been brought to the attention of operational staff and trainers, who are building it into training programmes. The measurement of time standards on a regular basis also reinforces the need to apply these recommendations. However, the wide variation in hotel and restaurant design does mean that it is desirable for managers at a unit level to customize the recommendations in the context of their specific hotel or restaurant. For instance, in the roadside diner context, travelling customers are particularly keen to get back on the road. They are unlikely to purchase a sweet item or coffee if they have had to wait too long for their main menu item. If both the main and sweet item can be served in less than 45 minutes, average sales per customer are likely to be significantly higher. Concern about waiting times was incorporated into menu design and so-called 'menu engineering'. It was known that in roadside operations certain combinations of menu items resulted in longer waiting times owing to the operational complexity of producing these items simultaneously. In revising and updating menus to reflect market and cost trends, these combinations have been avoided. There are now clear time standards established for the production of any given menu item to ensure that the overall meal time does not exceed the established standard. Perceptions have also been modified.

For instance, within the family restaurants it had not been the practice to give menus to customers waiting in the bar. This has now been changed to ensure that customers are 'occupied' during this waiting time. It is proposed that time standards be applied from the moment the customer enters the operation, and not just from the time he or she is seated at the table.

CONCLUSION

Managing capacity in foodservice operations is not a simple issue. The provision of food and beverages is highly complex with a number of stages, both in the production and the service processes, all of which have an effect on the volume of business and variety on offer. In addition, the limitations posed by the physical facilities are not always the key determinant of the potential capacity that can be achieved. In many cases the service specification will determine that inefficiency in the use of the facilities will be outweighed by the need to provide a certain level of service. The control of labour and material costs must also be taken into account in determining the potential volume of business which can be handled within the predetermined customer service specification. The start point of capacity, therefore, is the construction of the customer service specification and the determination of the potential level of demand for given service periods. This is followed by the organization of the service processes which are to be used. After this the production capacity can be determined, as this does not need to exceed the service process capability. This is summarized in Figure 11.3.

The food production system and service system are designed to match customer demand in volume terms, meet customer expectations in variety terms, and ensure that all stages of both systems are in balance. The operation's manager is still faced with managing variability in demand and variation in expectations. Thus for an existing operation the model in Figure 11.3 can be reversed in order to determine what potential can be met within a given customer service specification. It is also possible that the customer service specifications may need to be altered depending on the operation's capability. The review process does, however, enable decisions to be made on alterations to various parts of the service and production processes where particular

Figure 11.3   Capacity management cycle.

stages are limiting the capacity able to be met or where the limitations are directly affecting the ability of the operation to meet a particular customer service specification at a given volume of business.

REFERENCES

1. Thompson, J. D. (1967) *Organizations in Action*, McGraw-Hill, New York.
2. Cousins, J. (1988) 'Curriculum development in operational management teaching in catering eduction', in Johnson, R. ed., *The Management of Service Operations*, IFS Publications, pp. 437–459.
3. Jones, P. (1988) 'The impact of trends in service operations on food service delivery systems', *International Journal of Operations and Production Management*, Vol. 8, No. 7, pp. 23–30.
4. Cousins, J. and Foskett, D. (1989) 'Curriculum development for food production operations for the hospitality industry: a systems framework', *International Journal of Operations and Production Management*, pp. 77–87.
5. Lillicrap, D. and Cousins, J. (1990) *Food and Beverage Service*. Hodder & Stoughton, Sevenoaks.
6. Sill, B. T. (1991) 'Capacity management making your service delivery more productive'. *Cornell HRA Quarterly*, February, pp. 77–87.
7. Maister, D. (1985) 'The psychology of waiting lines', in Czepiel, J. A., Solomon, M. and Surprenant, C. S. (eds), *The Service Encounter*, Lexington Books, Lexington, Mass.
8. Jones, P. and Dent, M. (1993) 'Managing response time in hotel and restaurant operations', in Johnston, R. ed., *Service Superiority*, IFS Publications.

12

Improving Labour Productivity

Stephen Ball

INTRODUCTION

'Productivity' has been the battle-cry of successive post-war governments in their pursuit of a variety of economic, social and other objectives. In the early 1990s this cry acquired a new sense of urgency as economic growth faltered. The reasoning behind this high-level interest in productivity lies in the general belief that for nations and organizations alike their health and prosperity are dependent upon their comparative productivity. Productivity is a matter of great importance to all industries, and seeking improvements in productivity is a critical task for all managers, including foodservice operations managers, in both the private and public sector. The principal sources of productivity growth are individual organizations and their operations. They have the best opportunity for direct and swift productivity improvement and it is they who are increasingly being urged to give greater emphasis to productivity and productivity management programmes.

After explaining productivity and defining labour productivity this chapter aims to examine the importance of high productivity and the pressures for improvement in foodservice operations. An indication of productivity performance in foodservice operations will be provided. The chapter will explain reasons for poor performance and will briefly summarize those factors which may influence labour productivity. A model for managing and improving productivity will be outlined and finally approaches to adjust and control labour input for productivity gains discussed.

THE MEANING OF PRODUCTIVITY

Productivity is generally defined in systems terms and is basically stated as the relationship between the amount of goods and/or services obtained from a system and the amount of one or more of the input(s) employed in yielding this output. Thus:

$$\text{Productivity} = \frac{\text{output(s) obtained}}{\text{input(s) employed}}$$

This relationship remains the same regardless of the type of production system and may be derived for a single establishment, an operation within an organization, an organization, an industry, a sector or for the overall economy. For foodservice operations, as other operations, the concept can be expressed in either a partial or total form. Total productivity is the ratio of total outputs to the sum of all contributing and associated resource inputs; whereas in partial form, the ratio relates outputs to one class of resource input.[1] For example, labour productivity is represented as the ratio of output(s) to labour input.

For a number of reasons productivity in foodservice contexts lies beyond the scope of a simple quantitative input–output relationship. It must be linked with the quality of output, input and indeed the process itself. Quality has to be married to quantity. A 'trade-off' between either the quantity and quality of outputs or the quantity and quality of inputs may result in an adverse effect on productivity in foodservice operations.[2] Hence the basic definition of productivity should be expanded so that specific reference is made to both the qualitative and quantitative dimensions. Such a definition would be that productivity is the relationship between the quantity and quality of goods or services produced and the quantity and quality of resources used to produce them. This can be alternatively expressed as:

$$\frac{\text{Partial foodservice}}{\text{productivity}} = \frac{\text{f (quality of outputs, quantity of outputs)}}{\text{quality and quantity of a single class of resource, e.g. labour}}$$

The formula for total foodservice productivity would be similar but include all classes of resources. Table 12.1, adapted from Ball, Johnson and Slattery[3], gives examples of the range of foodservice productivity ratios.

Outputs of foodservice operations can be divided into two kinds: secondary and primary outputs. Secondary outputs are those which result from the conversion of inputs prior to selling or delivery to the customer. This is illustrated in Figure 12.1,

Table 12.1 Example ratios of foodservice productivity.

	Physical measures	Physical/financial measures combined	Financial measures
Labour measures	$\dfrac{\text{Kitchen meals produced}}{\text{No. of kitchen staff}}$	$\dfrac{\text{Restaurant revenue}}{\text{Time worked in restaurant}}$	$\dfrac{\text{Restaurant sales}}{\text{Restaurant payroll}}$
Raw material measures	$\dfrac{\text{No. of portions served}}{\text{Weight of commodity used}}$	$\dfrac{\text{No. of bar customers}}{\text{Cost of liquor sold}}$	$\dfrac{\text{Food revenue}}{\text{Food costs}}$
Energy measures	$\dfrac{\text{Total covers}}{\text{Total kilowatt hours}}$	$\dfrac{\text{No. of cooked meals}}{\text{Total cooking costs}}$	$\dfrac{\text{Food service operation revenue}}{\text{Total energy costs}}$
Total measure	$\dfrac{\text{No. of customers served}}{\text{Hour}}$	$\dfrac{\text{Total covers}}{\text{Cost of contributing resources}}$	$\dfrac{\text{Net profit}}{\text{Total operating costs}}$

FOODSERVICE INPUTS
|
production process
|
INTERMEDIATE OUTPUT
|
customer take-up
|
OUTPUT
|
Impact on customers
|
OUTCOMES

Figure 12.1 Model of foodservice operations.

where secondary outputs are identified as 'intermediate output'. The production of food in a restaurant production area would be an example. Primary outputs are those which have a 'sales' element, such as gross margin, customers served, menu items sold, or seating utilization. The choice of output, and indeed productivity ratio, is dependent upon the use to which it is put. A catalogue of ratios can be compiled by fitting outputs to associated inputs. Each ratio relates to different aspects of operating performance and to different organizational activities. From Figure 12.1 it can be seen that productivity can relate either to the relationship between foodservice inputs and intermediate (secondary) outputs or to that between foodservice inputs and (primary) outputs. Each of these ratios is different and has different measurement and improvement implications. It is important that the differences between these ratios are recognized to enable inputs and outputs to be more easily standardized, to achieve a constancy in the relationship between inputs and outputs, and to facilitate more accurate measurement of inputs and outputs.[4] The outcome factor in Figure 12.1 is significant as the effectiveness of transforming outputs into desirable customer outcomes is a matter of quality. This again shows how productivity interrelates with quality.

An understanding of the above concepts by foodservice operations managers is required if they are to realize the full benefits of productivity interventions. They should also note that all the outputs obtained should be used, consumed and/or purchased. If they are not, then productivity becomes worthless. A notorious example of this was found in the British coalmining industry in the early 1990s. Many mines were highly productive but coal stocks built to enormous levels as the markets for coal diminished.

LABOUR PRODUCTIVITY

The service sector has concentrated particularly upon the partial measure which links output quantities to amounts of labour input. Labour productivity has been the subject of a number of studies[5-8] in the foodservice industry too. This can be argued to be legitimate given that labour is present in almost all output-generating endeavours and that labour represents a significant proportion of the total operating costs of foodservice operations. Labour is also perceived as being a cost which can be largely controlled by management. Further reasons for focusing upon labour productivity are that labour measurements, such as hours worked, are normally readily available through EPOS systems, rotas and clock-in clock-out machines so that the calculation of labour costs is relatively easy. However, quality issues must not be overlooked. It should also be noted that the concentration upon labour productivity may have other shortcomings. Amongst these are that the relevance of other resource types may be obscured; it is incorrect to assume that all productivity improvements are the result of labour's efforts. It is difficult to imagine a type of output into which more than one input does not enter. In general, therefore, service industries must be wary of their preoccupation with labour productivity measurement. In the foodservice industry, the other main element of cost – raw materials – has equal importance and can be measured and managed by menu analysis and engineering techniques, as discussed in the next chapter.

Another problem with labour productivity measurements occurs when the labour input measure used is numbers of employees. Conclusions based on comparisons of such measurements are likely to be flawed given that full-time, part-time and casual staff are often included in the staffing complement of a foodservice operation. Ball, Johnson and Slattery.[9] when investigating labour productivity within the food and beverage departments of hotels operated by Commonwealth Holiday Inns of Canada, developed the concept of 'full-time equivalent employee' (FTEE) to overcome this difficulty. With this, for any particular time period, such as a month, the labour input can be standardized and expressed as FTEEs. FTEE is calculated as follows:

$$\text{FTEE} = \frac{\text{total hours worked for the month by all staff in a given department} \times \text{total working days for the month}}{\text{Number of hours in working day}}$$

PRODUCTIVITY PERFORMANCE IN FOODSERVICE OPERATIONS

Before considering in detail productivity in the foodservice sector, it is beneficial to place this in the context of service industries in general and the entire hospitality sector.

Productivity in Service Industries

Medlik[10] showed that output per head for service industries increased between 1979 and 1985 but at a lower rate (approximately one-half) than for the whole economy and a markedly lower rate (virtually one-quarter) than for manufacturing. Martin and Witt[11] state that this shows just how bad productivity rates in the service industries are, compared with manufacturing industries. A comparison of labour productivity between 1960 and 1984 in services in various national economies by the OECD[12] revealed that the average annual percentage increase of productivity in the UK service sector was better than that of the USA during each period investigated between 1968 and 1984. The UK rates were inferior to those of the USA between 1960 and 1968 and were worse than those of Japan, France and the Federal Republic of Germany for every period studied. When productivity of services is compared with that of manufacturing on an international front a service lag is apparent. Elfing,[13] for instance, has shown this to be the case from his investigations of British, US and European industry.

Overall, then, a gloomy picture of recent productivity in UK service industries emerges when evaluated on either an international or a domestic basis. Many reasons can be and have been offered for the poor productivity performance of services compared to goods manufacturing.[14] Most of these reasons are as applicable to foodservice organizations and their operations as they are to other services. The gap is commonly attributed to the nature of service products, service work and/or the service organization.

Productivity in the Hospitality Industry

Medlik,[15] using data collected by UK government departments, found that hotels and catering productivity actually declined at an annual rate of 0.7 per cent between 1979 and 1985. At the start of the period productivity levels were less than a third below the UK average and declined to two-fifths below the UK average in 1985. Predictions beyond 1985 looked unhealthy for hotels and catering, and 1990–93 has witnessed an economic recession in the UK with both hotels and catering being badly hit. It is likely that output and employment, and consequently labour productivity, have suffered. Data from the USA portray a similar picture to those for the UK.

Information on productivity levels and productivity growth in the UK foodservice sector is very limited, particularly, but not only, because of problems of defining the sector and to difficulties of establishing its volume of output. A Business Ratio Report[16] showed that average annual sales per member of staff in restaurants were £24,000, whereas the comparable figure for fast food chains was £15,900. However, productivity was growing faster in fast food. Another survey of large-scale foodservice operations[17] showed a wide variation in productivity rates. Table 12.2 shows that the greatest productivity levels were realized generally from cook-chill and cook-freeze methods, as factory-style methods are applied to traditional craft practices. The other significant feature is that differences in productivity levels within foodservice methods are as great as between them. This highlights the importance of other factors, such as size of unit, use of standardized recipes, degree of automation and degree of control over quality and costs, as well as productivity levels.

Table 12.2 Productivity in foodservice operations.

Category of unit	Method	Covers/day	Covers/labour hour
Production unit	Cook-freeze	13,000	28
Production unit	Cook-freeze	5,700	28.5
End kitchen (hospital)	Cook-freeze	350	2.5
End kitchen (school)	Cook-freeze	300	13
Central production unit	Cook-chill	1,630	25
Central production unit	Cook-chill	5,000	24
End kitchen (school)	Cook-chill	280	23
Hospital	Conventional	2,250	6.9
School	Conventional	1,060	10.7
Staff restaurant	Conventional	200	2
Staff restaurant	Conventional	4,500	17.6
Staff restaurant	Convenience	3,500	6.2
Staff restaurant	Convenience	180	6.8

Note: Lunchtime, evening meal = 1 cover
     Snack, e.g. breakfast, coffee/tea and biscuit = ½ cover
     Work hours of staff includes managers and supervisors

Extracted and adapted from Pekkola[18].

The National Restaurant Association[19] estimates that the US restaurant industry is only half as productive as manufacturing industries. Between 1980 and 1985 the 2.7 per cent per annum increase in average sales was more than offset by a 4 per cent per annum increase in labour use. Prior to this, Carnes and Brand,[20] when analysing productivity for eating and drinking places in the US, pointed to rises in such places as being at an average rate of about 2 per cent per annum less than the private economy between 1958 and 1976.

Productivity Levels in Individual Foodservice Firms

As well as considering the sector as a whole, it is also possible to draw some tentative conclusions about the productivity of individual firms. Table 12.3 includes productivity data for selected foodservice companies. These at best only serve as an approximation of the relative labour productivity. Because of data weaknesses inherent in company accounts, conclusions drawn from company data must be treated cautiously.[21]

Table 12.3 Labour productivity in selected foodservice organizations in the UK.

	Date of accounts	Profit/employee (£000)	Sales/employee (£000)	Capital/employee (£000)
BurgerKing (UK)	1990	0.50	15.59	21.48
McDonald's	1990	1.34	16.17	3.31
Pizza Hut (UK)	1990	0.70	18.78	8.82
Spud-U-Like	1990	0.24	16.35	1.32

Source: Company Reports.

REASONS FOR RELATIVE LOW LEVELS OF FOODSERVICE PRODUCTIVITY

Foodservice products, like service products in general, have two criteria which enable them to be distinguished from those of manufacturing organizations. These are claimed to be causes of the poorer productivity of services when compared to that of manufacturing organizations and are thus postulated to be likely causes of any gaps in productivity between foodservice and manufacturing organizations. The first of these is that the product is *perishable*. The finished product durability of hot food is usually only minutes before deterioration occurs. Likewise capacity is perishable; an empty restaurant seat is a lost opportunity and because it cannot be stored, it is lost forever when not used. The production of food and the utilization of capacity would not be a problem if only demand were constant. Alas, the largely uncontrollable and often unpredictable fluctuations in demand for foodservice products mean that without careful selection of food production methods food costs may either become excessive or customers dissatisfied as they have to wait for their orders to be met. The insensitivity of much of the labour cost to the demand for foodservice products also means that at certain times little can be done about the productivity of some employees.

The second differentiating factor is *intangibility*. This is associated with the direct contact experience between consumers and foodservice workers and makes the measurement of outputs frustrating and difficult. Foodservice work, unlike manufacturing, is nearly always undertaken in the presence of the consumer. The physical surroundings will have an important influence on secondary outputs or the outcome of the production process and upon the consumer's perception of the foodservice product. Because of this, the design of foodservice restaurants becomes important to the management of productivity. The presence of the consumers presents an opportunity for them to participate in the service process as a resource to do, to monitor and to promote the service. This is an opportunity which has been taken up by some foodservice operations.

Productivity in service sector work is probably lower than in manufacturing as services are typically labour-intensive and are often difficult to mechanize and automate. The ability and pace with which some foodservice operations, particularly traditional operations, have adopted labour-saving devices has often been restricted but the same cannot be said of modern operations such as most of the restaurant and fast-food chain operations which have adopted highly technocratic operating systems.

Another reason for lower productivity in services compared to manufacturing is that many service organizations and outlets are small, employing few people. This limits the introduction of machinery and the opportunities for division of labour. Again, whilst this might be applicable to many foodservice operations, it is not typical of all. McDonald's, Wimpy, branded restaurant operations in the BrightReasons group, TGI Friday's have all encouraged standardization and higher productivity through new technology and the systematic planning of each job. Productivity levels will also come under pressure in multi-unit operations as their numerous outlets make control formidable and certain scale economies very difficult to fully realize. These problems are exacerbated as chains increasingly internationalize. McDonald's, for example, has over 13,000 units worldwide and 500 in the UK. Such internationalization, however, has provided some impetus for 're-engineering the workforce'. BurgerKing found, through expansion into a number of different countries in Europe, that employment costs were very high, owing to the social and employment legislation of these states. New ways of working and new technology were introduced into these operating units in order to overcome this problem, with significant implications for productivity improvements in all their outlets.

While the above factors provide clues as to why foodservice productivity might be low, there is little empirical evidence to clarify their relative significance. Furthermore, the heterogeneity of foodservices makes generalizations difficult. Nevertheless it is probable that many of the above reasons do frequently apply. Indeed, Mill[22] claims that the labour-intensive nature of the hotel and catering industry generally and the undervaluing of employees impair productivity growth. Finally, Gamble[23] relates low productivity to the management style of hotel and catering managers, the low number of industry managers who hold formal qualifications, and the limited use of operations management techniques.

THE NECESSITY FOR PRODUCTIVITY IMPROVEMENT

The importance of productivity to foodservice operations is illustrated in Figure 12.2 by showing the consequences of declining and increasing productivity.

The pressures for productivity improvement in foodservice operations are numerous. First, there is the necessity to meet rising expectations of employers. In the case of

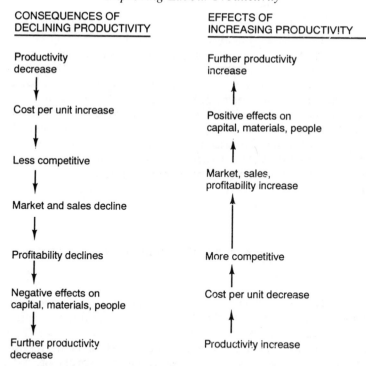

Figure 12.2 The effects of increasing and declining productivity.
Source: American Productivity Center.

profit-making operations this usually means increased profits. The relationship between profitability and productivity can be shown as follows:

$$\text{Profitability} = \frac{\text{output quantities}}{\text{input quantities}} \times \frac{\text{output selling prices}}{\text{unit costs}}$$

OR productivity × price recovery

The operation which relies only upon increasing its profitability by increasing its price recovery is dependent for survival upon its competition doing likewise. That which relies more or totally upon productivity is less affected by its competition. Secondly, productivity is important throughout the growth and development of an organization. Many writers,[24,25] though, claim that organizations should place a particular emphasis upon productivity, especially cost efficiencies, when they are approaching maturity. Some writers[26] consider that this emphasis is more appropriate when the organization is in decline. In the British fast-food sector, for example, there is evidence that the years of explosive growth are past and that it is reaching a phase of maturity. Consolidation, intensified competition and productivity will become more important across the sector. Thirdly, there is the need to combat both national and international competition. Another factor symptomatic of the latter stages of the product life-cycle which creates an increased pressure for productivity is increased competition. Competition within and between foodservice sectors will continue in the 1990s. As the amount of foodservice trade concentrated in the hands of chain operators and large companies expands, competition amongst them is expected to intensify.

A fourth pressure is the requirement in many foodservice operations to replace unproductive and obsolete equipment and facilities. The replacement of manual cash registers by EPOS systems in pub catering operations is an example, while another is the ways in which many hospital catering facilities have updated both facilities and food production and service equipment for productivity, safety, hygiene and other reasons. Finally, there is the need to meet rising customer and worker expectations. Customers continually seek improved service levels but at affordable prices. Employees continually demand better working conditions and wages. The UK government in the 1993–94 financial year proclaimed that pay rises for foodservice workers and other groups of workers in the public sector must be earned by greater productivity. The deteriorating demographic situation and the consequent competition for young workers has also made productivity important for certain foodservice operations.

MANAGING LABOUR PRODUCTIVITY IN FOODSERVICE OPERATIONS

One of the major tasks of all managers is to make work productive and the mark of an excellent manager is associated with their ability to extract all that is possible from a given set of resources and to improve upon that technology through time. Facility designers, equipment manufacturers, operatives and customers are just some of the groups who have a part to play in labour productivity improvement, but the major responsibility lies with management and especially operations management. One of their key objectives is to ensure the effective and efficient use of resources or, to put it another way, to manage productivity. Productivity, as already indicated, is a complex concept caused or influenced by a multiplicity of interrelated factors. Considerable theorizing has been directed at the factors affecting productivity, but broadly speaking the factors influencing the productivity of foodservice operations can be divided into external factors, such as political, economic, legal, social and technological changes, which are virtually uncontrollable by management, and internal factors which in turn can be considered either as soft or hard factors. The customer who participates in the production of foodservice and usually receives outputs *in situ* is a unique factor to foodservice and other service operations. These internal factors, summarized in Figure 12.3, are generally controllable, although some are more easily changed than others.[27] There are a range of ways in which these factors can be controlled and productivity improved. By putting these together, the manager can formulate a productivity strategy appropriate for the operation.

The analysis and comprehension of the factors influencing the productivity of a foodservice operation are vital to selecting the right strategy. Strategies for improving productivity have been classified as either contractive or expansive.[28] However, if one considers that productivity can be improved by changing the output to input ratio in one of five ways, as illustrated in Figure 12.4, then it is apparent that productivity strategies can alternatively be divided into five. This analysis of five possible strategies is particularly useful as it is possible to identify the external conditions that best fit each strategy and the specific techniques necessary to pursue each strategy.

Which strategy, and its approaches/techniques, will clearly be related to the specific type of foodservice operation being managed, as discussed above. But it may also be

INTERNAL FACTORS

HARD FACTORS

Amount and type of equipment and machinery

Quality and supply of raw materials

Nature of saleable physical product

Layout of operation

Working environment

Utilization of power

SOFT FACTORS

Organizational characteristics
 Reward systems
 Goal setting
 Leadership
 Structure
 Business system owner-
 operated, franchised

Work characteristics
 Job design
 Work methods
 Performance feedback
 Work schedules

Individual characteristics of
workers and customers
 Knowledge, skill, abilities
 Motivation
 Beliefs and values
 Attitudes

Figure 12.3 Model of productivity factors internal to foodservice operations.
Adapted from Prokopenko[27].

PRODUCTIVITY STRATEGY	WORKING EFFECTIVELY	WORKING SMARTER	MANAGING GROWTH	COST REDUCTION	PARING DOWN
Input/Output change for greater productivity	Increase output, decrease input	Increase output, maintain input	Increase output > increased input	Decrease input, maintain output	Decrease output < decreased input
STAGE OF THE SERVICE LIFE-CYCLE	INNOVATION	DEVELOPMENT	GROWTH	MATURITY	DECLINE
Main features of firm at each stage	Slow growth, one or two prototype operations	Growth by opening new outlets	Very rapid geographic growth	Saturation of sites	Close down less profitable units
Main features of operation at each stage	Trying out new ideas by trial & error	Adopt model, trial elsewhere	Adapt slightly in new locations	Adapt greatly to meet competitive threats	Revamp completely

Figure 12.4 The organizational life cycle and productivity strategies.

related to where the firm is on the so-called 'service life-cycle'. This cycle identifies different stages of development that an organization like a foodservice company or each of its restaurants undergoes. In each stage of development the problems and priorities change, the specific activities change and the input-output relationships change. Figure 12.4 also illustrates in simple terms how for one cycle of development the strategic factors and approaches relevant to the management of productivity in foodservice operations will be dependent upon the stage which has been reached.

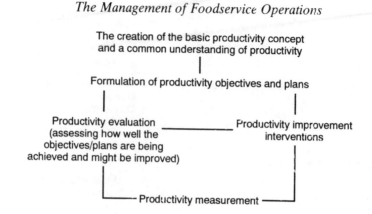

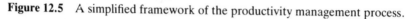

Figure 12.5   A simplified framework of the productivity management process.

It is important to recognize that the improvement of labour productivity in foodservice operations should be done within a productivity management framework. Ball[29] has developed such a framework, shown in Figure 12.5, and states that productivity improvement is but one of a number of elements which should be integrated in the productivity management process. Ball recommends that productivity should be formally managed through an organization-wide programme which he calls total productivity management.

Although there are broadly five productivity strategies, many of the approaches and techniques for improvement are common to more than one strategy. Those which are considered below focus on adjusting the labour input and work characteristics. The extent to which the labour input can be adjusted is conditioned very much by factors in both the internal and external labour markets.

Staff Scheduling

With foodservice demand often continually fluctuating in most operations, the number of staff required at any one time needs to reflect any ebbs and flows. If not, productivity and profitability are likely to be reduced for one of two reasons. First, there may be more staff on duty than is warranted by current business; therefore labour costs will be increased. Secondly, if there are fewer staff on duty than required, then lower sales, and perhaps customer dissatisfaction, are probable. Staff scheduling is crucial to labour productivity; thus the aim must be to schedule the correct number of staff at all times. Scheduling of staff is not especially onerous where demand fluctuations are small and fairly infrequent, for instance in hospitals caring for long-stay patients or in prisons. In contrast, where demand tends to fluctuate more frequently and widely, for example in high street operations, scheduling could be more problematic. However, past patterns of business activity can always be identified and used to forecast future demand.

Computer technology has facilitated this process. Bass Taverns is one example of a company that is using network technology to rota bar staff to work when it sells most. Forecasts along with productivity standards enable, as discussed in Chapter 5, variable-cost staff to be scheduled. Where scheduling is adrift the use of multi-skilled staff can provide some flexibility, for example where business demand is greater than that forecast.

Multi-skilling

The employment of multi-skilled staff and the cross-training of staff in foodservice operations enable managers to utilize staff more effectively. In addition, many foodservice jobs are of a repetitive nature and multi-skilling can improve the interest and motivation of staff. Multi-skilled staff have the ability to switch easily from one kind of task to another. However, they do require broader training than specialized workers and need manager and staff support to facilitate quick changes between kinds of tasks. In a traditional foodservice operation the multi-functioning of staff is unlikely owing to the considerable skill differences between service and production staff; whereas in fast-food chains multifunctioning is facilitated by the approach to training programmes which is identical for both production and service tasks.[30] Multi-functioning is also aided by the minimization of the skill content in each task.

Use of Part-timers, Casual Staff and Overtime

The covering of particular times by part-time staff has long been used in foodservice operations to reduce high labour costs. However, careful planning and utilization are important if problems are to be prevented. Training costs and costs associated with labour turnover are likely as more workers will be required than if only full-time workers are employed. There are also dangers of part-time staff being less committed and more unreliable. Fast-food operations have overcome these problems by having a large pool of part-time staff on call and by rewarding reliability and dispensing with those who are unreliable. Over 50 per cent of the workforce in Wimpy and Casey Jones, for instance, are part-time while as many as 80 per cent of McDonald's staff are part-time. It has been suggested that McDonald's employs these to cover unsocial hours without paying overtime and adjusts workers' hours as sales and staff members fluctuate. Casual staff are also used in foodservice operations to cover busy days or periods. The payment of such workers at basic rates rather than paying full-time staff overtime rates can again keep labour costs in check and enhance productivity. Uncontrolled overtime can lead to a spiralling of labour costs and retard labour productivity. But it can be used to reduce labour costs if overtime payments are less than what is required to pay an extra employee.

Flexible Working

One strategy used by a large and increasing number of British employers to adjust their labour input according to fluctuations in their business activity has been to introduce flexible working. This is basically a system of no fixed hours and, apart from possibly leading to higher unemployment, is generally considered to be of benefit to both employers and staff.[31] A variety of schemes exist to enable staff to work when they are most needed. Some arrangements force employees to work extra hours on days of high business activity and fewer hours on quieter days. Another scheme found in foodservice operations requires staff to choose hours and shifts from a range on offer. The voluntary selection of evenings and weekends means that staff are paid basic pay rates rather than overtime rates and therefore productivity measures based on labour costs are not damaged. Another approach to influence the labour input involves the allocation of an annual number of working hours to staff and is a movement away from traditional shifts and rosters. So, for example, a 39-hour week might be translated into 1,778 hours a year. Annual hours arrangements result in staff working longer hours and more days per week at certain times of the year but prevents the need for temporary staff, assures staff of more permanent positions and improves productivity particularly by allowing employers the flexibility to match working hours more closely to work demand. Such a system has enabled Euro Disney to improve its service by responding with more flexibility to variations in the number of customers visiting their theme park.

Work Study Techniques

Any methods of working within a foodservice operation which are less than efficient will increase the time taken to complete tasks and may affect the end output and thus reduce labour productivity. It is therefore beneficial for foodservice managers to study systematically work activities and methods of operation in order to improve both the efficiency and effectiveness when using labour and other resources. This is called work study. Work study can lead to lower labour and other costs and increase productivity through, for example, better use of people (workers and customers), raw materials or equipment and planning and control. Work study consists of a range of techniques which are associated with either *method study* – to determine the best ways of doing things in order to make improvement – or *work measurement* – to determine the time required for a suitably qualified worker to perform a task to prescribed standards.

Method study is normally limited to the study of operations and materials handling methods and is often used when new technology is introduced. The main objectives of method study are, first, to improve productivity by reducing costs whilst maintaining output, or to improve the value of outputs; and secondly, to improve working conditions.[32] These can be achieved by:

- improving product/service or system design
- improving the use of resources
- better layout of facilities
- reducing physical effort or energy required to perform work
- utilizing existing skills fully and developing new skills
- creating better physical working conditions otherwise known as ergonomics

Method study comprises a series of steps. Because of the complexities it would be impossible to study the total foodservice operation. The first step is therefore to select the activity or process to be studied. Secondly, all the relevant facts about the present work process are recorded and charted. Specific application of process chart activity to foodservice operations can be found in Kazarian[33] and Merricks and Jones.[34] The third step is to analyse the facts critically and carefully, followed by the development of an improved way of carrying out the activity. Fifthly, new methods are recorded and then re-examined to ensure that it is practical. Finally, the new method is installed and maintained.

Work measurement is particularly concerned with identifying and eliminating any ineffective time and setting time standards.[35] It is therefore natural that this should occur in all foodservice operations. The time standards that are set enable judgements to be made about staff performance, staffing levels and the costing of services. This has been used for many years in banquet service, albeit informally. In chain restaurant firms, there is an increasing emphasis on this approach linked to remuneration schemes.

Introducing Systems and Technology

The notion and origins of using technology and systems concepts to improve industrial productivity were referred to in Chapter 5. The recognition of their value and use in the service industry did not come about until much later than in manufacturing. Whyte,[36] for instance, explained the benefits to cooks and waiters of using a spike to collect restaurant orders. More recently, Levitt[37] used the example of McDonald's to argue that the systematic replacement of individuals with carefully planned technology could lead to greater productivity in the service industry.

Potentially technology and systems can produce productivity and other benefits for employers, managers, workers and customers of foodservice operations. But equally there could be disadvantages, and limitations upon the extent to which technology can be applied in foodservice operations. Evidence generally indicates that technological change should be considered beyond the purely technical aspects. Given that foodservice operations are socio-technical systems it is imperative that managers consider the effects that technology may have on both workers and customers. If technology is to increase productivity and realize other benefits and not be resisted, rejected, bypassed or overcome by workers or customers,[38] then consideration should be given to how workers (and possibly customers) use the technology, the environment in which it is to be used and the workers' and customers' attitude towards the technology.[39]

CONCLUSION

Productivity improvement is an important issue for foodservice operations. Traditionally, it is thought that labour productivity in the foodservice industry has been very low compared with that in many other industries. Recent evidence supports these thoughts. Indifferent productivity performance of foodservice operations undermines their competitive position, their viability and the living standards of those who work and invest in them. These, coupled with other mounting pressures, make the need for high productivity clear.

More and more foodservice operations are finding that either to survive or to stay ahead in the competitive world they must make the best use of all their resources, particularly their employees, and bow to the demands of their customers for enhanced service. This chapter focuses upon the use of non-standard forms of work such as part-time, flexible working, annual hours, and non-permanent contracts as a way of helping in this. Many other tools and techniques exist to help foodservice operations managers control and improve labour productivity – job design, work measurement, method study, labour scheduling, quality circles, the introduction of new technology and the development of payment systems are just a few. Some of these are referred to in this chapter while others are dealt with elsewhere.

There is no 'best' approach to productivity improvement: rather there are many routes to improved productivity and each should be viewed and implemented within a productivity management framework. Each approach should be considered in the context of the specific operation. The application of this framework to the total foodservice organization, or total productivity management, is recommended. This includes the formal management of productivity and the commitment and involvement of all people within foodservice operations.

REFERENCES

1. Ball, S. D. and Johnson, K. (1994) 'Productivity measurement – hotels', in Witt, S. F. and Moutinho, L. (eds), *Tourism and Management Handbook*, 2nd edn, Prentice-Hall, Englewood Cliffs, N.J.

2. Ball, S. D. (1993) 'Productivity and productivity management within fast-food chains: a Case Study of Wimpy International', MPhil dissertation.

3. Ball, S. D., Johnson, K. and Slattery, P. (1986) 'Labour productivity in hotels: an empirical analysis', *International Journal of Hospitality Management*, Vol. 5 No. 3, pp. 141–147.

4. Jones, P. and Lockwood, A. (1989) *The Management of Hotel Operations*, Cassell, London.

5. Kahrl, W. L. (1975) *Food Service Productivity and Profit Idea Book*, Cahners.

6. Pavesic, D. (1983) 'The myth of labor-cost percentages', *Cornell HRA Quarterly*, Vol. 24 No. 3, November, pp. 27–30.

7. Pedderson, R. B. *et al.*, (1973) *Increasing Productivity in Food Service*, Cahners.

8. Pine, R. and Ball, S. D. (1987) 'Productivity and technology in catering operations', *Food Science and Technology Today*, Vol. 1 No. 3, September, pp. 174–176.

9. Ball, S. D., Johnson, K. and Slattery, P., op. cit.

10. Medlik, S. (1988) *Tourism and Productivity*, BTA/ETB Research Services.

11. Martin, C. and Witt, S. (1989) *Productivity in Hotels*, Proceedings of the launch conference of the *Contemporary Journal of Hospitality Management*, April.

12. Akehurst, G. (1989) 'Service industries', in Jones, P. (ed.) *Management in Service Industries*, Pitman, London.

13. Elfing, T. (1989) 'The main features and underlying causes of the shift to services', *Service Industries Journal*, Vol. 9 No. 3, pp. 337–356.

14. Ball, S. D., op. cit.

15. Medlik, S., op. cit.

16. Business Ratio Report (1991) *Restaurant and Fast Food Chains*, ICC Business Ratios.

17. Sheppard, J. (1987) *The Big Chill: Report on the Implications of Cook-chill for Public Services*, London Food Commission Report No. 15.

18. Pekkola, M. (1983) *Productivity in Catering*, Report of Hotel and Catering Research Centre, Huddersfield Polytechnic.

19. Mill, R. C. (1989) *Managing for Productivity in the Hospitality Industry*, Van Nostrand Reinhold, New York.

20. Carnes, R. B. and Brand, H. (1977) 'Productivity and new technology in eating and drinking places', *Monthly Labor Review*, September, pp. 9–15.

21. Ball, S. D. op. cit.

22. Mill, R., op. cit.

23. Gamble, P. (1989) 'Profit and productivity', in *HCIMA Reference Book 1989/90*, HCIMA.

24. Crandall, F. N. and Wooton, L. M. (1978) 'Developmental strategies of organizational productivity', *California Management Review*, No. 21, pp. 37–47.

25. Thorpe, R. (1986) 'Productivity measurement', in Bowey, A. M. and Thorpe, R. *Payment Systems and Productivity*, Macmillan, Basingstoke.

26. Doyle, P. (1976) 'The realities of the product life cycle', *Quarterly Review of Marketing*, Summer.

27. Prokopenko, J. (1987) *Productivity Management: A Practical Handbook*, International Labour Office, Geneva.

28. Johns, N. and Wheeler, K. (1989) *Productivity and Performance Measurement and Monitoring*, Proceedings of International Association of Hotel Management Schools conference.

29. Ball, S. D., op. cit.

30. Johnson, K. (1992) 'Employment in fast-food operations', in Ball, S. D. (ed.), *Fast Food Operations and Their Management*, Stanley Thornes, Cheltenham.

31. Kelliher, C. (1990) 'Flexibility in employment: developments in the hospitality industry', *International Journal of Hospitality Management*.

32. Hill, T. (1991) *Production/Operations Management*, Prentice-Hall, Englewood Cliffs, NJ.

33. Kazarian, E. A. (1989) *Foodservice Facilities Planning*, Van Nostrand Reinhold, New York.

34. Merricks, P. and Jones, P. (1986) *The Management of Catering Operations*, Cassell, London.

35. Harris, N. (1989) *Service Operations Management*, Cassell, London.

36. Whyte, W. F. (1948) *Human Relations in the Restaurant Industry*, McGraw-Hill, New York.

37. Levitt, T. (1972) 'Production line approach to service', *Harvard Business Review*, September–October.

38. Gabriel, Y. (1988) *Working Lives in Catering*, Routledge & Kegan Paul, London.

39. Pine, R. and Ball, S. D., op. cit.

13

Menu Analysis

Peter Jones

INTRODUCTION

As we have seen in Chapter 3, the menu is central to the foodservice concept; it defines the product offering, establishes key elements of financial viability, namely price and contribution margin, and provides a powerful marketing tool. It is therefore not surprising that effective management of the menu can have a significant impact on operational success. Such menu management is usually carried out through some kind of menu analysis. In broad terms, menu analysis refers to a range of techniques and procedures that enable decision making with respect to pricing, dish costing, portion sizing, menu planning, and menu marketing.

It should be remembered that the philosophy of menu analysis is not new. Skilled *chefs de cuisine* in pre-Second World War kitchens regularly identified those dishes that were performing well and encouraged their sale. They also removed items from the menu that were not selling or were having an adverse effect on gross profit performance. In those days, there was a heavy reliance on fresh produce, as methods of preservation such as canning, freezing and chilling were very much in their infancy. Limited shelf-life and short seasonality of commodities led to the common practice in large hotel kitchens of emptying out store areas for daily cleaning and reviewing the state of each stored item. Foodstuffs still in good condition were returned to the stores, those that had deteriorated were binned. But those in need of eating were utilized by the chef, who designed a table d'hote menu for the day based around these items. To a very large extent this was one of the first instances of menu marketing and analysis. In the modern catering kitchen, the pressure to continue this practice has been removed by greatly improved storage conditions, changes to the nature and packaging of commodities, the ability to store safely for several days both semi-finished and finished dishes, and other new technologies. Totally original food production systems, based around central production units, cook-chill, cook-freeze or sous-vide, have revolution-ized menu management. Instead of food production having to match customer demand, finished dishes and meals can be stored in stock as a 'buffer' against variations in demand.

Likewise, the traditional menu concept of an à la carte menu supported by a table d'hote menu, typically found in hotel restaurants even today, has been modified to accommodate more narrowly defined restaurant concepts such as steakhouses, fast food restaurants and themed diners with very focused product ranges. Menus are also now part of national brands, with the same dishes and prices being marketed throughout the country, as in roadside dining chains and fast food outlets. Such chains are constrained by strong theming and marketing, with advertising and promotional activities planned over long time frames, making responses to menu analysis restrictive.

There are some sectors of the industry which have unique menu features that require a unique approach to menu analysis. For instance, many sectors – hospitals, some employee-feeding, in-flight catering, hotel package deals, university halls of residence – work to a cycle, offering a different set of dishes each day, rather than the wide range of dishes on an à la carte style menu. This is because they provide meals to a captive or semi-captive market, where there is a danger of menu fatigue, and where the meal may be included as part of a larger service package. In these sectors there is an emphasis on effective cost control and waste control through menu cycle planning, rather than the kind of menu analysis typically found in the commercial restaurant sector. There is a current trend of introducing branded concepts and products into contract foodservice, to make provision look more like what is offered on the high street. For instance, Compass have developed 'Famous Brands'. This approach may experience some difficulties as consumers may quickly become bored with this more branded delivery.

ALTERNATIVE APPROACHES TO MENU ANALYSIS

There are a number of different ways to analyse a menu, but each of the various techniques has limitations. Different types of foodservice operations also find some approaches more useful than others. Before examining specific techniques of menu engineering we need to define what is meant by the term 'menu analysis'. Jones and Atkinson's[1] review of the literature indicates that no definition exists. They propose that 'menu analysis' can be defined as *the systematic evaluation of a menu's cost and/or sales data for the purpose of identifying opportunities for improved performance.* Kasavana and Smith[2] prefer the term 'menu engineering.' which they define as *a quantitative model designed to provide a basis for analysing a menu's success both in terms of attracting clientele and in terms of profitability*. In practice, this term is then applied to one specific methodology for carrying out the quantitative analysis, namely 'portfolio analysis', even though the definition is relatively wide ranging. In our view, menu analysis is the generic term for any approach that seeks to improve menu performance, and menu engineering is a specific approach.

There are three main approaches to menu analysis. One approach is based on the analysis of *average spend*. There are at least two techniques used. The menu effectiveness technique advocated by Kreck[3] is based on comparing the 'menu average versus the guest-check average'. The frequency distribution technique, proposed by Miller,[4] is based on taking 'the average-check calculations one step further and converting them into a frequency distribution'.

The second main approach is *menu engineering*, developed by Kasavana and Smith.[5] This approach depends on the analysis of the popularity of each dish on the menu and the cost/selling price relationship or contribution margin. There have been several variations of this approach and it has been used as the basis for developing a number of computer software packages. We shall compare four alternative applications of this approach: those respectively, of Kasavana and Smith, Pavesic,[6] Uman,[7] and Merricks and Jones.[8] Although the techniques vary, all of these share the management of the 'micro-marketing mix' as their outcome.

The third main approach is based on intuition and experience rather than detailed quantitative analysis. Many independent restaurateurs review, amend and develop their menus without any reliance on hard data at all. Back in the 1970s, I practised this approach in running my own Brussels-based restaurant. Each month a new menu was developed, retaining popular items, replacing less popular ones, amending prices in line with costs and customer feedback. In those days, there was no information technology support for the restaurant, making detailed analysis difficult and time-consuming. These days, even though point-of-sale devices and food and beverage software enable quantitative data to be analysed, many operators continue to use their judgement as the basis for menu management. Recent research[9] suggests that menu prices are set using a number of parameters, including so-called psychological pricing, magic numbers, local competition and industry norms, as well as on the basis of pricing formulae and menu engineering.

MENU AVERAGE

Kreck proposes an approach to menu management based on 'menu effectiveness'. This compares the menu average with the average spend. To establish the menu average, all those dishes that play a similar role on the menu are grouped together. Such groupings are typically starters, main courses, side dishes, sweets or desserts, and so on. For each grouping the average price is established simply by totalling the prices of all dishes and dividing by the number of dishes. Once the menu average for each group is known, this can be used to establish the expected consumption pattern. Such a pattern might be that all customers will have a starter, main course, one side dish, and a sweet. The averages for these groups are then added together to establish what the expected average spend by the customer should be. This is then compared with actual average spend. This shows the true value that customers place on a meal in the outlet. The menu average should be close to this to ensure that dishes are priced around the range that customers wish to spend. If the menu average is higher than the average spend then the menu may be over-priced for the market being served. If the menu average is lower than the average spend, there may be the opportunity to increase some prices. Alternatively, it may be that the pattern of spend is less than that expected, highlighting the need to promote dishes other than main courses. Steakhouse restaurant chains focused their attention on patterns of purchase during the 1980s. For instance, one chain expected that for every 100 main dishes purchased there would be 80 starters, 73 sweets and 47 side dishes sold.

The main advantage of this approach is that it is relatively simple to apply and the information is readily available. Unlike other approaches to menu analysis it does not depend on compiling accurate records of dish costs and contribution margins.

However, this relative lack of sophistication means that it has limited uses. It helps in terms of identifying the range of price a dish should be put into and highlighting where the dishes should be promoted. But many menus may not be as easy to divide into groups of substitute dishes as proposed by the methodology. Certainly as the number of different possible courses increases, the proportion of customers having a dish from every course will decline. Even for a three-course menu, as our steakhouse example quoted above illustrates, a significant proportion of customers have only two courses. So perhaps for some people, starters and sweets are substitutes for each other. With more complex menus, working out substitution is even more difficult. A second problem is that although it identifies the difference between menu average and average spend, it does not explain the cause of this. The possible causes are customers buying fewer or more dishes than the expected pattern, the popularity of several dishes below or above the mean, or the popularity of just one dish below or above the mean. The action management should take is different for each of these possibilities, so that this approach by itself is limited.

Frequency Distribution Analysis

This technique takes the menu average approach 'one step further'. As Miller explains, managers who use average spend are making the assumption that there is a normal distribution around the average. That is to say, as many customers buy dishes less than the mean as those who consume dishes above the mean average. As we identified, this is not necessarily the case. By plotting numbers of customers and average spend on a graph, it is possible to identify the true frequency distribution of average spends. This may be 'normal', in which case the graph would have a bell-shaped curve. But it might also show two or more peaks, suggesting that two (or more) quite distinct customer groups use the outlet. Each group has its own average spend which when combined produce the overall spend. In this instance, moving menu prices nearer to the overall spend would satisfy neither group. The market segment with a low average spend would be priced out of the outlet; the segment with a higher average spend might be happy to see prices fall relative to their expectations, but the operator would not be maximising the sales opportunities offered by this group.

Although this analysis resolves one of the major shortcomings of the average spend approach, it does not necessarily provide the manager with very much more actionable information. Miller suggests that a major use of the graph is to show whether distribution is skewed towards one end of the range. Peaking towards the low end may 'indicate potential business problems', and peaking towards the high end 'missing an opportunity to increase profitability'. However, 'the graph reveals the dining patterns of your patrons, but it does not supply the reasons for the patterns'. In addition to this shortcoming typically associated with such measurement, a further inherent weakness of the frequency distribution approach is the assumption that patterns of distribution will be consistent and hence meaningful. First, eating patterns may be different in the summer than in the winter, with a switch from fewer, lighter salad items to more hot dishes. Secondly, actual patterns may not be as obvious in real-life operations as those used to illustrate methodologies in journal articles. The more average spend plotted the more complex the graph, and potentially the more meaningless. There is little evidence to suggest that this approach is being used extensively in the UK foodservice industry.

	Performance A	
	Good	Poor
Performance B Good	Standards* Signatures[t] Stars[‡]	Primes* Lead Items[t] Plowhorses[‡]
Poor	Problems* Hard to sell[t] Puzzles[‡]	Sleepers* Losers[t] Dogs[‡]

Performance A is based on some financial criteria with respect to dish performance, typically contribution or food cost.

Performance B is based on some criteria that typically include the number of dishes sold or relative popularity of each dish.

*David Uman – *Restaurant Business* (April 1983)
[t]David V. Pavesic – *Cornell HRA Quarterly* (November 1985)
[‡]Kasavana and Smith – *Menu Engineering* (1982)

Figure 13.1   Taxonomies for menu engineering.

MENU ENGINEERING

  The weaknesses of the average spend and frequency distribution techniques stem largely from their reliance on averages at a number of levels as the basis for analysis, i.e. sales of each dish and then of all dishes collectively. The nature of menu engineering is to compare the performance of each individual dish on the menu. The most frequently used criteria for comparison are the financial performance and sales volume of each dish. All the dishes are then placed according to these criteria into a matrix to illustrate their respective performance, as illustrated in Figure 13.1. Each of the quadrants of the matrix can be assigned a name to represent figuratively the nature of dishes in each quadrant. Various authors have assigned their own taxonomy to them, as shown in Figure 13.1. Effective management action is based on interpreting the reason for each dish's position and selecting one of three or four suitable solutions. Most authors agree on what these solutions should be. The objective is to modify the menu's composition in order to build on the positive items and reduce the negative ones.

  The action that can be taken based on positional analysis on the matrix can be summarized as follows:

Dishes with High Popularity and High Contribution:
  Do nothing
  Modify price slightly – up or down
  Promote through personal selling or menu positioning
Dishes with High Popularity and Low Contribution
  Do nothing
  Increase price
  Reduce dish cost – modify recipe
                   – use cheaper commodities
                   – reduce portion size
Dishes with Low Popularity and High Contribution
  Do nothing
  Reduce price
  Rename dish

Reposition dish on menu
Promote through personal selling
Remove from menu
Dishes with Low Popularity and Low Contribution
Do nothing
Replace dish
Redesign dish
Remove dish from menu

A 'solution' often ignored is the 'Do nothing' option. It should be remembered that the menu engineering methodology is designed to categorize dishes into good and poor performers. There will therefore always be those dishes with low popularity and poor financial performance. If every time the analysis was carried out, these dishes were removed without being replaced, the menu would end up with just one item on it!

Menu engineering tends to be considered only as an operation tool for managing profitability. Jones and Atkinson point out, however, that it is also clearly a marketing tool. They argue that the menu has long been established as the foodservice industry's equivalent of a brochure and price list. In effect it represents the operation's product range, specifies its prices, provides promotion opportunities, and is a significant distribution channel. The nature of menu analysis is that action designed to improve profitability impacts on all four Ps of the classic marketing mix. Depending on the results of the analysis, menu changes may be made to:

Product	Dish items will be added, removed or modified
Price	Prices will be modified or costs changed
Promotion	Dishes will be promoted by salesmanship, sales promotion literature/ campaigns, advertising, etc.
Place	Dishes may be delivered through an alternative 'distribution channel' such as a buffet or trolley.

Alternative Menu Engineering Techniques

Although the basic approach is standard, there are several menu engineering techniques, varying by the criteria used for differentiating between each dish's performance. The simplest approach has been advocated by Merricks and Jones. They use the actual number of each dish sold to establish popularity, indexed to 100 to enable comparison between different time periods, and the actual cash difference between dish cost and selling price (ex-taxes) to establish contribution. Since the cash difference is likely to be much greater on main-course dishes than starters, side dishes or sweets, they advocate separating out the different courses, so that like can be compared with like. This approach has been applied by this author in a number of settings and been generally effective in improving operational profitability. These settings included a cafeteria of a local authority catering service, pubs, and small cafés. All the operations had relatively small menus of between eight and twelve main-course items and could easily establish dish cost price, often because items were bought in ready-made from a supplier.

Uman uses a similar technique to Merricks and Jones. He too uses the unit contribution of each dish as one of the axes of the matrix, but rather than use the net number of dishes sold as a measure of 'popularity' he advocates using the 'total contribution margin'. The TCM is the number of dishes sold multiplied by its unit contribution. There seems to be no advantage in modifying the simple approach of Merricks and Jones in this way; in fact it tends to produce a less clear picture of what is happening since the relative position of a dish item on the TCM axis is affected by its unit contribution. It is therefore not immediately apparent, if a dish has a high TCM, whether this is due to the number of items sold or its unit contribution or both.

Kasavana and Smith propose a technique more sophisticated still. They do not discuss dividing the menu into sub-sections or dish categories. However, for the reasons stated earlier, it is clearly desirable to apply the technique only to groups of comparable dishes. They too use the contribution margin of the dish as one axis of their quadrant. They calculate 'popularity' by establishing what they call the menu mix percentage (MM%). This is the sales number of each dish divided by the total number of dishes sold expressed as a percentage. They compare the MM% against the MM% popularity rate for the menu. This rate is established by dividing the number of menu items into 100 per cent and then multiplying by 70 per cent. It should be noted that Kasavana and Smith do not advocate simply working out the average possible popularity, which would be found by dividing 100 per cent by the number of menu items. They state, 'it is important to recognize that a marketer would not consider an item low in popularity merely because it fell below the average'. Therefore by multiplying by 70 per cent they reduce the cut-off point between high and low popularity. However, they do *not* explain why 70 per cent is the most appropriate percentage for doing this. They state, 'The seventy percent rule referenced above has been established [*sic*] based upon extensive practical experience'. It may be that one of the reasons for this 'rule' is that they apply their technique to the whole menu. But, as identified above, some customers may choose not to have a starter or a sweet. If this were the case with a fair proportion of customers, a large number of items would then be categorized as low when compared against the simple average dish popularity. Restaurateurs should not forget that in addition to all the dishes they have on their menu, there is a dish called, 'nothing, thank you', which provides no sales and zero contribution margin.

Pavesic has advocated basing the menu analysis on axes defined as potential food cost (PFC) percentage and the average weighted contribution margin (AWCM). PFC is calculated by taking the weighted total food cost (i.e. cost of sales) and expressing it as a percentage of weighted total food sales (i.e. sales revenue). Dish items with a food cost percentage greater than this PFC are rated high, and items less than the PFC are rated low. The AWCM is calculated by dividing the total weighted contribution margin by the number of dish items on the menu. Dish items with a weighted contribution margin greater than this average for the menu are rated high, and items with a lower weighted contribution margin are rated low.

Comparison of Menu Engineering Techniques

As there are at least four different menu engineering techniques presented here, the obvious question is why? In fact each technique does slightly different things and each has its advantages and disadvantages. The first thing to say is that if the same set of data are compared it is clear that they each provide a different picture for the manager. If it is the case that the course of action to be taken is based upon the location of each dish in a specific quadrant and that these are similar courses of action for all four techniques, then managers would behave very differently according to which technique they had applied, *even though the circumstances are identical*. Hayes and Huffman[10] suggest that the fault lies with the technique itself, i.e. portfolio analysis. '[Such] methods suffer from a common flaw of matrix analysis. Because the axes on the matrix are determined by an *average* . . . some items *must* fall into the less desirable categories'. They suggest this leads to focused attention on the poor performers and ignores the impact that changes to one dish may have on other dishes. Jones and Atkinson also compare the effect of these four methods on a case example and conclude that 'foodservice managers should select from those methods which best suit their circumstances'. We therefore have to be clear about the nature of the information we are given by each technique and what circumstances are the most appropriate for using that technique. It may be that the particular case examples used by Hayes and Huffman or Jones and Atkinson to compare the different techniques are unrepresentative of the context that each particular technique has been developed for.

The approach advocated by Jones and Merricks has the advantage of being relatively simple to use and understand. Uman adopts a similar approach but uses total cash contribution rather than simple cash contribution. The rationale for this lies largely in the idea that what is really important for the manager to know is how actual cash contribution is being generated by a specific dish. Whilst this may be true, Jones and Atkinson believe that this added sophistication does not lead to any more sophisticated decision making, and it may impede the selection of the most appropriate course of action. Kasavana and Smith have a technique that is also close to the simple approach. Their menu mix percentage and 70 per cent rule takes into account the fact that average popularity may not reflect the pattern of sales effectively. This rule may not work well when different categories of dish, i.e. starters, main dishes, side dishes, are compared together. This approach may therefore be most appropriate in operations where the spread of prices between dishes on the menu, and the spread of contribution margins, is not too great. Pavesic uses a very different approach. This compares food cost percentage with weighted contribution margin, thereby targeting the manager's analysis on profitability. This is a valid aspect of menu engineering, but it ignores the impact that popularity has on performance, and as such provides more limited information for decision making. Also, by relating food cost percentage to contribution in the same analysis, there is a likelihood that dishes will polarize into two diagonally opposite quadrants. This is because food cost and contribution are likely to be inversely related to each other.

PROFITABILITY ANALYSIS

Bayou and Bennett[11] also carry out a review of alternative approaches to menu analysis. They identify three shortcomings of these methodologies: they tend to ignore different menu groups; they fail to differentiate amongst different meal times: and they focus on short-term profitability over long-run analysis. They suggest the 'profitability analysis' approach. This is based on the view that the profitability of a service entity is hierarchical. Typically in a foodservice operation there would be four levels, illustrated in Figure 13.2, as follows:

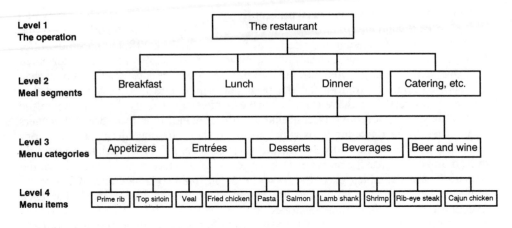

Figure 13.2   Levels of profitability analysis.
Reprinted with permission from *Cornell HRA Quarterly.*

1. The total operation
2. Meal segments, such as breakfast, lunch, dinner, special function
3. Menu categories, such as appetizers, main courses, sweets, beers and wines, hot beverages, etc
4. Specific menu items.

Each of these levels of activity should be analysed in different ways. Bayou and Bennett propose that levels 1 and 2, the restaurant and meal segments, should be analysed on the basis of an income statement in contribution format. This identifies the sales income for the operation as a whole, also broken down into meal segments, the variable or food cost for each of these, and hence the contribution margin. Direct fixed costs, which include salaries, utilities, maintenance and advertising, are then identified for both the restaurant as a whole and sub-divided to allocate to each meal segment. These costs, taken away from the contribution margin, establish what Bayou and Bennett call the 'segment margin'. Finally, all remaining fixed costs that it is not possible to allocate to meal segments, such as managers' salaries, rent, insurance and depreciation, are identified and allocated to the whole operation. This then enables the overall profitability of the restaurant to be established. Each of the three measures of profitability can be used for different types of decision making. The contribution margin should be looked at when pricing infrequent offers or developing special promotions; the segment margin enables a long-term analysis of every segment to eliminate cross-subsidization from one mealtime to another and ensure each contributes to the overall success of the business; whilst operating income makes sure that the operation stays in business over the long term.

For level 3, menu groups, the same kind of income statement analysis can be used. Many foodservice managers, both in pricing menus and monitoring costs, look at contributions by such menu groups, especially food cost and beverage cost percentages. Such analysis enables decisions about pricing menu groups around particular views of consumer psychology. For instance, there is a view that some consumers judge price on the basis of key items, usually main course items, so that margins and hence prices should be lower on main courses relative to starters and sweets. In the coffee shop business, one operator believes that tea or coffee is the key menu item that influences customers' price perceptions. Alternatively there is the view that consumers start reading the menu from the top so that starters should be more favourably priced as 'loss leaders'. Bayou and Bennett are unique in advocating that direct fixed costs, as described above, can also be allocated to menu groups. Finally at level 4, each menu item, it is possible to continue their approach of contribution analysis, or adopt one of the menu engineering approaches discussed earlier.

APPROACHES ADOPTED TO MENU MANAGEMENT IN THE UK FOODSERVICE INDUSTRY

All of the approaches to menu management discussed, with the exception of Merricks and Jones, have been developed in the USA. This is largely due to the size and scale of the American foodservice industry and the highly competitive nature of the business there. There are also specialist consultancy firms, such as The Menu Advantage, that advise independent and chain restaurateurs on improving profitability through effective menu analysis. Such consultants do not rely solely on point-of-sale data, purchase records and standard recipes. Changes are not introduced on to menus without a thorough review, which may include tracking a product from the time ingredients are received from suppliers through to the time it is consumed by customers. As well as observing such processes, all categories of staff may be interviewed along with a selection of customers in order to discover who orders the item and when; how it is perceived in terms such as healthy, exotic, rich, light; how long it takes to prepare; and how easy it is to prepare and keep in the context of the rest of the menu. Even after these extensive investigations, most chain restaurants will carry out trials of new menu items in test markets before changing their menus throughout the chain. For instance, the International House of Pancakes, based in California, trialled its new menu for ten weeks in ten of its outlets before introducing it into all 460 restaurants.[12] They found that profitability improved in nine out of the ten having carried out a menu analysis and repositioned the most profitable items in the centre of their menu card and highlighting certain items to promote them to customers.

Unfortunately there has been no large-scale survey of the UK foodservice industry aimed at finding out what approaches are actually used in operations in this country. Until such a study is carried out, a discussion on industry practice can only be based on the opinions and expertise of practitioners from across the industry. There is evidence to suggest that in the fast food sector, menu changes and pricing are based on strategic decisions rather than simply on analyses of operating performance. The addition or removal of a new menu item is often based on competitive or market analysis. In 1991 McDonald's had more menu items than any of its direct competitors, according to West[13] largely because of its leadership role in the sector and 'menu fatigue' experienced by McDonald's customers. Likewise price in the sector is more sensitive to competitor pricing policy than to menu analysis. In the USA during 1989 a major price war developed between the biggest burger chain operators, each desperately trying to hold on to market share. Typically, the price of main menu items, or 'signatures', is kept low in order to attract custom, with large margins on side items. So burgers have a contribution margin of around 60 per cent, whilst french fries contribute about 80 per cent gross profit.

Amongst theme restaurants, there is some evidence to suggest menu analysis is used. The chain My Kinda Town analyses sales volumes (popularity) of menu items and their respective contribution margins. However, changes to menus are not made frequently – about once every eight months or so – owing to the high cost of designing and printing menus. More frequent changes are made not through completely revising the base menu but by putting on 'specials' as one-off promotions or developing discount packages of various kinds, such as happy hours or two-for-one deals.

CONCLUSION

Menu analysis is not simply a mechanistic process of analysing cost and sales data in order to manipulate prices and products on the menu. It involves understanding in depth customers' needs and perceptions, the nature of the production processes within the operation, and the match between the menu and restaurant concept. Changes are not made lightly and if contemplated they are often tried out first. The 'do nothing' option is one that should always be kept in mind when using a technique that ranks items into apparent winners and losers. Clearly there are also major implications for foodservice managers of using each of the techniques described. Each gives the operator different signals about performance and what to do about it. Those techniques that are relatively simple to use may provide only rudimentary information that allows for decison making not much better than intuition. Those that are more sophisticated may be so time-consuming and complex to understand that the restaurateur makes errors in computation or misinterprets the data. Such computational issues are increasingly diminishing owing to the development of food and beverage software packages that provide a menu analysis function as part of the package. It should also be remembered that there are a very large number of foodservice operations for which menu analysis is not a suitable analytical tool at all.

As well as the inherent strengths and weaknesses of each method, there are some common aspects of their application and value that apply to menu analysis in general. First, all of these methods require large amounts of data to provide reliable and valid analysis. Therefore for single operations or small-scale operations, data must be collected over a reasonably long period. Secondly, menu engineering depends on the absence of variation in the product range over the time period being analysed. So menus must be planned and remain unchanged for a period of at least a few weeks. Thirdly, it is necessary throughout the analysis period to monitor closely commodity costs, yields and dish costs. The wider the product range and the deeper the product range the more there is multiple use of commodities, making such cost analysis complex and difficult. Fourthly, a series of analyses are required to ensure that the manager is reacting to real trends rather than short-term changes. For instance, the pattern of sales of menu items can be affected by the weather, with customers swtiching to ice creams and sorbets during hot weather and away from these in colder spells. And finally, managers must be aware that the portfolio methodology itself produces poor performers as well as good performers, and that equal attention should be given to all dishes. In this respect traditional skills of understanding customers' needs and behaviour are much more important than decision-making based on mathematical calculation.

Despite these problems, there are also some common benefits to menu engineering. Whatever the shortcomings of any specific technique, the analysis at least ensures the foodservice manager is carefully monitoring costs, sales volumes and spends. Likewise, the analysis of dish popularity enables the early detection of changes in consumer preferences and tastes and the speed of these changes can be evaluated from a series of analyses. This is a valuable source of marketing intelligence that may well help the management of the whole operation, not just the menu. The smaller the scale of the operation the simpler the method of menu analysis. There is little point in highly complex and sophisticated analysis of data that may be inaccurate to make decisions that are relatively easy to identify. For large-scale, multi-site operations with limited product range, such as the fast food sector, sophisticated, computerized menu analysis is to be expected.

REFERENCES

1. Jones, Peter and Atkinson, Helen (1994) 'Menu engineering: managing the foodservice micro-marketing mix', *Journal of Restaurant and Foodservice Marketing*, Vol. 1 No. 1, pp. 37–56.

2. Kasavana, Michael L. and Smith, Donald I. (1982) *Menu Engineering*, Hospitality Publications, Elsternwick, Victoria, Australia.

3. Kreck, Lothar A. (1984) *Menus: Analysis and Planning*, CBI Books, London.

4. Miller, Jack E. (1987) *Menu Pricing and Strategy*, Van Nostrand Reinhold, New York.

5. Kasavana, Michael L. and Smith, Donald I., op. cit.

6. Pavesic, David V. (1985) 'Prime numbers: finding your menu's strengths', *Cornell HRA Quarterly*, November, pp. 71–77.

7. Uman, David (1983) 'Pricing for profits', *Restaurant Business*, April, pp. 157–170.

8. Merricks, Paul and Jones, Peter (1987) *The Management of Catering Operations*, Cassell, London.

9. Carmin, JoAnn and Norkus, Gregory X. (1990) 'Pricing strategies for menus: magic or myth?', *Cornell HRA Quarterly*, November, pp. 45–50.

10. Hayes, David K. and Huffman, Lynn (1985) 'Menu analysis: a better way', *Cornell HRA Quarterly*, February, pp. 64–70.

11. Bayou, M. E. and Bennett, L. B. (1992) 'Profitability analysis for table service restaurants', *Cornell HRA Quarterly*, April, pp. 49–55.

12. Lydecker, Toni (1991) 'Money-making menus', *Restaurants and Institutions*, 27 March, pp. 96–112.

13. West, A. (1992) 'Fast food marketing' in Ball, Stephen (ed.) *Fast Food Operations and Their Management*, Stanley Thornes, Cheltenham.

14

Providing Service Excellence

Andrew Lockwood

INTRODUCTION

There is a growing realization across all sectors of industry that providing service excellence may represent the difference between success and failure. Manufacturing companies see service as a positive contribution to their competitive position.[1] It follows that in a business such as food and beverage operations, where staff-customer interaction is a major part of the total product, providing service excellence should occupy a position of prime importance. Some companies recognize the importance of service and incorporate it as part of their mission. For example, the Euro Disney Resort Hotels' mission is 'to be the highest quality service and hospitality organization in the world by creating an environment where all Cast Members and Guests are happy'. This mission is reproduced in a glossy business-card-size format distributed to every cast member. The card includes a list of the Euro Disney ten standards of excellence and also shows a diagram linking happy cast with happy guests and happy shareholders.

SERVICE AS KEY RESULT AREA

The Euro Disney diagram identifies the three parties involved in service interactions whose satisfaction is required to produce service excellence.

- *The customer*. A customer taking part in a service experience has two major expectations. First, the tasks involved in service should be carried out successfully – the food should be served at the right time, at the right temperature and so on. Second, he or she expects to be treated in an appropriate manner. What constitutes an appropriate manner will obviously depend on whether the customer is visiting BurgerKing, TGI Fridays or Simpson's-in-the-Strand.

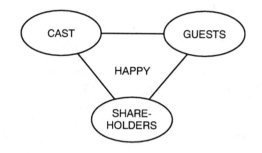

Figure 14.1 Euro Disney resort hotels' service mission.

- *The service provider*. Service contact staff interact with customers for a large part of their working day and these interactions are central to that employee's self-perception. Most contact staff have chosen that role fully aware of, and probably because of, the fact that their work will bring them into contact with people. For them to feel that they are doing their job properly will also involve two elements: the successful completion of the task and satisfying interpersonal interactions.
- *The organization*. The organization has three main requirements: first, that all customers should be satisfied with the service they receive; second, that its employees are satisfied with the work they do; and third, that the service has positive benefits for the organization for increasing sales, increasing profit or maintaining competitive advantage.

Providing service excellence involves achieving results in all three of these areas. It is no good if an operation has high profitability and satisfied employees if the customers go away disgruntled. Similarly, happy customers and happy staff are no good if the return to the organization is not sufficient.

The Customer Perspective

Tenner and De Toro[2] provide a synthesis of customer-based service attributes based on the models of Garvin[3] and Zeithaml, Berry and Parasuraman.[4] They argue that customers are looking for value in the products and services they purchase and use. They define value as the relationship between what customers get in exchange for what they give. However, value is not seen simply as a trade-off between price and quality. They introduce a third element of time or convenience into the equation. For example, people looking for very fast service may be prepared to sacrifice quality or pay a higher price to get what they want. Home-delivery pizza offers the customer added convenience over 'collect them yourself' fish and chips. There is no doubt, however, that the pizza is a more expensive option. They, therefore, split the customer wants into faster, better and cheaper. Rather than looking at product elements separately from service elements, they classify these into two components: deliverables and interactions. The deliverables define 'what' is provided for the customer and the interactions the 'how' of the style and behaviours of service. Applying these ideas to restaurant operations provides the framework shown in Table 14.1.

In order for any restaurant operation to provide service excellence, it will need to address each of the deliverable and interaction elements identified above against the

Table 14.1   A compendium of food and beverage service characteristics.

	Deliverables	Interactions
Faster	Availability, e.g. opening times Convenience, e.g. ease of use, absence of queues	Responsiveness, e.g. willingness to serve Accessibility, e.g. approachability of staff
Better	Performance, e.g. speed and effectiveness of service	Reliability, e.g. consistency of performance, honouring promises
	Features, e.g. extra service touches such as balloons for the children	Security, e.g. feeling safe, confidence in food handling
	Reliability, e.g. how consistent the standards are on repeat visits	Competence, e.g. staff have the skills and knowledge they need
	Conformance, e.g. how closely dishes meet their menu description	Credibility, e.g. the trustworthiness and honesty of staff
	Serviceability, e.g. how well problems are sorted out and corrected	Empathy, e.g. making efforts to understand customer needs, recognizing regular customers
	Aesthetics, e.g. appealing to the senses of sight, sound, taste and smell	Communications, e.g. listening to customers and adjusting language to meet customer needs
	Perceived quality, e.g. the reputation and image of the operation	Style, e.g. the politeness, consideration and friendliness of staff
Cheaper	Price	

Adapted from Tenner and De Toro[2].

expectations of the particular market segment the restaurant is aiming to satisfy. The basic parameters of the operation will have been set at the design stage, and operating standards will have been developed (as discussed in Chapter 6). The onus now is on consistently delivering to meet those standards and finding ways of improving the service provided to give extra benefit to the customer and competitive advantage for the organization.

The Server Perspective

In order for the service provider to deliver excellence in service, three elements need to be in place: the support of the rest of the operation to enable them to give good service, their own skills and ability in providing the service, and their willingness to provide service or service orientation. While both operational support and personal skills may be developed through management action, service orientation may be less easy to affect. The experience of training new food and beverage service staff suggests that some individuals are 'naturals' and seem to adopt the right approach straight away, whilst others find relating to customers just plain difficult. It is this basic predisposition of an individual in his or her inclination to provide service, to be courteous and helpful in dealing with customers that Hogan, Hogan and Busch[5] describe as service orientation. Cran[6] suggests that employees with higher service orientation will be more

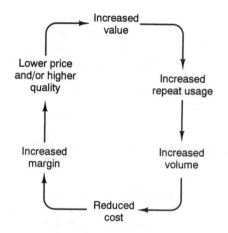

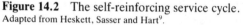

Figure 14.2 The self-reinforcing service cycle.
Adapted from Heskett, Sasser and Hart[9].

receptive to service training, will perform their work tasks more reliably and with lower levels of supervision needed, and will therefore be more organizationally effective than any counterparts because of their personal characteristics. It also follows that they are likely to achieve higher levels of job satisfaction from their service role than colleagues with a lower service orientation who do not perceive customer interaction as so fundamental to their personal make-up.

In their exploratory research across a range of service occupations, Dale and Wooler[7] have identified the key determinants of service orientation as sociability, technical curiosity, a need to know how things work, a 'fix-it' mentality, rule following (when appropriate), likeability and good adjustment (copes normally with life). If it is possible to identify these characteristics then it must make sense to incorporate them into selection procedures. Several methods are currently being developed[8] using tests to provide scores on these dimensions to inform managers as to the suitability of applicants for service roles. While it is obvious that service orientation is important for customer contact staff, the concept of the service chain would highlight its importance for all employees who contribute to providing eventual service excellence to the external customer, i.e. everyone.

The Organization Perspective

For the organization, the benefits of providing service excellence can be seen as a self-reinforcing process as described by Heskett, Sasser and Hart.[9] The benefits derive from the relationship between value to the customer on the one hand and profitability to the organization on the other. Value to the customer is a function of the quality of the service received in terms of both results and processes divided by the price and other costs involved in obtaining the service, such as travelling to a restaurant out of town. Profitability for the organization is a function of the profit margin on sales multiplied by repeat business as a return on the total investment. By providing service excellence, the profit leverage – value to the customer less cost to the provider – is enhanced and helps to establish the self-reinforcing cycle, as shown in Figure 14.2.

Taking TGI Fridays as an example, this restaurant chain is seen as offering excellent service that in turn enhances the value to the customer. This will encourage customers to visit the restaurant again and tell their friends about it. This will lead to greater volume of business that through economies of scale results in lower costs and greater profit margins. The chain can now either enhance quality further or reduce prices – both of which actions will result in higher perceived value so that the cycle goes round again.

CLASSIFYING THE SERVICE PROCESS

With the wide variation in styles of operation between different sectors of the industry, it would be inappropriate to use the same approaches to ensuring the provision of service excellence in all areas. An approach that is suitable for fast food operations will not necessarily be right in contract catering. Providing excellent service will have different problems in a roadside diner from those in an à la carte restaurant. One approach to exploring the differences between service operations has been suggested by Maister and Lovelock.[10] This is used as the basis for the illustration in Figure 14.3. Using the dimensions of the degree of service customization and the significance of customer contact as part of the operation to construct a matrix, four different types emerge.

The Service Factory

The service factory segment of the matrix is typified by very little or no customization of the service for individual customers and limited personal contact between customers and service staff. The throughput of customers in this type of operation is also likely to be high. Fast food hamburger operations fit easily into this type. The level of customization of the product is small. You can request deletions from the standard product e.g. no mayonnaise or gherkin, but, despite BurgerKing's 'you got it!' slogan, major amendments are not possible. Indeed, if every customer wanted to customize their burger, the basis of the design of the operation would be undermined and production would grind slowly to a halt. Interpersonal interaction does not form a significant part of the meal experience and is likely to be highly scripted or stylized. Likewise the provision of meals on airlines or in cafeterias exemplifies this kind of operation.

Mass Service

Operations in the mass service segment offer a highly standardized product but in a labour-intensive environment. Personal interaction between the customer and the service provider is a significant part of the service experience. As the name suggests, the throughput of customers in this type of operation is also likely to be high. An example here would come from the popular catering field offering a simple standard menu with limited choice such as roadside restaurants like AJ's or steak houses such as Beefeater. Here the emphasis on personal service plays a much greater part in the customer's overall satisfaction with the meal. Customers may well return to a Harvester Restaurant because they found the staff friendly and helpful, not just because of the food on the plate.

Service Shop

In a service shop, the emphasis is placed on adapting the service to meet the specific needs of the individual customer. Two examples from this segment illustrate the significance of customer contact in this sector. A sandwich bar that builds sandwiches to order to personal choice has limited service contact. An à la carte restaurant, on the other hand, has a much greater emphasis on personal contact but still with the product elements dominant.

Professional Service

It is the professional nature of the service offered in this sector that distinguishes it from the others. The levels of personal attention and customization are both high, giving extremely individualized attention. This segment is typified by lawyers, doctors or consultants and it is difficult to find their counterparts in the foodservice sector. However, although perhaps not truly constituting a 'profession', contract caterers offer a custom-designed service to their clients, and a catering consultant will spend many hours identifying and designing the contract operation to meet the client's needs. In a similar way, much time and effort go into preparing for a wedding reception in a banqueting operation or for a 'chalet' in an outside catering event.

This analysis has been described at the level of the operation but it is also possible to use this framework at the task or activity level within a single operation. Although an operation may fit in the service shop category – for example, a fine dining restaurant offering French cuisine – there will be elements of the service that will be better described as mass service – perhaps being served an aperitif in the bar – whilst there will be others that may impinge on the professional category – for instance, a wine waiter advising on the most appropriate wine to order to go with the chosen dishes.

ALTERNATIVE APPROACHES TO SERVICE EXCELLENCE

Each segment described above has an approach to service excellence that fits best with the style of operation, but within a single operation certain approaches may be more suited to certain tasks or activities than others. There are basically four alternative approaches to providing service excellence. Each of these focuses on different aspects, namely operations, interaction, flexibility and individuals. It is proposed that a combination of two of each of these approaches tends to be most appropriate for one of the four operational categories discussed above. This is illustrated in Figure 14.3.

The Operations Focus

This focus for service excellence concentrates on those aspects of the operation that will improve the overall efficiency of service, and that will make the operation run more smoothly and less liable to breakdown or interruption. The emphasis is on improving

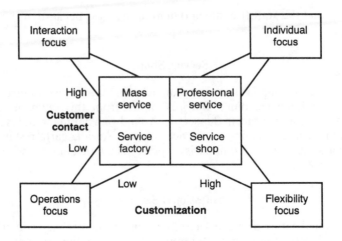

Figure 14.3 Alternative approaches to service excellence.

operating systems and procedures, improving employee knowledge and skills, and introducing new technology that will ensure that the operation runs as adeptly as possible.

One example of this approach is concerned with the time aspects of service. There is evidence from a wide range of industries that response time is a major area of concern to customers. A study by Jones and Dent[11] reviewed letters of complaint received by Forte. These showed that waiting time was a significant feature in many cases. Examples from such letters included statements such as 'table booked for dinner at 8.00pm. Eventually sat down at 8.45pm. No apology for delay'. or 'Having taken our seats in the restaurant we had to wait over twenty minutes before being given a menu and delays were experienced at all stages of the meal'. Recognizing the importance of this aspect of service to their customers, Forte instigated a survey of customers within their hotels and Harvester Restaurants using a questionnaire based on Maister's[12] propositions about the psychology of waiting lines. Over 70 per cent of all respondents were clearly concerned about waiting times. Results showed that waiting affects the mood of the customer and their willingness to spend. Significant principles identified from the survey were the need to let customers 'see things happening', to tell customers how long the wait would be, to keep the customer occupied while waiting, and to ensure that there was a smiling face and an apology 'at the end of the queue'. A follow-up analysis of service incidents resulting in poor response times identified the following critical points:

Arrival	wait to be acknowledged
Seating	wait to be seated
Order	wait for order to be taken
Drinks service	wait for order to be taken
Starter/main	wait for items to be served
Sweet/coffee	wait for order to be taken
Sweet/coffee	wait for items to be served
Payment	wait for bill
Payment	wait for account to be processed

Having identified the potential problem areas, it is then up to management to produce recommendations that will alleviate or remove these problems. These may include redesigning the service delivery system to reduce slow response, raising staff and management awareness of the areas of delay, improving service staff sensitivity to waiting customers' needs, attending directly to these needs of waiting customers by looking at queuing systems, providing distractions, removing uncertainty about what is happening and only promising what you can deliver.

Another illustration from this excellent research is worth noting. In Little Chef and Happy Eater, travelling customers are eager to get back on the road to continue their journey. The longer they have to wait for their main course, the less likely they are to feel they have time to have a sweet or coffee. If both the main course and sweet can be served in less than 45 minutes, the average sale per customer is likely to be significantly higher. This results in increased customer satisfaction due to the efficiency of the operation in speeding them on their journey and increased organization satisfaction in improving throughput and average spend.

The Interaction Focus

The interaction focus concentrates directly on the interaction between the customer and the service provider – the service encounter. This complex area has been the subject of considerable detailed research. See, for example, the collection of papers edited by Czepiel, Solomon and Surprenant.[13] However, its very complexity makes it difficult to understand and even more difficult to manage. Jones and Lockwood[14] provide a simple model that tries to identify the ways in which management can affect the delivery of service interaction, illustrated in Figure 14.4. Management's direct impact on the service encounter is limited, largely to the selection and training of employees and to marketing to customers. The manager does have influence over the roles employees play, the scripts they use, the design of the service delivery system, and the organizational culture, which indirectly affect the interaction.

The service encounter is primarily a meeting of two individuals – a dyadic encounter – but it is strongly influenced by the work environment within which it takes place. Although governed by the normal rules of social interaction, the service encounter has certain specific characteristics that make it unusual. The interaction is part of a work situation: the server is bringing the food to the customer not because they are friends but because the server is being paid to do that job. As a part of the job the server may be friendly but he or she does have a specific role to play that has been laid down. Whilst in this situation, service personnel must ignore their own status and respond to the customer as if the customer were of a higher status. Service is a personal action and employees must get very close to customers to take their orders, serve their food, clear plates and so on. In normal interaction this level of familiarity would be frowned upon. At the same time, the interaction will be task related and therefore somewhat predictable. For example, taking a food order from a customer will follow a similar pattern for everyone, but the specific details of the interaction will be different in each case.

An area where managers do have some influence is in the provision of scripts. The theoretical framework suggests that everyone holds structured knowledge about common events – like going to the doctor or visiting a restaurant – which can be triggered to help understanding and action. Both customers and service staff have a rough idea about how a restaurant meal should progress. As long as the actual

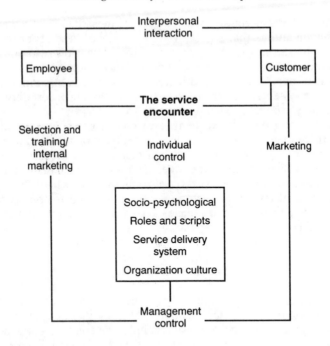

Figure 14.4   A model of management influence on service.

interaction follows this rough pattern then all will go smoothly. Deviations from the accepted customers' norm will result in problems and dissatisfaction. It is arguable that one reason for the lack of success encountered by Wendy's Hamburgers on their arrival in the UK was that customers expected a McDonald's-style approach and found a different series of scripts involving greater choice over their burger construction. Customers having only just got to know the fast food script, the Wendy's approach was unexpected and had a detrimental effect on customer perceived service quality. Providing service excellence will be a matter of fitting with the customers' expected script. Whereas a very tightly scripted approach may be the expected norm in fast food operations – the server says the same to each customer – in some formal up-market restaurants there may be a zero script – the customer does not expect the server to say anything. In TGI Fridays, the expectation is for a consciously unstructured approach where the server responds in different ways to each customer group.

The Flexibility Focus

In the interest of increasing the flexibility of manufacturing operations through such approaches as just-in-time, service operations are coming to see flexibility as an opportunity for differentiation and competitive advantage. For foodservice operations, where the customer is almost always present in the service process, flexibility provides a particular challenge. On the basis of work by Slack in the manufacturing sector, Silvestro[15] proposes three types of service flexibility: volume flexibility, delivery flexibility and specification flexibility.

Volume flexibility is the ability of the operation to match the demands of customers with the level of service output – an especially difficult task in food service where demand is so notoriously difficult to predict. The operation must be able to respond to changes in demand without suffering high wastage of either labour or materials. The operation must be able to provide the same quality of service whether catering for five customers or five hundred.

Delivery flexibility involves the ability to adapt the service process to meet different customer requirements for either an appropriate speed of response to a request for service and/or the total time taken to deliver service to the customer. For example, while customers in a high-class restaurant do not want to be rushed through their meal and indeed are paying for the privilege of spending as long over their meal as they want, they do not want to feel that they are waiting for service. Once they are ready for the plates to be cleared, sweets to be ordered or the bill to be brought, the operation must be able to respond. Similarly, although a fast food restaurant provides food quickly, customers do not want to feel that their meal has been assembled in a mad rush or that they are pressured to eat as quickly as the food was delivered. McDonald's ability to provide a child's birthday party, where nobody is in a hurry to rush everything through and the meal will therefore last around one and a half hours rather than the more normal ten to fifteen minutes, is a good example of flexibility in a very constrained operation.

Specification flexibility refers to the operation's ability to change the service process to meet individual customer needs for both goods and services. Fast food operations have limited opportunities to change the range of dishes they offer due to the constraints of their food production system. However, individual customer needs can be accommodated by removing or adding garnishes to the existing product or by the innovative introduction of new menu items. Steakhouse restaurants can cook the steak exactly the way the customer wants it. The salad bar allows the customer to select not only the items to be included in their salad but also the quantity and the type of dressing. Up-market restaurants may cook the food in front of the customers and involve them almost directly in the production process. This style of operation may also allow customers to ask for dishes that are not on the menu. Specification flexibility does not just cover the food on the plate but also involves the style of service and even the atmosphere of the restaurant. The choice of smoking or non-smoking areas is a form of flexibility.

The Individual Focus

In the type of service operation that requires service employees to use their own judgement, their professional expertise, as to how the customer's requirements can best be fulfilled, the focus for service excellence must move to the individual. It seems at first thought that this applies to very few situations in food service operations, but an example may help to illustrate the pervasive nature of this idea. Firnstahl,[16] the founder and chief executive officer of Satisfaction Guaranteed Eateries Inc. in Seattle, describes a process adopted in his chain of restaurants. Being concerned about the level of complaints he was receiving about his restaurants, he decided to give each food service employee the responsibility and the authority to do whatever it took to guarantee the satisfaction of the customer. If a customer had to wait too long for their starter, the server could give them a free drink. If the meal was a disaster, the server could cancel the bill completely. The important point here is that the decision about what to do was totally at the discretion of the service employee. No authority had to be sought from management to agree the compensation. At the same time, he introduced a procedure of calling the customers a few days after they had visited the restaurant to see if they had enjoyed their meal. If they said it was OK rather than excellent, they were immediately sent a letter of apology and a certificate for a free meal. Procedures were also put in place to identify and correct the system failures that caused the problems in the first place. Management took responsibility for correcting the errors but involved employees in finding the solutions. The results showed that at first employees were wary of using their new power and authority. Phone survey results were poor and the cost of putting things right was low because few problems were surfacing. Once employees began to believe in the system, the failure costs started to rise but phone survey results were still poor. Eventually, as more employees responded to the challenge the phone survey results showed dramatic improvement but failure costs were still high as system failures had still not been corrected. The final result showed low system failure costs as faults were eradicated from the system, resulting in high customer satisfaction.

The mass production philosophy of McDonald's and similar operations has worked well. The discretion of service staff is constrained by procedures and design. Most employees are young people paid minimum wages with high turnover. The organization structure is a pyramid of supervision and control. A new model of organization structure is emerging led by companies such as SAS, Taco Bell and Marriott, where the pyramid becomes a 'T' shape. Contact staff are the top of the 'T' supported by the rest of the organization and are expected to manage the service encounter at the point of delivery. This empowerment is based on a belief that employees want to do a good job and will do so if given the opportunity and the structure and resources to do so. Empowerment does not, however, mean that management abdicate their responsibilities and just let their staff get on with it. It does involve a conscious effort to build empowerment along three dimensions: alignment, capability and trust.[17] Alignment means that all employees know and are committed to the organization's mission, vision, values, policies, objectives and methodologies. The lack of a clear and clearly communicated direction will obviously invalidate efforts to encourage commitment. Capability involves employees having the abilities, skills and knowledge required for their jobs. They must also have the resources and support they need and that the organization must provide. The final element is mutual trust. Employees need to trust management and feel that management trust them. The policies and procedures of the organization need to reflect this trust. There may still be a feeling that control systems need to be in place to protect the organization against an unscrupulous few. These 'protections' destroy the trust for the whole operation. Recently a group of senior managers at Scotts Hotels were discussing empowering their receptionists to discount guest bills if the guest was dissatisfied in any way with their stay. They were discussing the limits that would be set for how much receptionists could knock off the bill. The managing director, who was chairing the meeting, was surprised but delighted when the hotel general managers unanimously and spontaneously agreed that there should be no limit and that the receptionists should be trusted to use their own discretion. The policy has worked well.

MEASURING SATISFACTION WITH SERVICE

To ensure that the strategies implemented are having the desired effect on service provision, some assessment of satisfaction with service needs to be put in place. There are many theories about customer satisfaction but one of the most widely quoted approaches is the expectancy disconfirmation theory.[18] According to this approach customers enter a restaurant with an expectation of what the experience is going to be like based on such things as their knowledge of restaurants in general, their use of similar restaurants, what their friends have told them and the establishment's own marketing. When the meal has been chosen and consumed, the experience is compared against the expectation. If the outcome matches the expectation exactly, then confirmation occurs. Positive disconfirmation occurs if expectations are exceeded – the meal was better than expected. Negative disconfirmation occurs if the outcome is less satisfactory than expected. This new experience is then added to all other experiences and may result in a change in expectations for the next meal occasion.

It is apparent from the above discussion that, as both the expectations and the perception of the meal experience are personal to each customer, the level of satisfaction will not be the same for every customer experiencing the same meal experience. Differences in the level of satisfaction from one customer to another, or from one meal occasion to another, can result both from changes in the customer's perceptions of the outcome of the experience and from changes in their expectations. For example, a general decline in customer satisfaction with your restaurant may not mean that you are not performing as well as you once did; it could mean that customer expectations have been going up. Indeed, the past few years have seen a general rise in customer expectations of restaurant food, and restaurant operations have had continually to improve their service simply to maintain the same level of satisfaction.

Approaches to the measurement of service satisfaction can be divided into three types: management audit; customer audit; and external audit. In a management audit, managers are asked to rate their establishment's performance on a series of factors felt to relate to customer satisfaction with the restaurant. Fitzsimmons and Maurer,[19] for example, have developed a 42-item questionnaire consisting of questions spanning the whole experience including approaching the restaurant from the car park, walking into the restaurant and being greeted, waiting for a table, being seated, ordering and receiving food and drinks, and finally receiving and paying the bill. This questionnaire is completed by managers on the basis of their perceptions of how the operation functions.

A customer audit can take many forms but is likely to use a questionnaire format to elicit customer satisfaction with the meal experience overall and on a number of product and service attributes felt to contribute to satisfaction. There are many different forms that these questions can take and each operation will need to design its own approach. Customers could be asked, for example, to evaluate the speed and efficiency of the service against a five-point scale ranging from very efficient but not too quick to very slow. They could be asked to score certain elements out of 10 or out of a 100, or to mark their satisfaction against a smiling face or a sad face.[20] By providing a series of demographic or profile variables – such as age, gender, number in the party, purpose of visit – the satisfaction scales for different types of customers and different meal times can be calculated. Using multiple regression with overall satisfaction as the dependent variable, the relative importance of specific attributes as independent variables can be calculated.

An external audit follows a similar procedure, but employs external specialists to make an assessment of the operation based on their experiences in it as a customer, working to a predetermined specification. This approach, which is widely used by organizations such as BurgerKing, Kentucky Fried Chicken and Harvester Restaurants, is commonly known as a mystery shopper programme.[21] If systematically designed, carried out and analysed, any of these methods of measuring customer satisfaction should provide management with a rich source of data for maintaining and improving the service offered by the restaurant.

SERVICE RECOVERY

Another potential source of valuable information about the performance of the operation can be provided by complaints from customers. Many foodservice managers believe that if they are not getting any complaints they must be doing well, but this may not be the case. Many customers are reticent about complaining and many operations make it difficult for their customers to complain. The result is that customers will leave the restaurant with their complaint or problem not sorted out and will simply not return to that restaurant in the future. At the same time they are likely to tell nine or ten other people what a bad experience they had, rather than the four or five people they would have told about their positive experiences. Whilst clearly it is best to satisfy the customer in the first place, it is very bad for an operation not to find out why its customers are dissatisfied. Having found out that a customer has a problem, the operation must then make every effort to put it right. This process of service recovery can represent a considerable source of benefit for the operation.[22]

It is not enough to wait for customers to bring their problems to the manager's attention. At all stages in the service, efforts must be made to monitor customer responses and elicit any complaints they may have. The service contact employee is the first line in this process but needs support from the organization. For example, Burger King in the UK has now placed a free telephone link in its stores direct to a customer service centre. All complaints are handled personally by staff at the centre and efforts made to rectify the problem. Records of complaints received can be analysed not only according to the store, as the source of the complaint, but also by type of complaint or by geographical area. This type of information not only allows the operation to sort out the customer's problem before it is too late but also provides valuable information on the parts of the operation that are causing service failures and therefore which need attention to improve the general level of service delivery.

CONCLUSION

Developing service excellence for any food service operation is a complex task but one that can bring great advantages in profitability and competitive advantage. It is well known that it costs much more money to create a new customer than it does to retain an existing one; estimates place it around ten times more expensive. Developing service excellence will ensure that existing customers are retained and encouraged to use the operation time and time again. This emphasizes the long-term nature of the contact between a restaurant and its customers – an emphasis on what has come to be called relationship marketing.[23]

As can be seen from the discussion above, developing excellence in any organization is not simply a matter of introducing one or two techniques or relying on a specific piece of equipment. It means a fundamental change in the way the organization operates.

Fitzsimmons[24] describes these organizations as world-class and suggests that to reach this status they should display the following attributes. They should be open systems ready to respond to their external environment. This implies that jobs should be designed with flexibility in mind, supported through a fluid organization structure. The emphasis throughout the operation should be on being part of a team with the focus being directly on satisfying the customer. Management should act not as supervisors and controllers but as coaches and facilitators, and technology should be seen to help in service delivery, not to replace human effort. The performance emphasis should concentrate on effectiveness and not only on efficiency. It is interesting to look at a range of organizations in the foodservice industry and attempt to assess them against these criteria. There are a number who are making efforts to follow these strategies but very few that could be said to have made it.

REFERENCES

1. Quinn, J. B., Doorley, T. L. and Paquette, P. C. (1990) 'Beyond products; services based strategy', *Harvard Business Review*, March-April.

2. Tenner, A. R. and De Toro, I. J. (1992) *Total Quality Management: Three Steps to Continuous Improvement*, Addison-Wesley, Reading, Mass.

3. Garvin, D. A. (1987) 'Competing on the eight dimensions of quality', *Harvard Business Review*, November-December, pp. 101–109.

4. Zeithaml, V. A., Berry, L. L. and Parasuraman, P. (1990) *Delivering Service Quality: Balancing Customer Perceptions and Expectations*, Free Press, New York.

5. Hogan, J., Hogan, R. and Busch, C. M. (1984) 'How to measure service orientation', *Journal of Applied Psychology*, Vol. 69 No. 1, pp. 167–173.

6. Cran, D. J. (1994) 'Towards validation of the service orientation construct', *Service Industries Journal*, Vol. 14 No. 1, pp. 34–44.

7. Dale, A. and Wooler, S. (1991) 'Strategy and organization for service', in Brown, S. W., Gummesson, E., Edvardsson, B. and Gustavsson, B. *Service Quality – Multidisciplinary and Multinational Perspectives*, Lexington Books, Lexington, Mass., pp. 191–204.

8. Samenfink, W. H. (1994) 'A quantitative analysis of certain interpersonal skills required in the service encounter' *Hospitality Research Journal*, Vol. 17 No. 2, pp. 3–16.

9. Heskett, J. L., Sasser, W. E. (Jr.) and Hart, C. W. L. (1990) *Service Breakthroughs: Changing the Rules of the Game*, Free Press, New York.

10. Maister, D. H. and Lovelock, C. H. (1982) 'Managing facilitator services', *Sloan Management Review*, Summer, p. 22.

11. Jones, P. and Dent, M. (1993) 'Improving service: managing response time in hotel and restaurant operations', in Johnston, R. and Slack, N. D. C. *Service Superiority: The Design and Delivery of Effective Service Operations*, Operations Management Association, Warwick, pp. 331–336.

12. Maister, D. (1985) 'The psychology of waiting lines', in Czepiel, J. A., Solomon, M. and Surprenant, C. S. (eds) *The Service Encounter*, Lexington Books, Lexington, Mass.

13. Czepiel, J. A., Solomon, M. and Surprenant, C. S. (eds) (1985) *The Service Encounter*, Lexington Books, Lexington, Mass.

14. Jones, P. L. M. and Lockwood, A. J. (1989) *The Management of Hotel Operations*, Cassell, London.

15. Silvestro, R. (1993) 'The measurement of service flexibility', in Johnston, R. and Slack, N. D. C. (1993) *Service Superiority: The Design and Delivery of Effective Service Operations*, Operations Management Association, Warwick, pp. 375–382.

16. Firnstahl, T. W. (1989) 'My employees are my service guarantee', *Harvard Business Review*, July-August.

17. Tenner, A. R. and De Toro, I. J. (1992) *Total Quality Management: Three Steps to Continuous Improvement*, Addison-Wesley, Reading, Mass.

18. Oliver, R. L. (1980) 'A cognitive model of the antecedents and consequences of satisfaction decisions', *Journal of Marketing Research*, Vol. 17, pp. 460–469.

19. Fitzsimmons, J. A. and Maurer, G. (1991) 'A walk-through-audit to improve restaurant performance', *Cornell HRA Quarterly*, Vol. 31 No. 4, pp. 95–99.

20. Pizam, A. (1994) 'Monitoring customer satisfaction', in Davis, B. D. and Lockwood, A. J. (eds), *Readings in Food and Beverage Management*, Butterworth-Heinemann, Oxford.

21. Newton, S. and van de Merwe, C. (1992) 'Quality assurance and the mystery guest programme in Harvester Restaurants', in Cooper, C. and Lockwood, A. (eds), *Progress in Tourism, Recreation and Hospitality Management*, Vol. 5, pp. 169–174.

22. Hart, C. W. L., Heskett, J. L. and Sasser, W. E. (Jr.) (1990) 'The profitable art of service recovery', *Harvard Business Review*, July-August.

23. Gronroos, C. (1991) *Service Management and Marketing: Managing the Moments of Truth in Service Competition*, Lexington Books, Lexington, Mass.

24 Fitzsimmons, J. A. and Fitzsimmons, M. J. (1994) *Service Management for Competitive Advantage*, McGraw-Hill, New York.

15

Controlling Costs

Paul Merricks with Peter Jones

INTRODUCTION

In Chapter 7 we looked at how control systems could be set up to enable actual performance to be compared with plans and targets. Three basic systems were discussed relating to the purchasing function, production kitchen and workforce. Plans and targets were identified in terms of financial budgets, food and beverage comparators, and labour cost comparators. In Chapter 9 aspects of physical security were discussed. But designing a system and ensuring secure premises do not of themselves guarantee that costs will always be under control – no system is foolproof. Four main areas of control need constant reviews and supervision. The purchasing function can be carried out only if there are effective *supplier relationships* that ensure that quality, service and prices are maintained. There also needs to be effective *stock control*, of consumable items in particular. There are two main causes of stock loss. Either employees do not carry out their duties correctly according to the standards established so that stock is wasted or becomes unusable, or stock is deliberately tampered with, pilfered or stolen. Thirdly, there can be waste and losses during the *production process*. Lastly, at the *point of service* there may be deliberate or accidental discrepancies between products or services sold and monies received.

As explained in Chapter 7, one of the first indicators that something may be wrong is the budget. The DoE report on school meals[1] referred to in Chapter 7 (see pp. 125–6) advocated budgetary control and provided an example of how costs could get out of control without such budgets. In one education authority it was found that food and labour costs combined ranged from between 90 and 190 per cent of income without any apparent explanation. A budget for each school would have shown the extent to which such cost performance was acceptable or not. In this chapter we shall look at budget variances, before going on to examine how control problems might occur in each of the four main areas. Both preventative action and corrective action are discussed.

Food Cost Report – week ending:.				
	%	£	%	£
Food sales	100	4997		
Budget food cost percentage	36			
Budget food cost		1800		
Potential food cost percentage	39			
Potential food cost		1950		
Policy variance			3 A	150 A
Actual food cost (from stocktake)		1848		
Actual food cost percentage	37			
Control variance			2 F	102 F
Total food cost variance			1 A	48 A

F = favourable variance, A = adverse variance.

Figure 15.1　Budget variances: a worked example.
Source: Merricks, P. and Jones, P. (1987) *The Management of Catering Operations*, Cassell, London.

MANAGING BUDGETS

Budgets are not primarily designed to ensure the most effective control of specific categories. In certain cases over-reliant or indiscriminate use of the budget as a cost control tool can lead to inappropriate corrective action being taken by management. At each stage of the process – purchasing, storage, production and service – there is the potential for such variances. For example, a restaurant budget usually includes a kitchen wage cost. Consider two alternatives: a deliberate policy change concerning the number of hours in the working week has resulted in a higher actual wage bill, or, secondly, that this variance has resulted from careless rostering and unnecessary overtime. In both cases, comparison with the budget will tell management that an adverse variance has occurred and that some corrective action is needed if the profit target is to be achieved. But the corrective action will not be the same in both cases. In the first case, management have approved extended working hours, perhaps in order to assure quality standards and sustain or increase sales volume. The 'corrective action' needed here is that sales should increase over budget in order to pay for the cost increase. However, the second example is a cost control problem whereby the corrective action of reducing hours would be appropriate. Simple budgetary control systems often cannot distinguish a policy problem, which usually requires creative profit improvement, and a cost control problem, which usually requires direct action on the cost category concerned. This is illustrated in Figure 15.1, which shows both policy and control variances, and their overall impact on performance.

If performance does not meet the expected standard, foodservice managers will need to investigate the causes of this 'variance'. Lepard[2] makes a very useful distinction between the budget food (or beverage) cost, the actual food cost and the potential food cost. The budget is the cost which the business intends to incur. The potential is the cost that should be incurred based on current purchase prices, selling prices, sales mix, standard recipes and portion sizes. The actual cost is derived from the trading account. A gap between the budget food cost and the potential food cost is termed a *policy variance*, which can be rectified by changing prices, portions, recipes or sales mix. A gap between potential cost and actual cost is a *usage variance* which can be rectified by control of wastage or attention to operating procedures. A particular difficulty is a variance caused by cost inflation. This can be tackled by including it in the original budget on the basis of a forecast of inflated costs over the year. Both costs and sales would include the inflation factor. However, variances can arise because actual costs rise faster or more slowly than forecast in the budget or because selling price increases fail to match real inflation. Information on such variances can either be derived from a periodic special exercise or be produced regularly as part of the budgetary control system. The former is usually more appropriate to small businesses, because it is costly to maintain the database necessary to provide the information for such inflation-related variance analysis. This is not to say that variance analysis is not appropriate for small businesses; far from it, but it needs to be considered carefully.

In larger businesses, variance analysis provides a very useful way of separating the responsibilities of different senior managers – where, for example, one manager is responsible for deciding on the implementation of selling price reviews and another is responsible for the negotiation of purchasing contracts and yet another is responsible for the efficient use of those materials. In this instance, variance analysis can provide a cost-effective way of planning and controlling these activities – but it is done at corporate, rather than unit, level.

MANAGING SUPPLIERS

If budgetary variances indicate a problem, especially related to the cost of supplies, it is necessary to work with suppliers in order to correct the problem. Such collaboration depends on having effective supplier relationships. As we saw in Chapter 7, the exact nature of purchasing will vary from one type of food service to another. For a franchise in a chain operation, supplier selection will not be an issue as suppliers will be specified as part of the franchise agreement. For an independent restaurateur in a large city, there may be continual review of suppliers and some switching from one to another. An institutional operator may have long-term contracts with suppliers, and supplier evaluation may take place only every one or two years. Finally, a small outlet, possibly some distance from urban areas, may have to rely on a single source of supply.

A major trend in the industry is the extent to which suppliers, especially food manufacturers are 'forwardly integrating' into foodservice. This is to say that suppliers are taking on many of the activities that were formerly carried out by the foodservice operator. Simple examples of this are ready-peeled and cut fresh vegetables, prepared bread and pizza doughs, and so on. In some sectors of the industry, the role of the foodservice operator may radically change as a result of this trend. In the in-flight sector for instance, food manufacturers such as Delta Daily Foods in The Netherlands are marketing 'food components' that can be 'assembled' in dishes by in-flight caterers almost in the same way that items are laid up on a tray. Some experts[3] are predicting that only first-class airline meals will continue to be produced by in-flight caterers, and that all other meals will simply be assembled from items supplied by food manufacturers.

Since supplier selection varies from one kind of operation to another, the relationship between foodservice operator and supplier will reflect this. But even a foodservice sector that adopts one main method of purchasing will have a range of possible supplier relationships. One example of the food purchasing process, developed by the School

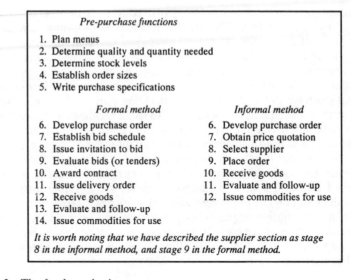

Figure 15.2 The food purchasing process.
Source: Jones, P. (ed.) (1990) *Restaurant and Foodservice Management*, Mount Saint Vincent University, Open Learning Programme.

Meal Service in the USA is illustrated in Figure 15.2. It shows that there are two types of relationship in the purchasing process, selected according to the types of commodities required. The *formal method* is for major purchase items from large-scale suppliers. The *informal method* is for less significant or less frequently purchased items from local suppliers. Effective supply depends on managing each stage of this process whatever the method, to ensure that the most satisfactory terms are agreed for both parties. Good relationships are possible only if both the supplier and the operator feel happy about the deal they have struck.

Features of Good Supplier Relationships

Reid and Riegal[4] surveyed the selection criteria and relationships of large-scale foodservice organizations with their suppliers. Most of the 61 organizations surveyed were company-owned retail restaurant chains, hence 60 per cent of respondents operated more than 100 units. Others were institutional foodservice operators – both private and government – and hotel foodservice operators. Nearly three-quarters of the respondents reported average unit sales of over $500,000 per year. The research showed that about 40 per cent of the foodservice organizations used 100 or fewer suppliers, while 20 per cent used over 500 annually. It made no difference if the organization was a retail, hotel or institutional foodservice. However, operators with larger annual sales had a larger number of suppliers. The operators were asked the number of suppliers they used; how many new suppliers they had; how often they used international suppliers; and aspects of supplier relation, such as how often the foodservice organization visited the supplier facilities.

The study investigated the basis on which the foodservice organizations selected their suppliers. Respondents were given a list of 20 supplier characteristics and asked to rate their importance. The six most important characteristics, across all types of organization, were:

- accuracy in filling orders
- consiste . quality level
- on-tim delivery
- willingness to work together to resolve problems
- willingness to respond in a 'pinch'
- reasonable unit cost

Institutional foodservice operators and the larger firms also were concerned about:

- reasonable minimum orders
- volume discounts
- frequency of delivery
- payment policies

The least important characteristics tended to be tangential services provided by suppliers such as:

- ability to sole source
- training in product use
- willingness to break a case
- provision of recipe ideas

Good supplier relations take some time to establish. The survey asked operators how many new suppliers they had added in the past year. All the organizations, especially government foodservice, reported an increase in the use of new suppliers. This is due to a wide range of factors, including the product range and geographical growth of the foodservice firms themselves. There was also growth on international suppliers, particularly among larger firms and hotel and retail foodservice organizations. Only the largest foodservice firms – about 10 per cent of the sample – actually visited more than three-quarters of their suppliers. This practice may not be necessary on an annual basis if firms have long-established relationships with their suppliers.

Supplier Negotiation

When dealing with suppliers, foodservice managers must be good negotiators and know something of the law. The basis of satisfactory negotiation is the concept referred to above: that both parties feel happy about the deal they have struck. As Figure 15.2 illustrates, such negotiation can be formal through a process of inviting tenders and reviewing bids, or informal by simply asking a range of suppliers to quote prices. Although the goal of minimizing the cost of purchases is desirable, this should never be achieved by accepting a lower-quality product. Successful negotiation gets a supplier to agree on a lower price for a specified quality. Most suppliers' methods of setting price allow some margin for negotiation, but there is always a price below which the supplier will not go. The foodservice manager needs to be aware of just how much latitude there is for cost reductions.

Suppliers are more likely to negotiate a price if they recognize that the foodservice manager is really price conscious. This price consciousness is most prevalent in industry sectors with very tight profit margins, such as institutional foodservice, or when purchasing expensive items like meat and fish. By 'shopping around' and learning the current range of market prices, foodservice managers can then demonstrate a price awareness to the suppliers. This supports their negotiating stance, helping them to obtain the best possible price. Even if suppliers cannot reduce prices further, foodservice managers may be able to negotiate more favourable credit terms or extend payment schedules. Alternatively, discounts may be agreed upon for bulk purchases or prompt payment.

Opportunity Purchasing

The price-conscious manager may also take advantage of opportunities for 'bargains' or 'specials'. These include receiving a discount on the purchase price if the manager promotes that product in the restaurant; taking advantage of introductory offers on new products; purchasing from a new wholesaler who is attempting to establish or widen the business by undercutting competitors; and purchasing items at lower prices when there is a glut of that particular product. But as with all bargains, the manager must be aware of the pitfalls. Both the quantity and quality of the goods supplied must still match established standards.

The first thing to consider is the effect that 'opportunity buys' may have upon the size of the order. Special offers from a supplier often depend upon the foodservice manger increasing the usual order size. This will save money on order costs, since the order frequency is reduced, but storage costs increase (as illustrated in Figure 7.3). If the increase in storage costs is greater than the money saved on the special offer, then the offer should be rejected. Many managers do not consider these factors when deciding whether to take advantage of a bargain. The savings made by purchasing a larger quantity would be regarded simply as an investment. But this 'investment' may be unwise, as can be illustrated with an example. Every month, a unit normally orders six cases of peaches at £50 per case. Then the unit receives a special offer; if it orders 12 cases then one of these will be free of charge. The total cost will therefore be £550 (11 months at £50). Normally £300 (six months at £50) would be tied up in canned peaches each month, so that to take advantage of the offer a further £250 is tied up or 'invested' for the month. Since this investment leads to a saving of £50, the return on the investment is 20 per cent. If this return is seen as adequate – which it almost certainly would be – then it is worth buying the peaches. However, there are other factors to take into account. For instance, over the next few months the price of the commodity may come down, or the restaurant may start to sell less of the commodity and be unable to use up the extra stock. The manager must also consider what effect the opportunity may have upon quality. He or she must determine whether the product can be stored for a long period and still maintain its quality. If the longer storage makes some of the product unusable, then the saving no longer exists.

In the Reid and Riegal study, firms were asked how they managed good supplier relations and how they ensured accurate supply and on-time delivery. The most frequently employed practice was through prompt payment, reasonable requests, and shared cost data. Also, firms were not reluctant to threaten to take their large amount of business elsewhere. Of relatively little use were long-term contracts with performance clauses or exclusivity contracts.

Managing Supplier Credit

When commodities or services are purchased, there are several different terms of supply which might be negotiated: payment may be made some time, often weeks, after the delivery has been made; it may be made at the time of the delivery, as in the case of cash and carry purchasing; occasionally payment may be made before the delivery occurs or discount may be made for payment within a certain time period. Within the limits imposed by the purchasing agreements, payment of accounts should be delayed as long as possible as this represents an interest-free unsecured loan to the business. Managers in foodservice businesses must keep careful control over suppliers' credit. The most useful way of measuring this is by monitoring the *average credit taken on purchases (ACTOP)*. This is established by dividing the average level of credit by the total annual purchases multiplied by 52 weeks to identify the granted, i.e. ACTOP. This is the equivalent of enough interest-free loans to pay for that number of weeks' purchases. By monitoring supplier credit, it is possible to identify when remedial action is necessary. If ACTOP dropped from three weeks to two weeks, the business might need to borrow from the bank. However, it might be possible to regain this credit by systematically reviewing each supplier account and establishing how long payment can be deferred. In many cases, regular payment is more important than payment on time.

INVESTIGATING STOCK CONTROL PROBLEMS

The second area of potential concern is the management of stock whilst in storage. Stock-taking serves a number of purposes. First, it establishes the value of stock according to one of the methods described in Chapter 7 (see page 116). Usually there will be some target stock value based on the level of sales turnover. This ratio aims to ensure that there are no stock-outs, whilst keeping the stock 'investment costs' to a minimum. This is often expressed as the number of days' stock held on average, i.e. sales revenue for the stock-take period divided by the average of the opening stock value plus closing stock value. Secondly, the level of stock turnover can be established by analysing categories of foodstuffs or single items. This ensures that within the overall target stock level, the different levels of sales for items is recognized. Slow moving items can be identified and appropriate action taken – either by returning them to the supplier, using them up in 'specials', and modifying the menu as part of the menu analysis process. Finally, stock-taking compares the actual value of the stock held with the value of the stock calculated from the stock record system. This enables the actual food cost or gross profit percentage to be established for comparison with the target, if necessary. In the event that stock-taking reveals a discrepancy between the stock records and actual stock held, this is a usage variance. If there is a discrepancy between target food cost and actual food cost, but no physical stock discrepancy, this is likely to be a policy variance or production control problem. The manager needs to carry out a systematic investigation of the causes of the problem.

In this section we shall review the causes of physical stock discrepancies and what to do about them. Stock shortages may be due to 'ghost' supplies, poor stock rotation, breakages or ullage, unauthorized consumption on the premises or theft. In fact there are so many different ways in which usage variances may occur that we can deal only with the most frequent causes here. So-called 'ghost' supplies refers to goods for which the foodservice manager is charged but which are never received. This can occur in a number of ways: the supplier can supply the correct stock level but overcharge; the supplier can charge the correct price but supply a quantity or quality lower than that specified on the purchase order; the delivery person can deliver less than the full order or substitute inferior goods for those specified. Even when goods inwards are carefully checked in an effort to prevent such malpractice, it is still possible to be defrauded. For instance, brewery draymen have been known to deliver the correct number of barrels to licensed premises, but to take out a full barrel along with the empty ones.

Unnecessary levels of wastage can occur for a number of reasons. Poor stock rotation may mean that perishable items deteriorate to the stage that they become unusable, whilst cans and jars may be held in stock beyond their 'use by' date. New deliveries should always be stored behind existing stocks to ensure that older items are used first. Stock may also become unusable because it is stored under incorrect conditions. The Food Safety Act has caused most foodservice operations to monitor their fridge and freezer temperatures more carefully to show due diligence.

Of most concern is a shortage, but the opposite result may also be a cause for concern. Having more stock than recorded suggests that records are not being kept correctly. This may be due to errors of recording supplies inward, goods returned to supplier, or issues to and returns from the production area, in which case systems may need to be tightened up and employees trained more effectively. The error may, however, be deliberate and derive from the fraudulent practice of employees bringing in their own 'stock', selling it and retaining the income.

CONTROLLING PRODUCTION QUANTITIES

Day-to-day food and beverage cost control depends largely on ensuring that production matches demand, so that for all menu or bar items the number sold is the same as the number made. This may seem obvious but there are a number of reasons why actual production is different to number sold, thereby causing usage variances. Such causes include producing the wrong number on the basis of poor forecasts of likely demand, producing items to the wrong standard so that some items are not saleable, selling items at the wrong portion size, deliberate fraud and accidents that lead to wastage.

It is clear that different sectors of the foodservice industry will face different problems with regard to matching supply with demand. Those sectors such as function catering, hospitals, in-flight and even floor breakfast service in a hotel where numbers of customers and orders for food and drink are placed some time ahead of the planned service time should be able to match demand and supply very closely. Similarly for those sectors that provide customers with items made to order, which in effect is how a bar operates. Those sectors that rely heavily on food and drink materials that are pre-prepared and pre-portioned, such as fast food chains, can more easily avoid wastage due to wrong portioning. And those operators that use sophisticated control systems and information technology, such as the licensed trade and fast food, can prevent deliberate fraud. Finally, some restaurateurs resort to making their menu as flexible as possible by writing it on a chalk board, so that if an item runs out they remove it immediately.

Assuming food items are not ordered in advance and that some dishes need to be prepared before service commences, there needs to be a systematic way to control production quantities in order to minimize over-production whilst ensuring no 'stock-outs': that is, the unavailability of an item. Such a system requires the recording of the sales history of items, the forecasting of portion sales, and determination of the daily production quantity. As we have seen, keeping sales histories is also needed to make menu analysis possible (see page 208) and forecasting of demand is carried out in order to schedule staff (see page 84). An efficient operation will therefore collect these data and use them in a number of different ways.

The sales history can be kept for all menu items, or only those that require production prior to the service, often just the main-course items. This record of sales frequency can be kept manually using a simple tally sheet, but increasingly is made through the point-of-sale electronic terminal. Whatever the method of compiling the record, it should be possible to analyse the data by day of the week or by operating period. For instance, using the former data set it may be that more fish items are sold on Fridays than on other days owing to religious observance; whereas using the data over a period may show trends with regard to increasing or decreasing levels of popularity of items. Some systems are sophisticated enough to record weather conditions on any given day, as food consumption patterns may be affected by this. It is also important to note if any day was unusual, perhaps because it was a public holiday or there was a transport strike, so that these data do not distort the next step – forecasting sales. Note also that the same data need to be collected in order to carry out menu engineering as described in the previous chapter.

There are a number of approaches to forecasting of greater or lesser sophistication. There is acceptance, however, that even the simplest forecast is more likely to be accurate than pure guesswork. The first step in forecasting food sales is to predict the total number of consumers for the forthcoming period. This is one of the main advantages of having a reservation system in a restaurant. If there is no such system, one of the simplest ways to predict sales is to take the average of the previous four periods. For instance, to establish the likely number of customers for a Monday lunch, the average of the four previous Monday lunches could be taken, so long as none of these was 'unusual' for any reason. This method is less accurate if there are quite wide variations in previous levels of activity. In this case it may be necessary to try to pinpoint the circumstances that surround busy periods when compared with quiet days – hence the value of noting the weather along with sales activity. Fast food restaurants, for instance, typically have lower sales per day when the weather is fine and sunny. In 1993, British Airways adopted a new approach to stocking meal trays on aircraft based on forecast, rather than on reservations. This was derived from the previous 13 weeks' activity for each specific flight. The second step in forecasting is to predict the sales level of each menu item. This can be done by using the popularity index of that item, i.e. the proportion each menu item is of total sales. So if on average a dish has an index of 0.15 (15 per cent of sales in the past have been this item), it can be forecast that 15 per cent of the total predicted sales will be of this item.

Sales histories having been used to establish total sales and dish forecasts, the daily production quantity can be identified on the production sheet. This lists each menu item, the forecast sales per item and the number of portions to be prepared. It is usually left to the chef to decide whether production quantity should match forecast exactly, or whether there should be a slight over-production in order to allow for inaccuracies of the forecast and ensure that stock-out does not occur. The sheet may contain more information if greater control is necessary, for instance by identifying the portion size, standard recipe, portions in hand, and adjusted production quota. Standard recipes serve a number of functions. As discussed in Chapter 6, they help to define the operating standard, and hence manage quality on an ongoing basis. They are a means by which employee performance can be defined and therefore measured against. Finally, from a control perspective, they should ensure that raw materials are used in such a way as to minimize wastage levels during the production process.

The effective control of the process that turns raw materials into finished meal or drink products requires two key elements. First, the relationship between, or 'yield' from, any given quantity of a commodity and the number of portions of a dish needs to be established. For some items the relationship or yield is simple. A 70-oz bottle of spirits serves exactly 32 measures of one-sixth of a gill. For others, especially where the ingredient may be used in a number of different ways, a standard recipe is needed in order to define exactly the quantity of raw materials needed. Secondly, the standard recipe controls not only the input quantities, but also the production process. This should ensure that the materials are handled in such a way as to ensure the right quality and quantity of finished products are produced. A typical example is that of roast meats cooked for precisely the right length of time at the correct temperature in order to ensure the joint yields a certain number of portions. The growth of chain operations and the trend, particularly in popular catering and in-flight catering, towards the purchasing of prepared and even pre-portioned materials have greatly reduced the need for yield testing and standard recipe development in foodservice outlets. Yield testing and standard recipes therefore have a number of advantages, as identified by Davis and Stone.[5] Yields and recipes assist with purchasing in that they help to define both the quality and appropriate sizes or weights of commodities. They enable the food orders to be written by translating production forecasts into commodity usages. They provide a second quality check, so that inferior goods accepted by the storeperson may be rejected at the production stage or as a check to ensure that goods have not become sub-standard whilst in storage. They should deter pilferage or theft during the production process. They are the means by which an accurate costing of a dish is established. And finally, in developing new menu ideas, recipes enable the relationship between existing dishes and new dishes to be explored to ensure that the variety of commodities needed to support the menu does not become too great.

CONTROLLING SERVICE AND SALES REVENUE

Just as production control involves a three-stage process, there are three basic standard procedures for revenue control. These are the recording of all food sales, pricing all sales correctly, and accounting for all receipts. There are a number of ways in which this can be achieved, depending on the level of sophistication necessary to obtain the desired level of control. All such revenue control systems require that the customer order is recorded in some way, each item on this order is priced for presentation to the customer as a bill, and that the cash or credit receipts match the total of bills for that period.

A triplicate check and separate billing system tends to be used in à la carte restaurants. The server writes the customer a check, one copy of which is retained by the customer, a second goes to the cashier, and the third to the kitchen. The extensive menu found in such restaurants makes pre-printed checks impractical. However, in steakhouses and other table service restaurants with limited menus, a duplicate, pre-printed check may be used that serves also as the customer bill. The pre-printing of the check makes it easier to read and use, as well as usable for billing purposes. Finally, in fast food restaurants the electronic point-of-sale (EPOS) device records all transactions, so that all orders and sales transactions are made by keystrokes on the EPOS system.

Just as there are a number of ways in the stores and in the production kitchen for losses to occur, the service or point-of-sale area may also be subject to unacceptable practices. Whether deliberate or in error, four main problems occur. First, the customer orders and receives items for which no record is kept. If done in error this results in items being 'sold' for which no income is received by the foodservice operator. If done deliberately, the server may obtain items without a written order by having an accomplice in the kitchen, bringing in his or her own stock or selling items short to create additional portions in order to 'charge' the customer and receive cash for such items. For instance, in the bar trade, just a slightly short measure of spirits may mean on a busy night that an 'extra' twenty or thirty measures may be sold by a dishonest barperson who then pockets the cash. Secondly, the customer's bill may be incorrect when matched against the items purchased. In sectors where an itemized bill is not always given, as in the licensed trade or fast food, a dishonest employee may overcharge deliberately. Point-of-sale displays, to ensure that the sum requested matches the amount entered are one way to prevent this type of fraud. Thirdly, the incorrect change may be given to the customer. If done in error, this problem is usually identified when the cash and credit notes are counted at the end of the trading session and matched against the bills. By that time it is usually too late to correct, and if the cash drawer is used by a number of employees it is not possible to discover who made the error. Some restaurateurs issue cash floats to employees and assign them the responsibility for matching income with receipts, expecting them to make up any shortages; or have strict guidelines assigning only one employee to each point-of-sale device for designated periods, as in the fast food sector. Finally, foodservice operations may be the victims of customer fraud. This may be in the form of 'walk-outs', whereby customers consume drinks or meals and leave without paying; credit fraud, as in the case when bills are paid for by using stolen cheques or credit cards; or fraud in the form of the passing of forged bank notes.

BEHAVIOURAL ASPECTS OF COST CONTROL

A budget may provide a suitable tool with which to control the overall profitability of a business. However, it is the employees such as cooks or waiters who have considerable discretion over the way costs are incurred, by, for example, their adherence to standard recipes and portion sizes. Managers have to achieve cost control through their staff, by breaking cost standards down into a number of specific and measurable performance standards, and by monitoring and correcting performance – or ensuring that their supervisors do so. Therefore, effective cost control is concerned just as much with supervisory skills as it is with financial skills. We also identified in Chapter 9 the horrifying research that suggests that at least one-third of employees in the industry may be deliberately dishonest.

Managers cannot personally control all of the costs associated with a foodservice operation. In larger operations, the foodservice manager may decide to devolve profit responsibility to some subordinate managers. For example, the food and beverage

Table 15.1 Influence on food costs of foodservice personnel.

Manager	Influence on food costs
Purchasing officer	Unnecessarily high prices paid Incorrect specification ordered Incorrect quality accepted Goods invoiced, but not received Materials stolen or spoilt from stores
Head chef	Incorrect material used Incorrect recipe used Materials stolen or spoilt Finished dishes wasted
Restaurant manager	Finished dishes spoilt or stolen Payment not received for dishes Change in sales mix

Source: Merricks, P. and Jones, P. (1987) *The Management of Catering Operations* Cassell, London.

manager of a large hotel may have several department heads responsible for the kitchen, stores, restaurant, coffee shop, floor service and banqueting. The manager in this example needs to decide what responsibility for cost control will be delegated to which subordinate. In certain cases, it may be appropriate to delegate responsibility for volume and gross profit as well. In the hotel example, responsibility for volume, gross profit, employment costs and other direct expenses may be delegated to the restaurant manager, but not to the floor service manager. Of course, authority should match responsibility and may involve the subordinate manager in authorization of costs, review of prices and the planning of sales promotion activities. If it is decided to devolve financial responsibility – either by delegating responsibility for several cost items or by setting up cost or profit centres – it is necessary to provide a financial planning and reporting system that takes account of these responsibilities. In practice this means participation in the budget preparation process, authorization of expenditure, control of costs and accountability for results.

Introducing responsibility centres involves some difficult decisions for the foodservice manager. A key question concerns the responsibilities for food costs: how should the responsibility be divided between a head chef, head storekeeper and the other managers? All of them have some influence on food costs but in different ways, as illustrated in Table 15.1. If any variance is significant and controllable, it should be isolated and reported in a way that highlights each manager's responsibility for the variance. However, separating these different variances is a difficult task, but without them the value of responsibility accounting in foodservice is somewhat diminished.

Managers' attitudes towards cost control have implications for the effectiveness of the system. Caplan[6] conducted a series of interviews with managers concerning their views on cost control. About half of the respondents put forward the viewpoint that control was necessary because employees, particularly operatives, were at worst deliberately lazy and wasteful and at best indifferent to cost-saving efforts. The other half put forward the view that managers (but not the operatives or supervisors) needed the information from a control system in order to reduce costs. Caplan's conclusion was that managers believe that control systems are there for them to exert control over other employees, rather than for other employees to exert control over their work. Caplan's research has also shown that managers' attitudes towards the reliability of the cost control system ranged from mildly cautious to openly distrustful and hostile. We have also found this to be the case in the catering business: where their unit's performance is below standard, some managers will take the opportunity to cast doubt on the reliability of the control system, rather than taking action to investigate and overcome potential problems.

Motivation theory also has some implications for cost control. People establish subjective expectations concerning their own performance. Repeated failure to achieve a goal will cause a person to lower their personal expectations. Conversely, people who have been successful in achieving goals in the past are likely to have higher expectations for future performance. There is untapped potential in the foodservice industry to harness operatives' enthusiasm for cost control. To take advantage of the motivational potential of cost control data it is necessary to provide feedback for operatives on cost performance compared with standard – ensuring that the goals are neither too low nor too high. Of course, employees' perceptions of what is important at work are largely shaped by the discussion between boss and subordinate. Some managers let control of costs slip away until a crisis is reached and then they have a purge on cost control. Managers who attempt to control costs by such methods are unlikely to achieve success. Employees tend to regard the 'purge standard' as an exception and after the purge is over they revert to the normal standard.

CONCLUSION

This chapter has focused on the practical issues of day-to-day control of the foodservice operation. It has tended to focus on managing the perishable stocks or 'consumables' of the operations, rather than the equipment and non-consumable items. This is partly because equipment security is looked at in Chapter 9, and partly because consumables, especially perishable foodstuffs, tend to be the most vulnerable stock items. A feature of this chapter is the huge number of ways in which the business may accidentally lose stock or money or deliberately be defrauded. Whilst the effective setting up of a control system is needed to make it possible to exert control, actual control only occurs if management operate the system as it was designed to be operated. Management must also accept that no system is entirely secure and that a determined thief or fraudster may find a way of beating the system, so that continual vigilance is needed. Every time a new way of exerting control is invented, new ways of overcoming this control are also invented.

The operation of bars is one area that leads the industry in devising new control systems and methods, largely because of the high volume of cash sales generated in the licensed trade. This sector has seen the introduction of bar coding as a means of control at point of sale. After a customer places an order for a drink, a hand-held bar code reader is used to record the item at the point from which it is dispensed. When the order is complete, the barperson downloads the data from the reader into a point-of-sale till; this totals the sale and shows the sum to the customer on a digital display. This means the barperson needs neither to remember the drinks prices nor add up the bill.

Furthermore, the system records the exact number of drinks items dispensed, their sales value and the income generated by each employee. Stock levels are adjusted accordingly and purchase orders established in order to return to par stock levels.

The sophisticated use of computer technology and bar coding has also been applied to the control of equipment stocks, most notably in the in-flight sector. The equipment handling and storage needs of these kinds of operation involve the stripping, washing and laying up with equipment of as many as 25,000 trays a day. New units at Heathrow providing meals for all British Airways short-haul flights, and another in Copenhagen for SAS, have applied the latest materials handling technology originally developed in car manufacturing plants. Part of this system means that equipment items are stored in bar-coded bins, so that when a certain type of item is needed it is automatically located within the storage system and delivered to where it is needed within the production unit. It is obvious that such sophistication is unnecessary in many other sectors of the industry. However, it is indicative of the fact that designers of control systems are increasingly applying not only information technology but also other technologies to the problems they face.

REFERENCES

1. Department of the Environment Audit Inspectorate (1983) *Education School Meals*, HMSO, London, March.

2. Lepard, N. and Cade, H., *Improving Food and Beverage Control*, Northwood.

3. Jones, Peter (1993) *Innovation in In-Flight Catering* (unpublished).

4. Reid, R. and Reigel, C. (1988) 'Foodservice purchasing: corporate practices', *Cornell HRA Quarterly*, Vol. 29 No 1, May, pp. 25–29.

5. Davis, B. and Stone, S. (1985) *Food and Beverage Management*. Heinemann, London.

6. Caplan, E. (1971) *Management Accounting and Behavioural Science*, Addison-Wesley, Reading, Mass.

16

Managing Quality

Nick Johns

INTRODUCTION

Management strategies for assuring and improving food service quality were discussed in Chapter 8. However, all strategies require good day-to-day management if they are to be effective, and almost by definition this means delegating responsibility for quality right down through the organization. Nevertheless, the systematic and detailed evaluation of the system, through HACCP (see below) or flow-process charting, may greatly help line managers take this responsibility. This chapter reviews theories that have made a major contribution to our understanding of service quality assurance during the past few years. It identifies the problems that tend to arise during service provision and examines various ways in which these may be addressed in practical terms. Measurement approaches such as audits, the costing of quality and customer surveys are presented and discussed. Another key aspect of quality management is the art of problem solving. The chapter therefore goes on to describe techniques and tactics which enable the foodservice manager to identify, prioritize and address service quality problems. Furthermore, delegation and the empowerment of employees are now accepted as important tools in the assurance and continuous improvement of service quality, so the chapter also deals with ways in which the day-to-day improvement of quality can be effectively delegated to and handled by foodservice staff.

CENTRALIZED V. DECENTRALIZED QUALITY ASSURANCE

The quality assurance process views foodservice as a 'product', produced by means of a series of steps or sub-systems. Broadly speaking, this is the approach taken by national quality accreditation bodies, such as the British Standards Institution.[1] Quality assurance consists in optimizing each sub-system, so that it contributes towards maximizing the overall quality of the product. A good example of such quality assurance is the Hazard Analysis and Critical Control Point (HACCP) procedure,[2] which is recommended for the management of hygiene and safety in foodservice systems.[3] Defects (hazards and risks) are removed by specifying and controlling the production/service process, as discussed in Chapter 9. Control systems are set up for monitoring and documenting each critical control point. This involves checking that the control standards have been adhered to every time the process was carried out. It also means recording the conditions under which each batch has been treated, so that the reliability of the process is assured.

The main thrust of HACCP is quality control testing of the system *processes*, not the *output* (i.e. the food product itself). Foodservice operators should test their product regularly, but food is a highly perishable commodity and by the time it has been tested or analysed it may no longer be attractive, or even safe, for consumption. Therefore practical quality management means assuring the quality of the food treatment process, not the food itself. HACCP's advantages are that it is logical and thorough. It is therefore very helpful when loss of quality would be serious, and is used by most large food manufacturing companies to assure the safety of their products.

Procedures similar to HACCP have been advocated for assuring food characteristics other than microbiological quality.[4] They may even have scope for managing the service encounter. In general, however, the HACCP approach is most suitable for processes which are either very product orientated, such as the production of sous-vide foods, or very large scale, such as the standardization of service in a chain of fast food outlets. Centralized quality assurance of this kind is cumbersome, with its insistence upon standard setting, monitoring and documentation for all critical processes. It is also rather inflexible, owing to the time it takes to make effective changes to processes, standards and procedures. In many service processes 'standards' may be very difficult to define and monitor, and in any case there may not be time for documentation.

An alternative system for monitoring and assuring quality service may be the concept of poka-yokes. This Japanese term can be translated as 'fail-safe devices'. They are used extensively in manufacturing industry quality control systems. Recently, Chase[5] has proposed that the concept be adapted and applied to services. Poka-yokes are designed into systems at each potential error point. Their purpose is to prevent such errors. He identifies six kinds of service poka-yoke, three relating to the service provider and three relating to the consumer of the service. This emphasis on the customer is particularly helpful, as Chase suggests that as many as two-thirds of complaints about service derive from the customers themselves making an error. The three service provider poka-yokes are:

1. *Task*. These poka-yokes are designed to prevent the service provider from delivering the service incorrectly, in the wrong order or too slowly.
2. *Treatment*. These poka-yokes are designed to ensure that the interpersonal contact between the provider and consumer is effective.
3. *Tangible*. These poka-yokes are aimed at ensuring that the environment in which the service act is carried out meets the specification.

The three customer poka-yokes are:

1. *Preparation*. The customer is provided with poka-yokes that ensure that he or she is adequately prepared for the service experience.
2. *Encounter*. Customers are assisted during the service to participate effectively in the encounter.

3. *Resolution.* Customers are provided with ways aimed at ensuring their satisfaction subsequent to experiencing the service.

In order to establish what poka-yokes to devise and implement, the foodservice operator must carry out a detailed flow process charting of the system. At each stage of the process, potential error points must be identified and an appropriate poka-yoke devised for ensuring non-failure. The application of this approach to roadside restaurants is currently being investigated.

An even more important consideration is the nature of service itself. The customer is a key contributor to the success and therefore the quality of the service encounter. This may make it impossible to identify critical control points in the service process, because they depend so much on interpersonal chemistry and may be different for every individual customer. If we view service in this light, the best way to ensure its quality is not to centralize control of the process, but to empower every 'front line' employee to manage the service encounter. This delegated, decentralized approach is now regarded as the best way to ensure quality in the smaller, predominantly service-orientated units which make up the bulk of foodservice establishments. It permits much more flexible management of complex service processes than can be achieved by a centralized approach. The rest of this chapter is devoted to understanding where quality problems may arise and the practicalities and techniques of ensuring quality through systems such as audits, quality costing, customer surveys, and quality management teams.

GAP THEORY

During the past ten years, marketing theorists have developed a number of models to describe service quality. Brogowicz and his co-workers[6] have assembled these into a single model, shown in Figure 16.1, which identifies five main areas where service quality problems are likely to arise. These five 'gaps' are shown as in Table 16.1. The five gaps indicate how management effort should be directed toward assuring service quality. In this text, we emphasize the importance of ensuring a match or fit between consumers' needs and the foodservice system developed to meet these needs.

The *positioning* gap develops if the product concept diverges from customer requirements, as may happen if fashions or demographic changes affect the market place. Such concept development was explained in detail in Chapter 2. Long-term control of the positioning gap can be achieved by regular top-level reviews of the established concept. This is usually done through both qualitative and quantitative market research, aimed at identifying customers' current wants and needs. The product concept should also take account of competitors' activities and the differentiating 'edge': the distinctive skills, assets and know-how of the organization. It will naturally also reflect the organizational objectives and goals.

The *specification* gap depends upon the quality of foodservice standards set by management. Standards may be either tangible or intangible. For example, Martin[7] suggests that service aspects fall into two categories, procedural and convivial, examples of which are shown in Table 16.2. Some of the more procedural standards set in the industry, such as the menu specification, layout and design standards, and productivity standards, have been discussed in Chapters 3, 4 and 5, whilst less tangible

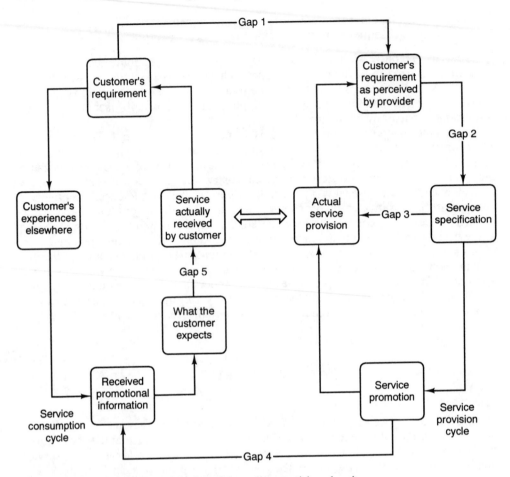

Figure 16.1   A simplified model of service quality provision showing gaps.

standards relating to service and quality were the subject of Chapters 7 and 8. The effectiveness of such standards depends upon how precisely they can be expressed and how well they can be communicated to the employees who must implement them. Tangible standards, such as maximum queue lengths, table waiting times or the temperature at which food is served, are generally easier to set. However, their contribution to the overall quality of service may be trivial compared with intangible aspects such as attitude or attentiveness. It is just as important to generate the correct company ethos and to encourage employees to set quality standards for their own work.

The *delivery* gap develops where employees do not, or cannot, produce a service to the standard required. All of the chapters in Part B of this book explore day-to-day operational issues that may impact on effective delivery. Poor delivery may be due to attitude problems, and it is essential that foodservice staff are committed to their work. However, poor performance may also result where the service environment is inappropriate for the job that is expected. For instance, queue length in a cafeteria is affected as much by the layout and type of service equipment as by employee attitudes or skill.

Table 16.1 The 'Five Gap Model' of service provision.

Gap No.	Name	Definition
1	Positioning	Between management perceptions of customer expectations and the expectations themselves
2	Specification	Between management perceptions of customer expectations and the actual service specified
3	Delivery	Between the service specified and that actually delivered
4	Communication	Between the service actually delivered and that externally communicated to customers (e.g. through advertising)
5	Perception	Between the service quality perceived and that expected by the customer

Table 16.2 Examples of service quality aspects.

Procedural aspects	Convivial aspects
Accommodation	Attitude
Anticipation	Attentiveness
Timeliness	Tone of voice
Organized flow	Body language
Communication	Tact
Customer feedback	Naming names
Supervision	Guidance
	Suggestive selling
	Problem solving

Adapted from Martin (1986)[7].

The fourth gap relates to promotional *communication*. This has an important influence upon customer perceptions of service quality, because for many operations it is the basis upon which customers build their expectations. It should therefore reflect the foodservice product accurately and faithfully. If gaps within the system have been minimized it will also reflect the product concept. Promotions should be reviewed regularly as part of the marketing audit, because they occupy a key role in measuring the relationship between organizational objectives, the mission, and the activities of front-line staff. The specification, delivery and promotion gaps of the service provision process can be identified and monitored by means of quality audits, discussed later in this chapter.

The difference between what customers expect and what they actually receive is generally regarded as the true measure of service quality.[8] This *perception* gap is the only one of the five gaps over which the foodservice organization has little or no direct control. The underlying assumption of quality assurance systems is that perceived service quality is most likely to be guaranteed by closing the other four gaps. The perception gap may be monitored by customer satisfaction questionnaires, or by market research surveys. Gap theory has certain implications for the design of such surveys, which will be discussed later in this chapter.

QUALITY AUDITS

A quality audit is a systematic appraisal of a service process.[9] A checklist of items is drawn up and compared by the auditor with each aspect of the service. It is a quick and effective way (often the only practicable way) to get an impression of service quality and it is therefore used by many types of service organization. Audits may be conducted either by in-house personnel or by specialized consultants. There are two main types: auditing by department, and customer perception audits.

Audit by Department

Audit by department is mainly concerned with the way in which the service conforms with management's perception of the operation, i.e. with gaps 1 and 2 of the service provision model (Figure 16.1). Audit checklists therefore tend to emphasize the departmental nature of the foodservice outlet. For example, they may involve a detailed study of kitchen hygiene or an evaluation of the behaviour, dress and attitudes of service personnel. If access is regarded as an auditable issue, it will tend to be associated with separate departments, e.g. the grounds and car park, or disabled facilities at reception. It may not be practicable for an outside consultant, or even an in-house specialist, to audit the whole service provided by a complex organisation.[10] For instance, in many foodservice establishments styles and standards may change during the day, becoming progressively more formal from breakfast through to the evening meal. The *ad hoc* nature of banqueting may make it inaccessible to the consultant auditor. The foodservice manager must therefore have a clear idea of what is required of the audit and make it clear to the auditor in a detailed brief. Audit priorities can be established using analytical techniques such as Pareto, fishbone and force-field analysis, discussed later in this chapter. These techniques allow quality problems to be identified in broad terms and traced to a particular department. It is then the auditor's job to pinpoint the cause.

Customer Perception Audits

An alternative auditing approach is to prepare a checklist that reflects the customer's view of the service experience. The service encounter can be regarded as a 'journey' through the series of events shown in Figure 16.2.[11] The auditor may follow this journey and report directly or solicit the views of customers at each stage. Alternatively, a group of customers may be informally asked to rate the issues (and likely deficiencies) at each stage of the 'journey'. Audit items often have space for rating the assessment ('very good', 'good', 'fair', etc.) rather than 'yes/no' responses. They may also have space for noting particular defects or for making general comments about the service. The customer perception approach is rapidly gaining ground in the hotel and restaurant industries,[12] because it simplifies the problem of what to audit. It also deals directly with

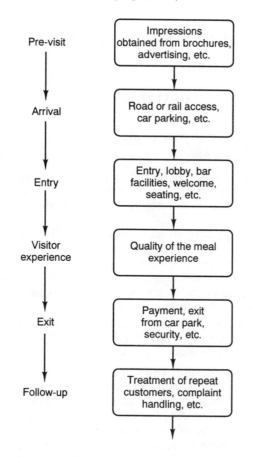

Pre-visit	Impressions obtained from brochures, advertising, etc.
Arrival	Road or rail access, car parking, etc.
Entry	Entry, lobby, bar facilities, welcome, seating, etc.
Visitor experience	Quality of the meal experience
Exit	Payment, exit from car park, security, etc.
Follow-up	Treatment of repeat customers, complaint handling, etc.

Figure 16.2 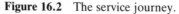 The service journey.

what is probably the most difficult part of service provision: matching it to customers' expectations. It can be used to investigate gaps 4 and 5 of the service provision model described above.

The 'mystery' customer, shopper or guest technique is used by some hospitality companies to monitor service standards. Merricks and Jones[13] describe an example of how the technique is used by a fast food/take-away chain. Mystery shoppers are trained personnel who buy a meal as a member of the public (i.e. without announcing themselves) and report the standard of service to head office. There is usually a precisely laid out shopping or dining procedure and observations may be reported on a standard form. Stopwatches may be used to measure the timing of service, and the food temperature may be determined with a probe thermometer. Mystery guest reports may therefore be very objective and precise, but there is limited scope for 'auditing' before the observer is detected.

All forms of quality audit tend to be controlled and resourced centrally within organizations, and so they are related more to centralized quality assurance systems than to devolved ones. There is some scope for giving employees a feeling of ownership of the auditing process, by allowing them to discuss the findings directly with outside consultants. With in-house auditing staff, a feeling of suspicion tends to prevail. Advantages and disadvantages of the various types of quality audit are summarized in Table 16.3.

COST OF QUALITY

Another potential measure of overall quality is the *cost* of quality. According to Wyckoff,[14] quality costs fall into four main categories:

Prevention	Costs of setting up standards and a system to maintain them, e.g. training staff, preparing purchase specifications, developing standard recipes, monitoring and documentation procedures (setting up costs).
Assurance	Costs of actually maintaining standards, e.g. resources required for inspection, measurement and documentation (staff time and administrative costs).
Internal failure	Costs due to waste or losses before the food reaches the customer, e.g. rejection of raw materials, losses due to faulty storage, foods rejected by the server (costs of waste and inefficiency).
External failure	Costs due to defective items reaching the customer, e.g. a free meal or drink offered to placate offended individuals (ultimately marketing costs and loss of repeat business).

Crosby[15] does not count the costs of setting up and maintaining a quality system as part of the cost of quality. These are costs which diligent management would have to bear anyway to set up an effective system. He defines the Price Of Non-Conformance (PONC) as the cost to management of not getting it right first time and every time. In other words, it is simply the cost of internal and external failure. Calculating the cost of quality in this way is of course difficult, because the value of lost repeat business and customer dissatisfaction, for example, is not easy to assess. However, many companies in the manufacturing sector already assign such costs to their service operations. The normal procedure is to decide standard costs for specific failure events and to multiply them by the number of such failure events. PONC calculations are usually carried out department by department, and individual managers are consulted as to what constitutes a 'non-conformance'.[16]

CUSTOMER SATISFACTION MEASURES

The most obvious way to assess the quality of a foodservice operation is by direct customer feedback. There are three accepted ways of obtaining this information: unsolicited compliments and complaints; comment cards; and customer surveys. Unsolicited compliments and complaints may be expressed both at the time of the meal experience and by letter afterwards. One survey[17] discovered that 60 per cent of all customers who sent letters of complaint had actually made an oral complaint at the time of the meal. One in three compliments were expressed, but only two in seven complaints. Whether guests actually express a complaint depends upon its seriousness, but also upon their own attitudes and personality. This type of customer response is

Table 16.3 Advantages and disadvantages of different quality audit styles.

	Advantages	Disadvantages
Audit by department	Provides a wealth of detail	Managers' priorities may not be the same as those of customers
	Easy for management to understand and design	Detail provided may be too complex for practical use
	Comparatively easy to trace a problem to a department	Results are qualitative and lack statistical rigour
	Data are *actionable*, i.e. non-conformance can be dealt with	
	Comparatively free of subjective bias from the observer/auditor	
	Front-line employees are likely to be receptive to discussions about the outcome	
Guest perception audit	Provides a wealth of detail	Comparatively difficult to design
	Reflects the customer's view of the service	May be subject to bias from the observer/auditor
	Gets to the heart of the service marketing issue	Data may need interpretation before action can be taken
	Front-line employees are likely to be receptive to discussions about the outcome	Management may find it difficult to relate to the findings Results are qualitative and lack statistical rigour
Mystery guest visit	Simple to design and administer	Provides very limited information
	Largely objective and free of observer bias	Measurements may bear little relationship to customers' perception of the service
	Numerous visits are practicable, and hence a statistically significant sample may be obtained	Front-line employees are unlikely to be receptive to discussion about the outcome

therefore a poor indication of non-conformance in a foodservice operation. Another objection is that responses are not likely to be statistically significant; there are usually not enough of them and they do not make a representative sample. Also, it is difficult to collect the comments as evidence, as many of them are made only orally, during busy periods. Even written evidence cannot give a systematic picture of the strengths and weaknesses of the operation.

Another approach to obtaining customer feedback is to leave comment cards on tables for customers to complete. Such cards should be easy to complete, yet provide the maximum of information. Phrasing of the questions is difficult, because ambiguities are apt to creep in. A customer might answer 'yes' to 'was the food properly prepared?', but be dissatisfied with the meal overall. Comment cards usually solicit yes/no answers or scale ratings, such as 'good', 'fair', 'poor'. These are easy to analyse, but may provide little clue about the actual source of problems. On the other hand, customers may avoid free 'comment on' responses because they are too time consuming. Recent research[18] mentioned earlier in this chapter suggests that customers perceive service quality as the difference between what they were expecting and what they actually experienced. Barsky[19] has developed and evaluated cards which asked customers to rate their experience as better than, the same as, or worse than expected. Barsky's statistical analysis is encouraging and this approach is more logical than simply asking whether the experience was 'good' or 'fair'. It is likely that this style of card will gradually come into more general use. However, customer comment cards suffer from the same general drawbacks as the unsolicited comments described. They are passive approaches, relying upon the customer's willingness to respond. They can make no claims to reliability or accuracy, since they do not provide a statistically significant or representative sample size.

Customer surveys are a proactive attempt to measure satisfaction and service quality and to provide feedback. Like any market research they may be qualitative and quantitative. Qualitative surveys may be carried out formally by a specialist organization; but many restaurateurs simply approach customers informally to solicit their opinions. The value of a survey depends on the level of information and analysis which can be obtained from it. Quantitative studies using questionnaires or trained interviewers may be carried out outside the restaurant in order to discover customers' perceptions and motivations. Studies aimed at determining the perceived quality of the service should be carried out within the restaurant, i.e. as close as possible to the time and place of the meal experience. Survey questionnaires and comment cards assume that customers perceive foodservice quality as the sum of a number of different quality attributes: food quality, friendly service and so on. Analysis of such data is normally achieved by first subjecting the questionnaire items to factor analysis, to identify common factors amongst them. Item scores which make up each factor are then added together to form a factor index and the factor indices are subjected to multiple regression to discover their weightings: that is, the extent to which they contribute to overall quality. An overall quality index is then prepared by multiplying the factor indices by their weightings and adding them together. These processes are shown in Table 16.4.

The example in Table 16.4 is simplified to give an idea of the process. A real survey would of course be expected to produce more factors, more weightings and a more complex calculation of the overall quantity index. Collison and Turner[20] have actually determined the weightings of different contributors to the meal experience. Their results are shown below expressed in the form of multiple regression equations:

Study 1   285 Customers; 9 Meal Occasions
Whole meal = 0.57 + 0.43 (entrée) + 0.21 (sweet) + 0.21 (starter) + 0.14 (potato).
(i.e. b_0 (regression constant) = 0.57, b_1 = +0.43, b_2 = +0.21, b_3 = +0.21, b_4 = +0.14

Study 2   115 Customers; 9 Meal Occasions
Meal experience = 0.96 + 0.57 (food) + 0.17 (environment) + 0.12 (service)
(i.e. b_0 (regression constant) = 0.96, b_1 = +0.57, b_2 = +0.17, b_3 = +0.12

Table 16.4 Analysis of questionnaire comment card data.

A. Example items and factors

Item	Mean item score	Factor	Factor index
The food was served at the correct temperature	5.3	1 (Food)	12.9
The food looked attractive	3.2	1 (Food)	
The food had a pleasant taste	4.4	1 (Food)	
The service was timely	4.1	2 (Service)	7.5
The service was friendly	3.4	2 (Service)	

B. Example multiple regression

Total quality = β_0 + β_1 (Factor 1 quality) + β_2 (Factor 2 quality) + β_3 (Factor 3 quality) + etc.
(Sum of all items)   (sum of Factor 1 items) (sum of Factor 2 items) (sum of Factor 3 items)
                     scores   scores   scores

where β_1, β_2, β_3 etc. are the weightings which relate the factors to the total quality.

C. Example calculation of overall quality index

Item	Mean item score	Factor	Factor index	Weighting	Overall index
The food was served at the correct temperature	5.3	1 (Food)	12.9	$\beta_1 = 0.86$	15.22
					(= 12.9 x 0.86 + 7.5 x 0.55)
The food looked attractive	3.2	1 (Food)			
The food had a pleasant taste	4.4	1 (Food)			
The service was timely	4.1	2 (Service)	7.5	$\beta_2 = 0.55$	
The service was friendly	3.4	2 (Service)			

TECHNIQUES FOR QUALITY MANAGEMENT TEAMS

Chapter 8 dealt with the sort of team structures which may be set up in order to gain a continuous improvement in service quality. Such teams require considerable support, because unfamiliar skills are often required. The quality improvement process usually follows the problem-solving sequence shown in Figure 16.3. A number of techniques can be used to support these activities, and foodservice managers should be aware of them as a source of practical help in problem-solving and as an important part of the quality training of employees. There are basically three kinds of technique: problem identification, problem prioritization and problem location.

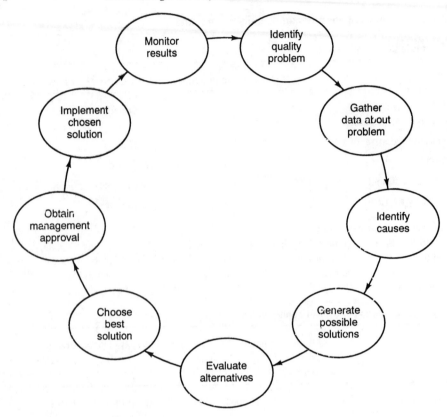

Figure 16.3 The quality improvement process.

Problem Identification Techniques

One may wonder why it is necessary to identify problems to solve. Yet employees approaching the problem-solving challenge 'cold' are frequently at a loss as to where to start. They also tend to identify the problem as being somewhere else in the operation rather than directly with themselves. Food production staff blaming service staff, and vice versa, is a classic symptom of poor quality, identified by Whyte's research[21] as long ago as 1948. Problem identification techniques enable the members of a quality circle or quality action group to focus upon workplace problems. They also ensure a proactive approach to quality improvement, as opposed to managers merely responding to such problems as come along. Problem identification techniques include brainstorming, mind mapping and force-field analysis. All these techniques can be used in other contexts, but they are also important ingredients of successful quality improvement systems.

The brainstorming technique can be used to generate a large number of ideas quickly. It is widely used in marketing, strategic assessment and other areas of business practice. In quality management it can be used to identify problems to be solved, causes of quality problems and potential solutions. Effective brainstorming requires a group of between five and twelve individuals. Those chosen should be able to make some particular type of contribution, e.g. those who supply the materials for, receive the products from, or carry out a particular job. The basic rules are that all members enjoy equal status in the group and there must be no criticism or comment on the ideas as they are generated. The group should elect or appoint a leader who will lead the session and facilitate the process. It must then define the problem or area to be brainstormed. The leader must ensure that everyone understands why they have been asked to help and allow everyone a turn at providing ideas. The group should strive for quantity of ideas, which should be written down on a flip chart or OHP so that everyone can see the list grow. The list of ideas can either by analysed and discussed immediately, or prioritized using a technique such as paired comparison, discussed below.

Another useful technique is mind mapping, which models the association between loose ideas and a particular theme. It can be used by a group or an individual to clarify thinking, capture ideas, determine the scale of a situation or opportunity and trigger action where it is required. The first step is to decide on the problem or opportunity which needs clarification and write it in the centre of a large sheet of paper or flip chart. Sub-themes and issues related to the central theme are then captured by brainstorming. Words which simply describe these issues are written down and joined to the central theme by lines to build up a spider's web of relationships. Finally the mind map is reviewed and at least three sub-themes selected for action.

Force-field analysis is another focusing technique, which aims to identify restraining and driving forces within the system. It can help to pinpoint causes of existing or potential non-conformance and improve the ability of the system to achieve conformance. Force-field analysis usually involves an organized team of individuals with an identified leader who chairs and co-ordinates the sessions. The analysis process begins with the current quality position being defined in terms of driving forces which work towards meeting quality requirements and restraining forces work against them. All the forces which may affect the present or future quality position are brainstormed and a list is drawn up. The forces are then summarized as arrows on a diagram. Those above the line represent restraining or opposing forces, whilst those below are positive or driving forces. The relative effect of each force is denoted by the length of the arrow, and the whole diagram can be used to identify quickly which force patterns need changing in order to maximize quality. The example shown in Figure 16.4 is a force-field analysis of the factors influencing queue length in a self-service operation.

Problem Prioritization Techniques

Paired comparison is a technique used to obtain team consensus of priorities where a number of quality problems of apparently equal merit have been identified. The quality problems are listed and a copy of the list made available to each team member. Then each member individually compares each item in the list with every other item and decides which is the more important of each pair. All members count the number of times each item has been selected as the more important. Scores are then collated for the whole team and the highest score is the overall democratic decision.

Pareto analysis aims to identify the most frequent causes of quality problems. It consists of listing potential causes of quality problems and measuring how often each occurs over a sample time period. A histogram can then be prepared, showing the frequencies of the various causes in descending order. The example in Figure 16.5 shows the frequencies of various types of kitchen accident. Typically the first or first plus second bars of the histogram account for about 80 per cent of the problems; for

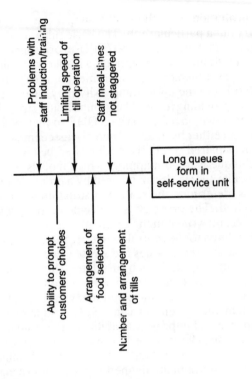

Figure 16.4 A force-field diagram.

example, the commonest types of occupational accidents in kitchens are knife cuts and dry burns. The Pareto chart identifies the main causes and enables them to be prioritized for action.

Problem Location Techniques

Flow charting offers a way to set out the foodservice process in the form of an action sequence. Quality problems and causes may frequently be located on the chart, making it possible to determine and position preventative action. Flow charting involves determining and listing the steps of the process. They are then sequenced and drawn as a series of rectangular boxes joined by arrows. Each step should be named as a process using a verb and a noun, e.g. 'peel potatoes' and key action steps (those needing special attention or care in order to ensure conformance of output) should be clearly marked. Flow charting can contribute positively to understanding the sub-systems involved with both production and service aspects of food service. Analysis and evaluation of flow charts is part of the HACCP system of quality assurance discussed above.

Cause and effect, or 'fishbone', analysis is a technique for locating the root causes of quality problems in specific departments or activities. A typical 'fishbone' diagram is shown in Figure 16.6. It was obtained by identifying the 'effect' to be considered (in this case a billing delay). This was then placed in the box to the right of the diagram. The

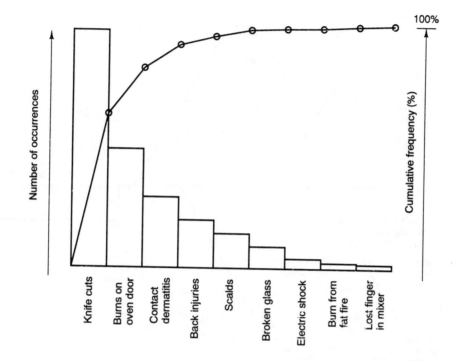

Figure 16.5 Pareto chart of accident occurrences.

branches to the left of the diagram were then labelled with likely locations of the root cause; those most usually used are methods, manpower, machines (equipment) and materials. The team preparing the diagram then brainstormed possible causes of the effect and wrote them on the respective branches. The fishbone diagram shows that most of the root causes lie on the personnel (manpower) and equipment (machines) branches. The team's next step will be to prioritize the causes and decide what course of action should be taken.

CONCLUSION

This chapter examines the management techniques that are required to support the management of quality in a foodservice operation. In broad terms, quality management consists of three key activities:
- Setting standards for production and service
- Communicating quality standards to employees
- Monitoring the quality of the service delivery process

One way to integrate these activities is through centralized quality assurance systems such as Hazard Analysis and Critical Control Points (HACCP). This may be quite

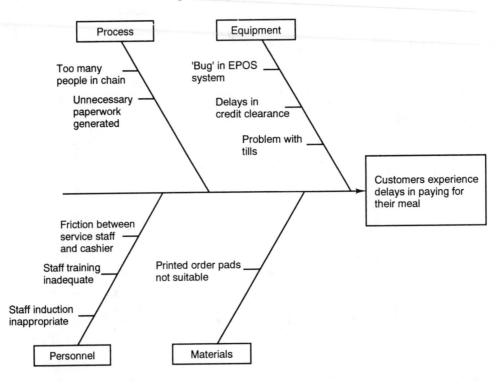

Figure 16.6 Cause and effect diagram.

satisfactory for food production activities and even large-scale standardized service operations. However, the management of more personal service quality is fraught with difficulties, owing to the perishability of food products and the intangible nature of service. It may be that the concept of service poka-yokes can address this issue.

Recent theories of service delivery indicate that quality management strategies should address the 'gaps' which can develop at particular stages of the service delivery system. Each of these poses specific management challenges. In much of the foodservice industry, effective quality strategies are likely to involve a decentralized approach in which front-line employees are empowered to take a high level of responsibility for service quality. This has consequences for the foodservice manager, in terms of training and communication. Various ways of measuring service quality are discussed, including quality audit models, as well as formal and informal customer feedback mechanisms. An alternative approach to monitoring quality is the setting of targets for the price of non-conformance, for instance by measuring the cost of lost business.

Numerous techniques are available for solving quality problems. It is important that these are understood by management, and even more important that they are communicated to employees. Solving quality problems involves identifying root causes of problems, prioritizing them for action and locating them within the foodservice system. It is important for managers to realize that the solution of quality problems is in the hands of service staff, and that in order to do the job they need the tools and techniques.

REFERENCES

1. British Standards Institution, BS 5750: Part 0: Section 2, p. 3.

2. Johns, N. (1991) *Managing Food Hygiene*, Macmillan, Basingstoke.

3. World Health Organization (1992) *Report of the International Commission on Microbiological Specifications for Foods: The Hazard Analysis, Critical Control Point System in Food Hygiene*, WHO Doc. No. VPH/82.37, Geneva.

4. Jones, P. (1983) 'The restaurant, a place for quality control and product maintenance', *International Journal of Hospitality Management*, Vol. 2 No. 2, pp. 93–100.

5. Chase, Richard and Stewart, Douglas (1993) 'Failsafe services'. Paper given at the Operations Management Association's Eighth International Conference, Warwick Business School, May.

6. Brogowicz, A. A., Delene, L. M. and Lyth, D. M. (1990) 'A synthesised service quality model with managerial implications', *International Journal of Service Industries Management*, Vol. 1 No. 1, pp. 27–45.

7. Martin, W. B. (1986) 'Defining what quality service is for you', *Cornell HRA Quarterly*, February, pp. 32–38.

8. Parasuraman, A., Zeithaml, V. A. and Berry, L. L. (1985) 'A conceptual model of service quality and its applications for further research', *Journal of Marketing*, Vol. 49 No. 4, pp. 41–50.

9. Willborn, W. (1986) 'Quality assurance audits and hotel management', *Service Industries Journal*, Vol. 6 No. 3, pp. 293–308.

10. Haywood, K. M. (1983) 'Assessing the quality of hospitality services', *International Journal of Hospitality Management*, Vol. 2 No. 4, pp. 165–177.

11. Whittle, S. and Foster, M. (1991) 'Customer profiling: getting into your customer's shoes', *International Journal of Bank Marketing*, Vol. 9 No. 1, pp. 17–24.

12. Fay, A. (1991) 'Auditing hotel employee performance', *Journal of Property Management*, Vol. 56 No. 6, pp. 26– 28.

13. Merricks, P. and Jones, P. (1986) *The Management of Catering Operations*, Cassell, London.

14. Wyckoff, D. D. (1984) 'New tools for achieving service quality', *Cornell HRA Quarterly*, November pp. 78–91.

15. Crosby, P. B. (1984) *Quality without Tears: The Art of Hassle-Free Management*, McGraw-Hill, New York.

16. Johns, N. (1994) 'ICL Kidsgrove: snapshot of a changing culture', in Teare, R. Atkinson, C. and Westwood, C. (eds) *Achieving Quality Performance*, Cassell, London.

17. Lewis, R. C. (1983) 'When guests complain', *Cornell HRA Quarterly*, August, pp. 23–31.

18. Parasuraman, A., Zeithaml, V. A. and Berry, L. L., op. cit.

19. Barsky, J. D. (1992) 'Customer satisfaction in the hotel industry: meaning and measurement', *Hospitality Research Journal*, Vol. 16 No. 1, pp. 51–73.

20. Collison, R and Turner, M. (1988) 'Consumer acceptance of meals and meal components', *Food Quality and Preference*, Vol. 1 No. 1, pp. 21–24.

21. Whyte, W. F. (1948) *Human Relations in the Restaurant Industry*, McGraw-Hill, New York.

Index

A.I.D.A. 20, 55
asset performance 10, 112
assets 143–159
average spend 111, 205

Bass Taverns 80, 198
Benihana 11, 33
boundary role stress 167–169
BS 5750 128, 133
branding 47, 205
budgeting 110, 231, 232–233
built environment 145–146
BurgerKing 37, 47, 81, 82, 131, 146, 158,
    164, 193, 194, 220, 227

cafeterias 9, 72, 124, 179, 248
capacity 9, 60, 83, 174–187
casual staff 91, 199
chain of standards 100–101
Citizen's Charter 128, 134
competitive environment 24
concept development 12, 18, 34–39
consumer behaviour 18, 19–24
continuous quality improvement 132
contribution margin 208
control systems 12, 104, 107–126, 231–244
COSHH 152
cost allocation 120, 121–122
cost control 231–244
cost of quality 252
cost structure 107–108, 111
customer demand 10, 46, 174
customer facilities 73–75
customer satisfaction 104, 160, 226–228, 249,
    252–255

decoupling 6, 175
demand forecasting 84–85, 186, 238–239
design 35, 49, 59–77, 82, 96–97, 105, 108,
    139

economic order quantity 113
employee feeding 12, 19, 110, 205
employee performance 10, 160–173
empowerment 131, 166–167, 226, 247
energy management 156–158, 189
equipment 81, 147–148
ethics 57
European Foundation for Quality
    Management 135–137

fast food 6, 12, 40, 83, 84, 91, 125, 150, 195,
    238, 239
fire 148
fishbone analysis 258
flexible working 199
flow process charting 4, 64, 103, 247, 258
food courts 72–73
food delivery system 8
food manufacturing system 8
Food Safety Act 144, 149, 152, 238
force field analysis 258
franchising 18
fraud 155, 241
frequency distribution analysis 207

Gardner Merchant 47, 97
gap theory 247–249
gaze motion theory 54

HACCP 149–150, 246, 258
Harvester Restaurants 98, 104, 222, 227
health and safety 37, 61, 144, 149
home delivery 11, 95, 217
hospital catering 12, 19, 41, 104, 182, 205,
    238
human resource management 162
hygiene 61, 68, 69, 104

income 10

inflight catering 9, 12, 145, 205, 238, 239, 244
information technology 56, 81, 124–125, 198, 238
insurance 155–156
integrated foodservice systems 8
Investors in People 128, 133

job description 90, 163, 164
job design 86–88, 163
job enlargement 90
job enrichment 90
job rotation 89–90
job satisfaction 161, 219
job specialization 12, 88–89

Kentucky Fried Chicken 81, 114, 227
key result areas 5, 10, 11, 13, 15
kitchen design 61–71

labour costs 78, 121–124, 160, 189
layout 12, 49, 59–77, 82, 87, 105
location analysis 12, 18, 39–41

McDonalds 15, 35, 42, 47, 80, 98, 131, 145, 165, 193, 194, 199, 213, 225
maintenance 147–148
market research 18, 24–32, 46, 96
market segmentation 18, 32–34, 96
market structure 24, 39
market testing 38
mass service 220
menu 10, 45–58, 63, 80, 174, 204–215, 237
menu analysis 204, 205
menu design 52–55, 55–58
menu engineering 206, 208–211
menu planning 12, 48–52, 55–58, 105
motivation 88, 160, 161–165, 243
multi-skilling 199
mystery shoppers 57, 96, 227, 251, 253

new product development 19, 51

operating standards 94–106, 113
opportunity purchasing 236
organizational culture 170–172
organizational life cycle 197
output standards 101

Pareto analysis 258

performance measurement 118–120
pest control 152
Pizza Hut 15, 81, 98, 165, 171, 193
point of sale 81, 196, 231, 239, 241
poka-yoke 246
policy variance 232
post-operational control 109, 121, 123
potential commodity usage 119
potential sales volume 119
pre-operational control 108, 121, 123
primary research 28–30
problem identification 256–257
problem location 258–260
problem prioritization 257–258
process standards 101, 240
production control 117–118
production kitchen 9, 61–71
production strategy 80
production systems 5, 83, 112, 175–177, 204
productivity 10, 12, 99–100, 160, 183, 188–203
productivity standards 85
professional service 221
profitability analysis 211–213
psychology of waiting lines 184–186, 222
purchase specification 113
purchasing control system 113–114

quality 10, 12, 127–139, 240, 245–261
quality assurance 12, 129–131, 246
quality circles 130
quality control 12, 129, 151
quality inspection 12, 115, 128–129

rates of pay 121
relationship charting 63–64
restaurant design 71–75
revenue control 240–241
reward systems 165–166
roadside dining 12, 41, 145
role stress 167–169

sales mix 80, 174
sampling 30–31
sanitation 150
school meals 12, 32, 41, 125, 234
scripts 223
secondary research 25–28
security 115, 145–146, 153–155
self-service 11, 72, 74
service 10, 98–99, 183–184, 216–230
service design 4, 14, 35

service encounter 169, 218, 223
service factory 220
service recovery 228
service shop 221
service system 6, 177–180, 219
site selection 12, 41–42
social skills 169
space allowances 61–63, 65, 71–72
spoilage 149
staff scheduling 198
staff turnover 89, 160
staffing levels 12, 78–93, 110, 200
staffing structures 91
standard recipes 95, 117, 239–240
stock control 112, 115, 231, 237
stock levels 113
stocktaking 116
stores 112
strategic operations 10, 12, 15, 175
suppliers 112, 114, 231, 233–237
systems analysis 3, 4, 8, 15

target cost percentage 118, 122
teamwork 169–170, 255
technology 81, 110, 175, 201

TGI Fridays 15, 22, 48, 55, 170, 181, 194,
   220, 224
theft 155, 241
total quality management 12, 131–133
trade area 40
Trades Description Act 57
training 162, 217
travel catering 12

usage variance 232

value cost leverage 95, 219
variable costs 91, 110, 198
vending 11, 12, 62, 179

welfare catering 12, 110
Wendys 14, 224
Wimpy 14, 194, 199
work centres 63–65, 66–68, 87
work measurement 86, 200
work study 200
workflow 68, 72, 82

yield 51, 240